RELIGIOUS SCHOOLS
IN AMERICA

GARLAND REFERENCE LIBRARY
OF SOCIAL SCIENCE
(VOL. 338)

RELIGIOUS SCHOOLS IN AMERICA
A Selected Bibliography

Thomas C. Hunt
James C. Carper
Charles R. Kniker

GARLAND PUBLISHING, INC. • NEW YORK & LONDON
1986

Library of Congress Cataloging-in-Publication Data

Hunt, Thomas C., 1930–
  Religious schools in America.

  (Garland reference library of social science ;
vol. 338)
  Includes indexes.
  1. Church schools—United States—Bibliography.
I. Carper, James C. II. Kniker, Charles R. III. Title.
IV. Series: Garland reference library of social
science ; v. 338.
Z5814.C57H86 1986   016.377'0973   86-12118
[LC427]
ISBN 0-8240-8583-3 (alk. paper)

Printed on acid-free, 250-year-life paper
Manufactured in the United States of America

DEDICATION AND ACKNOWLEDGMENTS

We respectfully dedicate this reference book to those professors of ours whose own commitment to scholarship most impressed and influenced us. In particular, Thomas Hunt cites the contributions of Herbert M. Kliebard and the late Edward A. Krug of The University of Wisconsin; James Carper wishes to acknowledge Richard W. Smith of Ohio Wesleyan University and Charles E. Litz of Kansas State University.

We acknowledge with thanks the help of Mrs. Mila Moore in typing both the manuscript itself and all related correspondence, and of David Cavalier, who worked on the indexes. Finally, the editors wish to express their gratitude to the Division of Curriculum and Instruction and the College of Education at Virginia Tech for the support they provided.

Thomas C. Hunt
Blacksburg, Virginia
James C. Carper
Mississippi State, Mississippi
Charles R. Kniker
Ames, Iowa

CONTENTS

INTRODUCTION

The role of religion in schooling in the United States
has provoked considerable scholarly interest and public
debate. With a few notable exceptions, most of the
attention has been focused on the relationship of religion
to public education. Since the late 1970s, however,
researchers, policy makers, and the general public have
become increasingly interested in religious schools, which
account for 85 to 90 percent of the enrollment in the
private sector.

This interest is in large measure part of the current
concern for private education. Several factors account for
the growing interest in private schools in general and
religious schools in particular. First, the Reagan
administration's emphasis on educational choice and advocacy
of tuition tax credits and vouchers has drawn attention to
private education. Second, as reports decrying the
condition of public education have multiplied, interest in
private education has increased. Third, James Coleman's
widely publicized and debated report, Private and Public
Schools (1981), has prompted scholarly interest in the
characteristics of private schools. Fourth, United States
Supreme Court decisions in Bob Jones University v. United
States (1983), Mueller v. Allen (1983) and Aguilar v.
Felton (1985) have rekindled debate over public policy
concerning religiously-affiliated schools. Finally,
Americans seem more receptive now than at any other time in
recent history to private schools.

This selected bibliography deals with private schools
that are religiously affiliated (about 75 percent of the
total). It is divided into several sections. There is,
first, a chapter on the most influential general books on
religion and schooling. The second section is comprised of
summaries and analyses of court decisions and commentaries

on the issues of government aid to religiously affiliated schools and of government regulation of these schools.

It is the third section, however, which constitutes the major thrust of this book. Here the reader will find entries of the schools operated in the United States by seventeen religious groups, alphabetically arranged. Each is assembled by a person most knowledgeable of those schools. The entries are annotated, with two exceptions. The Catholic schools, by far the most numerous with a vast literature, are arranged according to substantive topic. Brief bibliographic essays precede the Episcopal listings.

The fourth, and final section, is made up of three chapters related to: 1) statements on religious schools by both public school educators and religious school advocates; 2) formal and informal interactions of public and religious schools; and 3) the concept of the education of the public by religious and public schools.

Definitions in this field are a constant problem, especially since we present both historical and contemporary references. We realize, for example, that the term "parochial school" has a different meaning for many twentieth century writers than it did for nineteenth century authors and speakers. The term "religious day school," in the minds of some, refers to all-day, Monday through Friday, denominationally-sponsored schools, while it may mean an after public school program once or twice a week to others. As a rule of thumb, we have opted to use the term in the annotation that the authors used in their work. Statistically, since most "nonpublic" schools are religiously oriented, that term is sometimes used as a generic term. We recognize, however, that in recent literature, the terms "private schools" and "nongovernmental schools" are growing in popularity.

This is a selected bibliography on K-12 schooling. Sources on higher education were included only if they contained a reference to elementary or secondary schools, a rather common phenomenon in the academies of the nineteenth century. Contributors were asked to include only the most salient works, whether book, article, dissertation, essay review, report, or thesis. Authors, where feasible, divided their chapters into "Historical" and "Contemporary" sections, determining the dividing line at an appropriate date. Geographically, with few exceptions, the book is confined to the United States.

This book follows the publication of a previous edited work, Religious Schooling in America, which appeared in 1984. To our knowledge, no other reference work focuses on religiously-affiliated schools. This work, accordingly, pulls together a wealth of reference material, mainly on religious schools, and provides a much-needed resource for those interested in religious schooling, whether scholar, student, policy-maker, or interested citizen.

THOMAS C. HUNT
Blacksburg, Virginia
JAMES C. CARPER
Mississippi State, Mississippi
CHARLES R. KNIKER
Ames, Iowa

Religious Schools
In America

CHAPTER 1
MAJOR WORKS ON RELIGION AND AMERICAN SCHOOLS
Donald E. Boles

1. American Association of School Administrators. Religion in the Public Schools. New York: Harper and Row, 1964.

   Evaluates the impact of the Schempp decision on public school programming, and suggests methods of using the Bible in the study of literature and history.

2. Barr, David L., and Nicholas Piediscalzi, eds. The Bible in American Education: From Source Book to Textbook. Philadelphia: Fortress Press, 1982.

   Shows through the use of historical essays that the exclusion of biblical study cannot be assured as a norm for public education. Also explores appropriate ways to include the Bible in everyone's education.

3. Boles, Donald E. The Bible, Religion, and the Public Schools. Ames: Iowa State University, 1965.

Studies the evolution of the controversy over
Bible Reading and other religiously oriented
programs in the public schools along with
pertinent court decisions and conflicting views
of religious and educational groups.

4.   Boles, Donald E. The Two Swords. Ames: Iowa
     State University, 1967.

Presents the major state and federal court
decisions involving church-state-schools issues
including a brief historical sketch of the
issues, and public reaction to the decisions as
reflected in newspaper and journal accounts.

5.   Brickman, William W. and Stanley Lehrer, eds.
     Religion, Government, and Education. New
     York: Society for the Advancement of
     Education, 1961.

Contains 13 articles that provide a view of
public and private education prior to the Schempp
decision.   Includes selections by leaders of
private religious schools, a chronology of
church-state events in the United States, and an
article on religious schooling in other
countries.

6.   Butts, R. Freeman. The American Tradition in
     Religion and Education. Boston: Beacon
     Press, 1950.

Provides a historical perspective (from a
liberal position) that is to guide future policy
makers of church and state issues.   Focuses on
the principle of separation in the original
states, in the new nation, and in the 19th
century.   Discusses, in the final chapter, public
funds for sectarian schools and sectarian
religious practices and non-sectarian activities
in public schools.

7. Carper, James C. , and Thomas C. Hunt, eds.
    Religious Schooling in America. Birmingham:
    Religious Education Press, 1984.

    Underscores the importance of religious
    schools in the history of the country. Suggests
    that their existence may be enhanced by the
    prominence of issues relating to the separation
    of church and state currently. Includes
    histories of six denominational schools, followed
    by articles on relation of public schools to
    religious schools and current issues, such as
    tuition tax credits.

8. Cord, Robert L. Separation of Church and State:
    Historical Fact and Current Fiction. New
    York: Lambeth Press, 1982.

    Concludes, based on primary historical
    documents, that the U.S. Supreme Court has erred
    in its interpretation of the First Amendment.
    Favors "moderate accommodation. "

9. Dolbeare, Kenneth M. , and Philip E. Hammond. The
    School Prayer Decisions: From Court Policy to
    Local Practice. Chicago: University of
    Chicago Press, 1971.

    Reviews key court decisions and efforts to
    implement them on the local and state level in
    the face of major public resistance in many
    areas.

10. Fellman, David, ed. The Supreme Court and
    Education. New York: Teachers College,
    Columbia University, 1960. 3rd edition,
    1980.

    Analyzes thoroughly court decisions dealing
    with religion and education and demonstrates a

variety of inconsistencies running throughout
them.   Concludes that the Wall of Separation is
frequently breached in practice.

11.   Gaffney, Edward McGlynn, Jr. , ed.   Private
       Schools and the Public Good: Policy
       Alternatives for the Eighties.   Notre Dame,
       IN: University of Notre Dame Press, 1981.

       Explores the pros and cons of tuition tax
credits, basic educational vouchers, and grants
for private schools, especially as they effect
racial and ethnic minorities and handicapped
student enrollments in private schools.

12.   Greene, Evarts B.   Religion and the State: The
       Making and Testing of an American Tradition.
       New York: New York University Press, 1941.

       Presents the main outlines of the European
tradition of church-state relations, the
transplanting of that tradition in the United
States, and the process of liberalization
leading to the principle of church-state
separation.   Discusses the problems that still
remain.

13.   Howe, Mark DeWolfe.   The Garden and the
       Wilderness: Religion and Government in
       American Tradition.   Chicago: University of
       Chicago Press, 1965.

       Analyzes, in meticulous detail, state and
federal court decisions touching on nationalism,
the Fourteenth Amendment, political and
religious liberties, and concepts of equality in
their relationship to problems of church and
state.   Focuses in particular upon the
interaction between religious liberties and
political liberties.

14. Johnson, Harry C. , Jr. The Public School and
    Moral Education. New York: Pilgrim Press,
    1980.

    Describes the proper role of moral education
    in the public schools, following a discussion of
    religion and moral education programs.

15. Konvitz, Milton R. Religion, Liberty and
    Conscience. New York: Viking Press, 1969.

    Studies the complexity of attempts to
    interpret the Free Exercise clause in cases of
    non-religionist conscientious objectors to war
    and their claims to freedom of religion and
    concludes that conscience is primarily
    religious; thus, to "protect religion fully it
    is necessary to protect rights of conscience
    generally."

16. Kraushaar, Otto F. American Nonpublic Schools:
    Patterns of Diversity. Baltimore: The Johns
    Hopkins University Press, 1972.

    Describes the historical development of the
    variety of schools that are non-governmentally
    controlled. Argues that there are major
    differences between schools that have been
    labeled "parochial," "nonpublic," "private," and
    "sectarian."

17. Kurland, Philip B. Religion and the Law: Of
    Church and State and the Supreme Court.
    Chicago: Aldine Press, 1962.

    Offers a solution to what is considered the
    Court's failure to interpret the First Amendment
    sensibly. Argues in favor of the "neutral
    principle," i.e., religion may not be used as a
    basis for classification for purposes of
    governmental action, whether that action be the

conferring of rights or privileges or the
imposition of duties or obligations.

18.   Malbin, Michael J.   _Religion and Politics: The
      Intentions of the Authors of the First
      Amendment._   Washington, DC: American
      Enterprise Institute, 1970.

      Utilizing research from the First Congress
      Project at George Washington University, argues
      that Congress did not mean the Establishment
      Clause to require strict neutrality between
      religion and irreligion.   Claims that framers
      viewed the Free Exercise clause in a way that
      would deny anyone had a right to claim an
      exemption from a valid, secularly based law
      because of a religious objection.

19.   McCollum, Vashti.   _One Woman's Fight, 1951-1961._
      Boston: Beacon Press, 1961.

      Details, step by step, the fight by Mrs.
      McCollum resulting from harassment of her son
      for refusing to participate in religious
      programs in the public schools through a local
      appeal to an Illinois school board to the U.S.
      Supreme Court's decision in a landmark case.

20.   Michaelsen, Robert.   _Piety in the Public School._
      New York: The Macmillan Company, 1970.

      Examines the high points in the history of
      the relationship between religion and the
      American public schools.   Focuses on the
      dynamics of American religion and the possible
      role of the public school as America's
      "established church."

21.   Morgan, Richard E.   _The Politics of Religious
      Conflict._   New York: Pegasus, 1968.

Utilizes conceptual tools of modern political
science to analyze the civic conflict called the
politics of church and state. Suggests possible
developments in the 1980s.

22. Pfeffer, Leo. Church, State and Freedom.
     Boston: Beacon Press, 1966.

Demonstrates that the origin of the public
school not only antedates the principle of
separation between church and state, but argues
that public education may owe its very existence
to the fact that it antedates the doctrine of
separation.

23. Pfeffer, Leo. God, Caesar and the Constitution.
     Boston: Beacon Press, 1975.

Surveys church-state relations through the
eyes of a "strict separationist" and discusses
the key court decisions in the context of social
history, including the questions left unanswered
by the Court.

24. Pfeffer, Leo. Religion, State and the Burger
     Court. Buffalo: Prometheus Books, 1984.

Gives a penetrating analysis of the Court
under Chief Justice Burger and notes a trend
toward greater "accommodation" since the
election of Ronald Reagan and his appointment of
Sandra Day O'Connor to the Court.

25. Sizer, Theodore R. , ed. Religion and Public
     Education. Boston: Houghton Mifflin
     Company, 1967. (2nd edition: Washington:
     University Press of America, 1982.)

Includes a series of articles that attempt to
clarify what is legally permissible and
pedagogically sound in light of the recent

series of Court decisions (particularly the
school prayer decision of 1962 and the Bible
reading case of 1963).

26. Sorauf, Frank. The Wall of Separation: The
Constitutional Politics of Church and State.
Princeton, NJ: Princeton University Press,
1976.

Examines 67 church-state cases in appellate
courts in the U.S. between 1951 and 1971 in an
analysis of law and public policy during that
era with an epilogue covering additional cases
from 1971 to 1974.

27. Stokes, Anson Phelps, and Leo Pfeffer. Church
and State in the United States. 3 volumes.
New York: Harper, 1964.

Traces church-state relations in the United
States from colonial times to midtwentieth
century. Demonstrates that the primary area in
which the battles have been fought is the public
school.

28. Van Alstine, George. The Christian and the
Public Schools. Nashville: Abingdon Press,
1982.

Argues that Christian schools are too limited
to meet the essential needs of today's students,
since they tend to be reactions to desegregation
orders and perceived permissive secularization,
and are not based on a positive educational
foundation. Urges more responsive involvement
by Christian parents and educators in
educational systems that involve all citizens.

29. Warshaw, Thayer W. Religion, Education, and the
Supreme Court. Nashville: Abingdon Press,
1969.

Examines U. S. Supreme Court decisions on religion and schools from 1925 to 1977 with major concern with what exactly the Court has affirmed or denied including brief quotations from the majority opinion. Concludes with a questionnaire.

30. Wood, James E. , Jr. , ed. Religion, the State and Education. Waco, TX: Baylor University Press, 1984.

Includes essays expressly devoted to public education as well as to church schools, to religion in public schools and to religion in state universities, with special attention given to models of religion studies developed for the public schools from two state programs.

CHAPTER 2
FEDERAL COURT DECISIONS CONCERNING
GOVERNMENT AID TO AND REGULATION
OF RELIGIOUS SCHOOLS
Robert W. Pearigen

31. Bradfield v. Roberts, 175 U. S. 291 (1899).

Upholds federal assistance for the
construction of a hospital that was operated by
a religious order, the Catholic Sisters of
Charity. Based upon the "contract for secular
services" theory, the Court held that because
the beneficiary of the federal grant was a
nonreligious corporation, distinct from the
Sisters who were shareholders and its operators,
and because its primary objective was health
care, there was no violation of the
Establishment Clause of the First Amendment.

32. Quick Bear v. Leupp, 210 U. S. 50 (1908).

Holds that money from the U. S. Treasury paid
to Indians for tuition in sectarian schools was
legally spent. The Court determined that the
money came not from federal funds, but rather
was money simply held in trust by the U. S. and
belonging to the Indians from federal
compensation for land. Thus, at the direction
of the Indians, the funds could be spent for
tuition at church schools.

13

33. <u>Meyer</u> v. <u>Nebraska</u>, 262 U.S. 390 (1923).

Declares unconstitutional a 1919 Nebraska
statute that prohibited the teaching of any
subject in any language other than English and
the teaching of a foreign language prior to
ninth grade in either a public or a private
school. Recognizes the power of the state to
compel attendance at some school, but rules that
the law in question interferes with the rights
of teachers, parents, and pupils.

34. <u>Pierce</u> v. <u>Society of Sisters</u>, 268 U.S. 510
(1925).

Rules unconstitutional a 1922 Oregon law that
required children to attend public schools
through the eighth grade. Asserts that the
state may reasonably regulate private schools,
but may not deny children the right to attend
private schools or preclude their operation.
Claims that parents have a fundamental right to
direct the "upbringing and education" of their
children.

35. <u>Farrington</u> v. <u>Tokushige</u>, 273 U.S. 284 (1927).

Declares unconstitutional 1925 Hawaii
legislation and accompanying regulations that
prohibited students from attending foreign
language schools until they had completed second
grade in the public schools, limited attendance
to certain hours, and effectively controlled the
content of instruction at these schools.
Asserts that the Hawaii law deprives parents of
the Fourteenth Amendment right to direct the
education of their children.

36. <u>Cochran</u> v. <u>Louisiana State Board of Education</u>,
281 U.S. 370 (1930).

Rules constitutional Louisiana's practice of
furnishing secular textbooks to all school
children in public and private schools,
including sectarian schools. Denying a
Fourteenth Amendment challenge, the Court
determined that the texts were of general
benefit to the community, of particular benefit
to the child, and did not provide support to
parochial schools.

37. Everson v. Board Education of Ewing Township,
     330 U.S. 1 (1947).

Upholds, by a five to four vote, a New Jersey
statute authorizing reimbursement of parents for
costs incurred in busing children to both
private, sectarian schools and public schools.
The opinion by Justice Black, which recognized
that the Establishment Clause of the First
Amendment should be made applicable to the
states by the Fourteenth Amendment, provided the
first definitive explanation of the meaning and
parameters of the Establishment Clause. Using a
metaphor of Thomas Jefferson, Black insisted
that the First Amendment erected a "wall of
separation between Church and State" which must
be kept "high and impregnable." In this
instance however, the wall was not breached
because the state had a legitimate interest in
the safe transportation of all school children;
an interest that was neutral rather than
supportive of religion and an interest that was
aimed at benefitting the child and not the
school or parent.

In dissent, Justice Jackson argued that the
majority opinion calling for an uncompromising
separation of church and state was completely at
odds with its conclusion.

38. <u>McCollum</u> v. <u>Board</u> <u>of</u> <u>Education,</u> 333 U.S. 203
    (1948).

    Declares religious instruction classes in
    Champaign, Illinois, which brought
    representatives of several religions into the
    public school classrooms, unconstitutional.
    Although the classes were arranged on a
    voluntary, released time basis, they were
    violative of the separation of church and state
    because they were held on public school property
    and because the state's compulsory attendance
    law brought the pupils into the situation.

39. <u>Zorach</u> v. <u>Clauson,</u> 343 U.S. 306 (1952).

    Rules that a released time program for
    students to participate in religious instruction
    and training off the premises of the public
    schools in New York City is constitutional.
    Public funds are not expended, nor are public
    facilities used. The program requires merely an
    accommodation of student's schedules to their
    outside religious instruction.

    Justice Douglas wrote that to deny
    accommodation of religion would make church and
    state "aliens to each other, hostile, suspicious
    and even unfriendly."

40. <u>Abington</u> <u>School</u> <u>District</u> v. <u>Schempp,</u> 374 U.S.
    203 (1963).

    Adjudges that government mandated reading of
    Bible verses at the opening of each day in
    public schools, or the recitation of the Lord's
    Prayer as in the companion case of <u>Murray</u> v.
    <u>Curlett,</u> are unconstitutional breaches of the
    religious neutrality of states. Even when
    attendance is not compulsory, the supervision by
    public school personnel violates the First

Amendment. The Court articulates a two-part
test of state neutrality which stipulates that
any governmental program involving religious
activity (A) must have a secular, legislative
purpose and (B) must have a primary effect which
neither advances nor inhibits religion.

Justice Brennan's detailed concurring opinion
discusses areas of public policy where
accommodation of religion is necessary, as in
the military service or in legislative
assemblies.

41. Flast v. Cohen, 392 U.S. 83 (1968).

Broadens the base of potential challenges to
federal expenditure by holding that a federal
taxpayer has standing to sue against federal
statutes when the statute involves the tax and
spend power of Congress and when there is an
allegation that a specific limitation on
congressional taxing and spending has been
violated. In this instance, a taxpayer alleged
that the expenditure of federal funds under the
Elementary and Secondary Education Act of 1965
violated the specific limitations of the
Establishment Clause.

42. Board of Education v. Allen, 392 U.S. 236
    (1968).

Upholds, by a six to three vote, the free
loan of nonreligious textbooks to private and
parochial school students at public expense.
The books loaned were part of the secular
education of the student and were thus
beneficial to the child, not the religion.
Furthermore, the program was administered
without a prolonged or detailed supervisory
relationship between the state and religious
schools.

43.   Walz v. Tax Commission, 397 U.S. 664 (1970).

  Rules that a New York City law permitting tax
exemption for nonprofit religious, educational
or charitable enterprises is constitutional.
The Court, adding a third element to the test of
neutrality articulated in Schempp, insists that
the end result of the governmental policy must
not excessively entangle the church and state.

44.   Johnson v. Sanders, 319 F. Supp. 421 (D. Conn.
  1970), aff'd, 403 U.S. 955 (1971).

  Adjudges that a Connecticut statute
reimbursing religious schools for a portion of
their expenses for texts and teachers salaries
was unconstitutional. Although the funds were
directed toward enhancement of secular subjects,
the Court determined that this assistance was
tantamount to state sponsorship of sectarian
student bodies and that it fostered excessive
entanglement between church and state.

45.   Lemon v. Kurtzman and Early v. Dicenso, 403 U.S.
  602 (1971).

  Declares unconstitutional programs whereby
states paid money to nonpublic schools to
reimburse them for furnishing secular
educational services to students. A
Pennsylvania law (Lemon) reimbursed private
schools for the costs of teachers' salaries,
texts and instructional material used for
secular courses, and a Rhode Island statute
(Early) authorized 15% annual salary supplements
to private school teachers of secular subjects.
The Court held that the statutes (A) advanced
the cause of religion and (B) fostered excessive
entanglement due to the degree of surveillance
necessary in the administration of the programs.

46. Brusca v. State of Missouri, 332 F. Supp. 275
    (E. D. Mo. 1971), aff'd, 405 U. S. 1050 (1972).

    Rejects the plaintiff's assertion, based upon
    the First Amendment and the Equal Protection
    Clause of Fourteenth Amendment, that the
    Constitution required state subsidization of
    nonpublic education. The Court held that the
    First Amendment does not compel states to assist
    parents in providing parochial education for
    their children, and that exclusion of religious
    schools from state funding does not violate the
    parents rights.

47. Wolman v. Essex, 342 F. Supp. 399 (D. C. S. D. Ohio
    1972), aff'd, 409 U. S. 808 (1973).

    Rules that a general tuition grants law
    whereby the state reimbursed parents for
    parochial school tuition is unconstitutional.
    The court insisted that filtering public funds
    to denominational schools through the avenue of
    tuition reimbursement for parents does not cause
    the funds to lose their public character.

48. Lemon v. Kurtzman II, 411 U. S. 192 (1973).

    Permits the continuation of payments pursuant
    to the contracts established before the Lemon I
    ruling, although a program for state
    reimbursement to parochial schools for secular
    services had been declared unconstitutional in
    Lemon v. Kurtzman (1971). While additional
    contracts between the state and parochial
    schools were impermissible, principles of
    fairness and equity necessitated the honoring of
    previously contracted obligations.

49. Levitt v. Committee for Public Education and
    Religious Liberty, 413 U. S. 472 (1973).

Invalidates a New York statute which allowed
the state to subsidize nonpublic schools for
administering state-devised and state-mandated
testing programs and record keeping. The First
Amendment forbids allocation of funds directly
to parochial schools. The reimbursement under
consideration constituted a subsidy of an
integral part of the educational program which
could not be easily distinguished or severed
from the schools' religious function.

50. Committee for Public Education and Religious
    Liberty v. Nyquist, 413 U.S. 756 (1973).

Strikes down, by a six to three vote, three
financial aid programs for nonpublic schools in
New York. The programs involved (A) state
grants for maintenance and repair of facilities
and equipment, (B) tuition reimbursement grants
to low-income parents with children enrolled in
nonpublic elementary and secondary schools, and
(C) income tax credits to middle-income parents
who paid tuition for private schools. Justice
Powell maintained that the programs served to
unconstitutionally advance religion. The
programs also engendered political divisiveness
and thus created potentially excessive
entanglement.

The dissent insisted that tax credits were
not direct aid to sectarian schools and should
be allowed the same legitimacy as transportation
(Everson) and textbooks (Allen). The dissent
also suggested that indirect assistance to
private schools would limit the economic and
demographic strains on public education.

51. Sloan v. Lemon, 413 U.S. 825 (1973).

Rules a Pennsylvania statute, passed to avoid
the "entanglement" problem of Lemon I, which

allowed the state to reimburse parents with
children in nonpublic schools for tuition
expenses, unconstitutional, even though the
public funds were granted to parents rather than
the sectarian schools. Such assistance is
considered a violation of the "primary effects"
test of the Establishment Clause.

52. Norwood v. Harrison, 413 U.S. 455 (1973).

Rules that while the Establishment Clause
allowed a degree of state aid to
nondiscriminatory religious schools, nonetheless
that states may not loan textbooks to students
attending racially exclusive private schools.

53. Leutkemeyer v. Kaufman, 364 F. Supp. 376 (W.D.
Mo. 1973), aff'd 419 U.S. 888 (1974).

Holds that while states are permitted the
option of financing transportation for students
in nonpublic schools, they are not
constitutionally required to do so. The court
rejected the contention that the Equal
Protection Clause of the Fourteenth Amendment
secured for private school children an
unequivocal right to state supported
transportation. The state may erect an even
higher "wall of separation" than is required by
the Establishment Clause.

54. Wheeler v. Barrera, 417 U.S. 402 (1974).

Avoids ruling on whether or not the
Establishment Clause would allow Title I of the
federal Elementary and Secondary School Act of
1965 to subsidize special education programs for
educationally deprived children in nonpublic
schools. The Court ruled merely that the Title
I requirement that comparable services be given
to private school students did not compel state

use of Title I teachers in private schools
during regular school hours.

55.   Meek v. Pittenger, 421 U.S. 349 (1975).

Upholds, in a six to three decision,
Pennsylvania's textbook loan program, based upon
the "child benefit theory," but struck down the
program for the loan of instructional material
and equipment and the provision for auxiliary
services to private schools. The loaning of
equipment and the providing of services to
nonpublic schools was viewed as advancing
religion, fostering entanglement between church
and state and generating political divisiveness
in the community.

56.   Runyon v. McCrary, 427 U.S. 160 (1976).

Upholds the use of 42 U.S.C. 1981 to prohibit
private schools from denying admission solely on
the basis of race. Asserts that the law does
not infringe upon parents' free association or
educational rights.

57.   Wolman v. Walter, 433 U.S. 229 (1977).

Reviews a complex Ohio statute which provided
various forms of assistance to nonpublic
elementary and secondary schools. (A) By a six
to three vote the Court upheld the loan of
secular textbooks based upon the child benefit
theory. (B) By the same vote the Court upheld
state funding of secularly devised standardized
tests as long as the private school pays for the
administration of the test. (C) By an eight to
one vote, state supported diagnostic services
for private school children was upheld because
the diagnostician was a public employee with
limited contact with the students. (D) In a
seven to two vote the Court upheld therapeutic

services provided by public employees on public
property. In each of the above programs the
three prong-test was met. That is, each program
had a secular purpose which did not advance nor
inhibit religion and which did not foster
entanglement.

However, (E) by a six to three vote the Court
held invalid the loan of instructional material
and equipment because of its effect of aiding
sectarian education, and (F) by a five to four
vote the Court held that public support for
field trip transportation could not be
administered without promoting religion and
fostering excessive entanglement.

58. Filler v. Port Washington Union Free School
     District, 436 F. Supp. 1231 (E.D. N.Y. 1977).

     Upholds provisions of a state statute which
     authorized diagnostic services, in nonpublic
     schools, performed by physicians, dentists,
     dental hygienists, or nurses. However, based
     upon Wolman v. Walter, the court ruled that
     remedial or therapeutic services performed by
     psychologists or speech therapists must take
     place in a religiously neutral location.

59. Members of Jamestown School Committee v.
     Schmidt, 427 F. Supp. 1338 (D. R.I. 1977).

     Invalidates a state law which authorized
     public transportation beyond school district
     boundaries for students attending sectarian
     schools. The court ruled that this statute,
     unlike the law in Everson, benefitted only
     children in private schools and thus was a
     violation of the Establishment Clause.

60. School District of Pittsburgh v. Pennsylvania
     Department of Education, 33 Pa. Cmwlth. 535
     (1978).

Sustains a Pennsylvania law that required
school districts to provide free transportation
to private school students for distances up to
ten miles beyond the district's boundary, even
if no public school students are bused beyond
the district boundaries. In their appeal to the
Supreme Court, the plaintiffs insisted that such
legislation resulted in the state extending
greater benefits to sectarian school students
than to public school students. The Supreme
Court dismissed the appeal for want of a
substantial federal question (442 U.S. 901).

61. National Labor Relations Board v. Catholic
    Bishop of Chicago, 440 U.S. 490 (1979).

Declares that schools operated by a church to
teach both religious and secular subjects are
not within the jurisdiction granted by the
National Labor Relations Act, so they are not
subject to the NLRB's authority. By a five to
four margin the Court ruled that there was no
evidence that Congress intended the NLRB to have
such jurisdiction, and that there would be a
significant risk of infringement of the Religion
Clauses of the First Amendment if the Act
conferred jurisdiction over church-operated
schools.

62. Committee for Public Education and Religious
    Liberty v. Regan, 444 U.S. 646 (1980).

Upholds, by a five to four vote, the
constitutionality of a New York statute which
appropriates public funds to reimburse church
sponsored and secular private schools for
performing state mandated testing and reporting
services. Although nonpublic personnel are
involved in the administration and grading of
these tests, the tests concern only secular

academic matters; thus there is little risk the
tests can be used for religious purposes.
Furthermore, the recordkeeping and reporting
services are not part of the teaching process
and, therefore, cannot be used to foster an
ideological perspective. Viewed in light of
Meek and Wolman, these reimbursements serve the
state's legitimate secular goals, without any
real risk of being used to advance religious
views or entangle the church and state.

63. St. Martin Evangelical Lutheran Church v. South
     Dakota, 451 U. S. 772 (1981).

     Interprets the Federal Unemployment Tax Act
     as not applicable to a church-operated school.

64. Bob Jones University v. United States, 461 U. S.
     574 (1983).

     Upholds the revocation of the tax status of
     Bob Jones University. Asserts that free
     exercise of religion does not prohibit the
     government from dealing with private acts of
     racial discrimination.

65. Mueller v. Allen, 463 U. S. 388 (1983).

     Upholds, by a five to four vote, a Minnesota
     statute which allows tax deductions for parents
     with children in either public or nonpublic
     schools. Tax deductions are permitted for the
     cost of transportation, tuition, secular
     textbooks, and other educational related
     expenses. Unlike Nyquist where the Court
     disallowed deductions by parents with children
     in private schools only, the Minnesota
     deductions were available to all parents. The
     secular legislative purpose of education is
     enhanced without advancing sectarian schools in
     particular and without entangling the church and
     state.

The dissent claimed that the practical effect
of the deduction was not financially neutral
because only parents with children in private
schools, 95% of which are religiously
affiliated, incurred expenses large enough to
encourage deductions. Calling the plan an
indirect subsidy of tuition payments for private
education, the dissent insisted the plan had the
"direct and immediate" effect of advancing
religion.

66. School District of the City of Grand Rapids v.
     Ball, 473 U.S. ____ (1985).

Invalidates, in a five to four decision, the
use of state funds to finance remedial and
enrichment courses in nonpublic schools.
Although conducted in classrooms located in
private, primarily religious schools, all
religious symbols were removed from the
classrooms involved in the program and the
courses were taught largely by public school
employees. Nevertheless, the Court determined
that the program had the principal effect of
promoting religion because teachers might become
involved in inculcating religious beliefs and
because any state support of sectarian
institutions conveys a message of symbolic union
between government and religion.

67. Aguilar v. Felton, 473 U.S. ____ (1985).

Rejects, in a five to four decision, a New
York program which used federal Title I funds to
send public school employees into nonpublic
schools to teach remedial mathematics and
English to educationally deprived children from
low-income, primarily inner-city families.
Although the city had adopted a strict
monitoring system to ensure that Title I funded

teachers did not become involved in
intentionally or inadvertently inculcating
religious beliefs in their students, the Court
concluded that such monitoring would inevitably
result in the excessive entanglement of church
and state.

CHAPTER 3
GOVERNMENT AID TO RELIGIOUS SCHOOLS
COMMENTARY AND ANALYSIS
Robert W. Pearigen

Part I: Historical

68. Blum, Virgil C. Freedom in Education. Garden
    City, NJ: Doubleday and Company, Inc. , 1965.

    As a supporter of public subsidization of
parochial schools, Father Blum purports to show
the moral, philosophical, educational, and
juridical basis for such support. Direct
subsidies, tax credits and vouchers would
guarantee competitive improvement among
educational institutions and would foster
freedom of choice for parents. By disallowing
public aid to private schools, the Supreme Court
would be denying the civil rights and freedom of
conscience of parents, as well as engendering
student conformity to mass opinion and
encouraging a state-enforced orthodoxy of
secular humanism.
Brickman, William W. and Stanley Lehrer, eds.
    Religion, Government and Education. New
    York: Society for the Advancement of
    Education, 1961.

* See item 5.

69. Brown, William E. and Andrew M. Greeley. Can
    Catholic Schools Survive? New York: Sheed
    and Ward, Inc., 1970.

    Insists that Catholic schools are the most
    important mission of the church and that they
    must survive without public assistance. Any
    type of public aid, including tax credits or
    vouchers, would threaten the independence of the
    church school and compromise the religious
    values taught in the classroom.

70. Buchanan, Sidney. "Government Aid to Sectarian
    Schools: A Study in Corrosive Precedents."
    Houston Law Review 15 (1978): 783-838.

    Examines the Supreme Court's incremental
    movement from the "high wall" of separation
    between church and state in Everson v. Board of
    Education to the "blurred wall" in Wolman v.
    Walter. Advocates a return to the position
    espoused by Justice Rutledge in his Everson
    dissent. Rutledge claimed that any aid to
    religious schools was, in actuality, aid to
    religion and therefore unconstitutional.
    Buchanan suggests that parochial schools'
    principal reliance should be on faith and
    voluntarism, not government.

    Butts, R. Freeman. The American Tradition in
    Religion and Education. Boston: Beacon
    Press, 1950.

    * See item 6.

71. Choper, Jesse H. "The Establishment Clause and
    Aid to Parochial Schools." California Law
    Review 56 (1968): 260-341.

    Reviews history of governmental financial aid
    to religious schools and proposes that direct or

indirect public assistance is constitutional as
long as it does not exceed the value of the
secular educational services offered by the
schools. This proposed standard is examined in
light of the operation of parochial schools and
in contrast to other theories concerned with
public aid, religious schools, and the First
Amendment.

Cord, Robert L. Separation of Church and State:
    Historical Fact and Current Fiction. New
    York: Lambeth Press, 1982.

* See item 8.

72. Cushman, Robert F. "Public Support of Religious
     Education in American Constitutional Law."
     Illinois Law Review 45 (1950): 333-356.

     A highly regarded constitutional scholar
closely examines the Supreme Court's
interpretation of the First Amendment in Everson
v. Board of Education and McCollum v. Board of
Education. Concentrating on the child-benefit
theory and the issue of released time programs,
Cushman questions the Court's interpretation and
use of the Framers' intentions.

73. Freund, Paul A. "Public Aid to Parochial
     Schools." Harvard Law Review 82 (1969):
     1680-1692.

     Advocates strict adherence to the principle
of neutrality articulated in Board of Education
v. Allen but supports general welfare services
for children in all schools, whether public or
private. Examines the problem of public aid to
parochial schools by considering the principles
of religious voluntarism, mutual abstention, and
governmental neutrality as embodied in the First
Amendment. While generally an advocate of

judicial self-restraint, Freund insists that
political divisiveness on religious issues can
be forestalled only by the courts' articulating
a clear constitutional rule.

74. Gabel, Richard J. Public Funds for Church and
     Private Schools. Washington, DC: Catholic
     University of America, 1937.

     Exhaustive, 800 page history of public aid to
     private and parochial schools in America from
     the colonial period to the mid-1930's. Defends
     the use of public resources for sectarian
     schools.

75. Gianella, Donald A. "Religious Liberty,
     Nonestablishment, and Doctrinal Development.
     Part II. The Nonestablishment Principle."
     Harvard Law Review 81 (1968): 513-590.

     Recognizes that the issue of government aid
     to private schools is confusing because both
     sides have conflicting claims to free exercise,
     equality, and neutrality under the First
     Amendment. Furthermore, the doctrine of "strict
     neutrality" is difficult to apply in an
     increasingly active, complex governmental
     operation. In this extensive, scholarly
     analysis of the nonestablishment issue, the
     author concludes that limited forms of aid may
     be permissible and that indirect child benefits
     have the best chance of passing the Court's
     test.

76. Gunther, Gerald. Cases and Materials on
     Constitutional Law. 11th ed. Mineola, NY:
     The Foundation Press, Inc., 1985.

     Standard, comprehensive casebook. Includes
     excerpts from important Supreme Court decisions,
     introductory notes and essays, and bibliographic

material.   Chapter Fourteen, "The Constitution
and Religion: Establishment and Free Exercise,"
deals with the issue of public aid to religious
schools.

Howe, Mark DeWolfe. The Garden and the
    Wilderness: Religion and Government in
    American Constitutional History. Chicago:
    University of Chicago Press, 1965.

* See item 13.

77. Huegli, Albert G., ed.   Church and State Under
     God. St. Louis: Concordia Publishing House,
     1964.

     Impressive collection of essays by
     distinguished scholars analyzing the political,
     social and theological implications of church-
     state relations.   In particular, chapter seven,
     "Church Schools and the Church-State Issue" by
     Arthur Miller, discusses parochiaid from an
     accommodationist perspective.   Miller suggests
     that private schools should not be allowed to
     suffocate financially.   Thus, he proposes that
     nonpublic schools should be eligible for
     publicly recognized social services such as
     transportation, aptitude tests, lunch programs
     and civil defense measures.   However, private
     schools should not be subsidized for
     instructional programs, such as teachers'
     salaries, textbooks, and building construction.

78. Jellison, Helen M., ed.   State and Federal Laws
     Relating to Nonpublic Schools. Washington,
     DC: U.S. Department of Health, Education,
     and Welfare, 1975.

     A comprehensive, 1975 study of federal
     programs, state constitutional provisions, and
     state laws effecting or contributing to the
     maintenance of nonpublic schools.

79. Katz, Wilber G. Religion and American
     Constitutions. Evanston, IL: Northwestern
     University Press, 1964.

     Argues that the courts should be guided by a
     rule of neutrality which is not hostile to
     religion and which permits the possibility of
     limited forms of parochiaid. Based upon a
     series of lectures delivered at Northwestern
     University, the author exa⁊ines in a concise,
     articulate, and normative fashion, the
     historical and contemporary conflicts between
     sectarian and non-sectarian influences.
     Government policy should not be shaped so as to
     discourage parental choice.

80. Kauper, Paul G. "The Supreme Court and the
     Establishment Clause: Back to Everson."
     Case Western Reserve Law Review 25 (1975):
     107-129.

     Insists that the Supreme Court is following
     an unnecessarily rigid interpretation of the
     Establishment Clause and endorses a more
     accommodationist, benevolent attitude toward
     state aid to private schools. Stresses that the
     Court should be more cautious in determining who
     has claims for free exercise and equal
     protection rights in our pluralistic society.

81. Kirby, James C. "Everson to Meek to Roemer:
     From Separation to Detente in Church-State
     Relations." North Carolina Law Review 55
     (1977): 563-575.

     Traces the Supreme Court's progress from the
     "no-aid dictum" of Everson v. Board of
     Education to the accommodation of later cases
     and argues that the current state of limited,
     provisional aid is satisfactory. Suggests that

the prevailing law is one of detente between the
views of Madison, Jefferson, and Roger Williams.

82. Kliebard, Herbert M., ed. Religion and
    Education in America: A Documentary History.
    Scranton: International Textbook Co., 1969.

    Useful documents and primary sources related
    to the church-state issue. Includes writings of
    Madison, Jefferson, Mann, congressional debates
    over the First Amendment, Catholic position
    papers, and Supreme Court decisions up to 1968.

83. Kurland, Philip B. and Gerhard Casper, eds.
    Landmark Briefs and Arguments of the Supreme
    Court of the United States: Constitutional
    Law. Frederick, MD: University Publications
    of America, Inc., 1980, 1982, 1983.

    Multi-volume, ongoing collection of landmark
    Supreme Court decisions and the briefs and
    arguments presented by the litigants before the
    Court. Included in the collection and
    applicable to the question of public aid to
    religious schools are: Everson v. Board of
    Education (vol. 44); Wolman v. Walters (vol.
    96); and Mueller v. Allen (vol. 134).

84. Kurland, Philip B. "Of Church and State and the
    Supreme Court." University of Chicago Law
    Review 29 (1961): 1-96.

    Comprehensive and scholarly examination of
    numerous issues and Supreme Court decisions
    concerning church-state relations. Kurland
    proposes his well-known principle of neutrality
    to ensure First Amendment objectives: "The
    freedom and separation clauses should be read as
    stating a single precept; that government cannot
    utilize religion as a standard for action or
    inaction because these clauses, read together as

they should be, prohibit classification in terms of religion either to confer a benefit or impose a burden. " Kurland's notion of neutrality leads him to the conclusion that limited aid to private schools is not unconstitutional as long as it is nondiscriminatory.

Kraushaar, Otto F. American Nonpublic Schools. Baltimore: Johns Hopkins University Press, 1972.

* See item 16.

85. Lannie, Vincent P. Public Money and Parochial Education: Bishop Hughes, Governor Seward, and the New York School Controversy. Cleveland: Case Western Reserve University Press, 1968.

Excellent study of the New York school controversy which had a significant bearing on the development of Catholic education in the nation. Centers on the Catholic Church's dynamic Bishop Hughes who condemned public education as protestant sectarianism bent on destroying Catholicism and divorcing education from moral teaching.

86. LaNoue, George R. Public Funds for Parochial Schools? New York: Office of Publication and Distribution of the National Council of Churches of Christ, 1963.

Comprehensive examination by a strict separationist of the historical background, legal issues, and public policy considerations of the First Amendment church-state question. Insists that public tax support for private schools would violate the taxpayer's control of tax money, undermine individual religious liberty, and engender a proliferation of sectarian schools to the detriment of public education. Rejects the notion that equal protection or free exercise principles are violated when parochial schools are prohibited from securing public funds.

87. LaNoue, George R. "Religious Schools and 'Secular Subjects.'" Harvard Educational Review 32 (1962): 255-291.

Interesting analysis of the ways in which religion is integrated into the allegedly secular material in parochial school textbooks. Concludes that the subject matter and material presented in sectarian schools is not truly secular, and that government programs of aid to religious schools in the guise of assisting secular subjects violates both constitutional principles and sound public policy.

88. Larson, Martin A. When Parochial Schools Close. Washington, DC: Robert B. Luce, Inc., 1972.

Traces the development of public and private, secular and sectarian education in America. Making use of extensive statistical research, the author concludes that the closure of parochial schools and the subsequent incorporation of their pupils into the public schools does not create the adverse economic and educational dislocations often suggested by those supporting parochiaid. Suggests that private schools often drain enthusiasm and resources from public schools and that when private schools lose, the community unites to support public schools.

89. Manning, Leonard F. "Aid to Education--Federal Fashion; State Style." Fordham Law Review 29 (1961): 495-552.

Examines the evolving standards articulated
by the Supreme Court concerning public aid to
private schools. Argues there is nothing in the
Constitution which forbids public aid.
Furthermore, if the government is charged with
lending its assistance to schools satisfying the
educational needs of the community, and if
church-related schools satisfy those needs and
requirements, it is irrelevant whether church-
schools also happen to teach religion. The
Court is breaching the wall of separation by
preferring irreligion over religion.

90. McCluskey, Neil G. Catholic Viewpoint on
    Education. Garden City, NJ: Doubleday and
    Company, Inc., 1959.

    One of the most articulate spokesman of the
    Catholic Church, exhaustively explains the
    reasons for a separate and politically
    independent school system. Concerned that
    public schools, in an effort to remain
    religiously neutral, have undermined normative
    values and contributed to a "secularist cult,"
    McCluskey argues the necessity of viable
    parochial schools. While basic public subsidies
    (grants for salaries and building construction)
    should be neither offered by the public nor
    accepted by the church schools, the students in
    parochial should be eligible for educational
    grants directly related to general welfare
    benefits (health services, transportation,
    testing and guidance services, and tax credits).

91. McGarry, Daniel D. and Leo Ward. Educational
    Freedom and the Case for Government Aid to
    Students in Independent Schools. Milwaukee:
    The Bruce Publishing Company, 1966.

    Fifteen articles by highly regarded scholars
    covering various aspects of the public aid

question.   The essays, all sympathetic to some
form of public assistance, deal with the
historical and philosophical background of
public aid in pluralistic America as well as in
other nations.   In addition, the economic,
social, and constitutional questions are
examined, and a local community's effort to
secure public assistance for private schools is
explored.   Bibliography included.

92.   Morgan, Richard E.   The Supreme Court and
       Religion.   New York: The Free Press, 1972.

       Narrative account of the Supreme Court's
       First Amendment decisions through 1970.
       Examines these decisions in their historical,
       political, legal, and social setting.

93.   Murray, John Courtney.   We Hold These Truths.
       New York: Sheed and Ward, Inc., 1960.

       Highly regarded and innovative articulation
       of a Catholic doctrine of religious liberty as
       it relates to the experience and ideology of
       American democracy.   Recognizing the "lay"
       character of the state under the First
       Amendment, Murray insists that the state is
       responsible for ensuring religious liberty but
       it is not obligated to aid the religious
       education of the child.   On the other hand,
       Murray rejects an exaggerated doctrine of
       separation and calls for the accommodation of
       the spiritual needs of religious people.   In
       chapter Six, "The School Question," Murray
       states that while public support for sectarian
       schools is not required, it should be allowable.
       For the state to foreclose any occasion to
       support private schools, would be to establish
       the religion of secularism.

40   Religious Schools in America

Pfeffer, Leo. Church, State and Freedom.
Boston: Beacon Press, 1967.
* See item 22.

94. Powell, Theodore. The School Bus Law.
    Middletown, CT: Wesleyan University Press,
    1960.

    Case study of busing as a method of public
    assistance to sectarian schools in Connecticut
    in 1956-57. Analyzes the role of religious
    groups as a political force and suggests how
    such groups can influence public policy without
    generating political divisiveness.

95. Schwarz, Alan. "No Imposition of Religion: The
    Establishment Clause Value." Yale Law Review
    77 (1968): 692-737.

    Insists that the Court should adopt an
    interpretation of the First Amendment which
    unifies the Free Exercise and Establishment
    Clauses. Suggesting that the Court must be more
    precise in balancing the various claims of
    equality, neutrality, secular purpose, and aid
    to religion, Schwarz proposes that the First
    Amendment should be read to prohibit only aid
    which has as its "motive or substantial effect
    the imposition of religious belief or practice."
    Under this "no-imposition" standard,
    accommodation and aid to private schools is
    permissible.

96. Slough, M. C. and Patrick D. McAnany.
    "Government Aid to Church-Related Schools:
    An Analysis." Kansas Law Review 11 (1962):
    35-75.

    Informative, largely unbiased, historical
    examination of the issue of church-state

relations. Outlines issues beginning with the colonial period and ending with McCollum vs. Board of Education, and considers arguments in both support and opposition to public assistance.

Sorauf, Frank J. The Wall of Separation: The Constitutional Politics of Church and State. Princeton: Princeton University Press, 1976.

* See item 26.

Stokes, Anson Phelps and Leo Pfeffer. Church and State in the United States. 3 vols. New York: Harper and Row, Publishers, 1964.

* See item 27.

97. Stravinskas, P.M.J. "The Constitutionality of Federal Aid to Parents of Nonpublic School Children." Catholic Lawyer 27 (1982): 301-315.

Thoughtful interpretation of how the First Amendment should be applied to the Federal assistance debate. The author calls for the courts to examine the historical facts which he believes support the constitutionality of federal aid.

98. Swanson, Auston D. and Joseph A. Igoe, eds. Should Public Monies Be Spent to Support Nonpublic Education: A Review of the Issues and Practices. Danville, IL: Interstate Printers and Publishers, Inc., 1967.

Helpful review of the historical development and the philosophical issues (in a pro-con format) concerning public support for nonpublic schools. Also examines mid-1960's status of governmental assistance on a state by state

basis, as well as public support in other
countries.

99. Swomley, John M. , Jr. *Religion, the State and
    the Schools.* New York: Pegasus Press,
    1968.

    Warning by a strict and total separationist
    that any public support to religious schools
    imperils the independence of the church and the
    neutrality of the state. Insists that public
    subsidization of even the allegedly secular
    programs of sectarian schools involves the
    coercion of nonbelievers through taxation to
    benefit a faith they have not accepted.
    Concerned about the sectarian spirit of the
    hierarchy of the Church, Swomley proposes that
    education is essentially a function of the
    state.

Part II: Contemporary

100. Alexander, Kern and K. Forbis Jordan.
     Constitutional Reform of School Finance.
     Lexington, MA: Lexington Books, 1973.

     Analysis of various issues of public and
     private school finance. Part II, concentrating
     on public aid to nonpublic schools, evaluates
     the recommendations of President Nixon's
     Commission on School Finance for the
     strengthening of private schools through tax
     credits and vouchers. Various forms of
     educational vouchers are examined and positions
     both supporting and opposing such vouchers are
     presented.

101. Arons, Stephen. "The Separation of School and
     State: *Pierce* Reconsidered." *Harvard
     Educational Review* 46 (1976): 76-104.

Argues that the Free Exercise Clause of the
First Amendment and Pierce vs. Society of
Sisters are rendered meaningless unless parents
can afford private education for their
children. Tuition tax credits for elementary
and secondary education are constitutionally
permissible. Such credits would have the
direct effect of providing parents a choice in
the education of children, while having only an
indirect and incidental effect on the religion
sponsoring the educational institution.
Parents unable to exercise choice are subject
to state-sponsored educational socialization.
Furthermore, the Equal Protection Clause of the
Fourteenth Amendment should be read to prevent
the double taxation inherent in a system in
which parents pay private school tuition
without the option for tuition credits.

102. Canavan, Francis. "The Impact of Recent Court
      Decisions on Religion in the U. S." Journal
      of Church and State 16 (1974): 217-236.

Criticizes court decisions which limit or
prevent public aid to private, parochial
schools. Such decisions tend to segregate
considerations of morality and religion from
public life and the political dialogue. They
also result in an increasingly secular culture
and the eroding of government authority to
protect public morals and the community
conscience.

103. Choper, Jesse, H. "The Religion Clauses of the
      First Amendment: Reconciling the Conflict."
      University of Pittsburgh Law Review 41
      (1980): 673-701.

Criticizes the Court for not providing an
adequate standard to determine when an
accommodation of religion, as required under

the Free Exercise Clause, constitutes
impermissible aid proscribed by the
Establishment Clause. As a way of resolving
the tension between these two First Amendment
principles, Choper proposes a standard that
"the Establishment Clause should forbid only
government action whose purpose is solely
religious and that is likely to impair
religious freedom by coercing, compromising, or
influencing religious beliefs." Also
criticizes the Court for its recent, simplistic
tendency to focus on whether public aid to
sectarian schools generates political
divisiveness in the community.

104. Cogdell, Gaston. What Price Parochiaid?
      Silver Springs, MD: Americans United for
      Separation of Church and State, 1970.

      Argues that the adverse effects of
      government aid to parochial schools will be
      strongly felt by both the church and the state.
      Parochiaid creates potential governmental
      control over the church, threatening the
      independence of the church and generating
      hostility and anti-clericism. Any type of
      financial assistance (whether direct public
      subsidies, tax credits, or tax deductions) is
      compulsory public support for church activity
      and thus violates the First Amendment.

105. Coons, John E. and Stephen D. Sugerman.
      Education by Choice: The Case for Family
      Control. Berkeley and Los Angeles:
      University of California Press, 1978.

      Sympathetic to state governmental assistance
      in providing parents with the means to send
      children to private schools. Public support is
      necessary, particularly to low-income families,
      if parents are to have a true choice in

educating their children. Examines
theoretical concerns and practical issues
with regard to tuition vouchers.

106. Crockenberg, Vincent A. "An Argument for the
      Constitutionality of Direct Aid to Religious
      Schools." Journal of Law and Education 13
      (1984): 1-18.

      Insists that the Supreme Court has
      overreacted in its position that public aid to
      private schools will create political
      divisiveness in the community. The religious
      divisiveness argument is both empirically and
      historically doubtful. Furthermore, the Court
      has distorted the Establishment Clause in
      declaring public assistance unconstitutional.

107. The Fleishman Report on the Quality, Cost, and
      Financing of Elementary and Secondary
      Education in New York State. New York:
      Viking Press, 1973.

      Three-volume, extensively researched and
      documented study and recommendation concerning
      the quality, governance, organization, and
      financing of elementary and secondary schools
      in New York. Volume one contains chapters on
      aid to nonpublic schools and concludes that
      public funds, tax revenues, and tuition
      vouchers should not be used to support
      sectarian schools. Although short-term
      economic factors suggest the necessity of
      continuing incidental aid, in the long run,
      government assistance to private schools is
      neither desirable nor warranted.

108. Frey, Donald E. Tuition Tax Credits for
      Private Education: An Economic Analysis.
      Ames, IA: Iowa State University Press,
      1983.

With the constitutionality of tuition deductions and potential tax subsidies having been settled in <u>Mueller</u> v. <u>Allen,</u> the author suggests the need to shift the debate to the wisdom and policy implications of such programs. Issues addressed include the loss of governmental revenue under a tax credit program, the possibility of increased racial segregation, and the potential decline in public support for public schools. The study includes the historical and legal background of tuition tax allowances and an econometric study of the private education market.

Gaffney, Edward McGlynn Jr. , ed. <u>Private Schools and the Public Good: Policy Alternatives for the Eighties</u>. Notre Dame: University of Notre Dame Press, 1981.

* See item 11.

109. Gey, Steve. "Rebuilding the Wall: The Case for a Return to the Strict Interpretation of the Establishment Clause." <u>Columbia Law Review</u> 81 (1981): 1463-1490.

Criticizes the Court for dismantling the "strict separation" doctrine of <u>Everson</u> v. <u>Board of Education,</u> for failing to develop an adequate replacement standard, and for generating two decades of decisions which are contradictory, confusing and unsupportable. Suggests a theory of "strict neutrality" which would clarify the issue and prevent any public aid, whether direct or indirect, from being given to private schools.

110. Goldberg, George. <u>Reconsecrating America</u>. Grand Rapids: William B. Eerdmans Publishing Co. , 1984.

Highly critical of the Supreme Court's decisions on church-state relations, particularly those rulings concerning government support of parochial schools, prayer in schools, and religious symbols in public places. Attacks the Court's interpretation of the First Amendment as misguided, confusing, destructive of the financial solvency of religious education, and an unreasonable excising of all religious references from public schools.

111. "Government Neutrality and Separation of Church and State: Tuition Tax Credits." Harvard Law Review 92 (1979): 696-717.

Examines the First Amendment principles of neutrality, voluntarism and separation of church and state and concludes that government tax and spend policies burden the principles of voluntarism and neutrality by creating incentives for parents to select secular, public schools rather than private schools. However, excessive public aid would violate the separation principle. Suggests ways of balancing these First Amendment rights by disallowing direct grants but permitting tuition tax benefits.

112. Gunther, Gerald. Cases and Materials on Constitutional Law. 11th ed. Mineola, NY: The Foundation Press, Inc., 1985.

Standard, comprehensive casebook. Includes excerpts from important Supreme Court decisions, introductory notes and essays, and bibliographic material. Chapter Fourteen, "The Constitution and Religion: Establishment and Free Exercise," deals with the issues of public aid to religious schools.

113. Hopson, Mark D. "State Aid to Parochial
      Schools: A Quantitative Analysis."
      Georgetown Law Journal 71 (1983): 1063-1089.

      Suggests that the Supreme Court, in
      addressing the primary effects of parochiaid
      constitutionality, considers two analytical
      categories: qualitative and quantitative.
      Qualitative analysis considers the type of aid
      and how the aid is distributed. Quantitative
      analysis involves how much aid is given and to
      whom it is provided. Argues that greater
      attention should be given to quantitative
      analysis and the guarantee of quantitative
      neutrality so that public aid is permitted only
      when it is not disproportionate to the size of
      the group to whom it is given.

114. James, Thomas and Henry M. Levin, eds. Public
      Dollars for Private Schools: The Case for
      Tuition Tax Credits. Philadelphia: Temple
      University Press, 1983.

      Scholars from a variety of
      disciplines--economics, history, political
      science, public policy and education--examine
      the issues surrounding government reduction of
      tax liability as a partial reimbursement for
      tuition costs. Arguments for public aid
      (preventing double financial burdens,
      increasing parental choice, enhancing the
      quality and diversity of education) are
      balanced against arguments opposed to public
      assistance (undermining the wall of separation,
      creating social-economic stratification and
      racial isolation, and denial of common
      education and socialization for students).

115. Kelly, George A. , ed. Government Aid to
      Nonpublic Schools: Yes or No? New York:
      St. John's University Press, 1972.

From a 1971 symposium, these essays are
generally sympathetic evaluations of parochiaid
on questions of public policy, legislative
control and constitutionality. Highly critical
of the findings and the personnel composition
of the New York state sponsored Fleishman
Report (which concluded that aid to parochial
schools is unwarranted).

Kurland, Philip B. and Gerhard Casper, eds.
    Landmark Briefs and Arguments of the Supreme
    Court of the United States: Constitutional
    Law. Frederick, MD: University
    Publications of America, Inc.

* See item 83.

116. LaNoue, George R. , ed. Educational Vouchers:
      Concepts and Controversies. New York:
      Teacher's College Press of Columbia
      University, 1972.

Useful collection of essays by supporters
and opponents of a voucher system of education.
Juxtaposing the relevant political, economic,
and legal questions, the authors debate a
change from using taxes to finance public
education to a system providing tuition
vouchers to parents who then purchase education
for their children in the marketplace of
diverse schools.

117. Leitch, David G. "The Myth of Religious
      Neutrality by Separation in Education."
      Virginia Law Review 71 (1985): 127-172.

A thorough discourse on the problems of
separation and neutrality between government
and religion. Argues that the complete
separation of church and state is impossible
and that a system of education which purposely

excludes traditional religion violates the
First Amendment's neutrality requirement.
Suggests that the rigid, separationist
interpretation of the First Amendment should be
abandoned in favor of an interpretation that
requires integrating religion, along with other
ideological competitors in our comprehensive
value system, into the pluralistic marketplace
of education.

118. Lowell, C. Stanley. The Great Church-State
     Fraud. Washington, DC: Robert B. Luce,
     Inc., 1973.

     Strict separation between church and state
     serves financial and functional purposes for
     both the church and the state. Highly critical
     of the various disguises (child-benefit theory,
     textbook loans and others) by which government
     subsidizes, and subsequently uses, the church
     as an instrument of socialization. In the end,
     there is a compromising of the secular
     integrity of the government and the spiritual
     significance of the church.

119. McCarthy, Martha M. A Delicate Balance:
     Church, State and the Schools. Bloomington:
     Phi Delta Kappan Educational Foundation,
     1983.

     Comprehensive, but concise, summary and
     analysis of the legal developments and
     implications of church-state relations through
     1983. Examines Supreme Court decisions and
     their progeny at the lower federal court and
     state court level on the issues of
     transportation aid, publicly loaned textbooks,
     diagnostic and remedial services, state
     prescribed testing, and tuition tax relief.

120. McCarthy, Martha M. "Separation or
     Accommodation?" Harvard Educational Review
     51 (1981): 373-394.

     Asserts that First Amendment guarantees are
     being compromised and threatened by
     increasingly active state legislators who, in
     turn, are being increasingly pressured by
     religious groups. Suggests that as legislative
     assemblies are being more assertive, the courts
     are becoming lenient in permitting public aid
     to private schools.

     Pfeffer, Leo. Religion, State and the Burger
         Court. Buffalo: Prometheus Books, 1984.

     * See item 24.

121. Schotten, Peter M. "The Establishment Clause
     and Excessive Governmental Entanglement:
     The Constitutional Status of Aid to
     Nonpublic Elementary and Secondary Schools."
     Wake Forest Law Review 15 (1979): 207-249.

     Focusing on the Supreme Court's "excessive
     entanglement" test, the author criticizes the
     fragmented, ill-conceived, and unpersuasive
     rulings since Walz v. Tax Commission. Insists
     that the Court is unfortunately engaged in
     incremental, legislative-style policy making
     without the benefit of legislative information
     or tools. Fears that the unworkable tests used
     by the Court in church-state litigation has
     exposed its inability to articulate valid
     constitutional standards.

122. Sullivan, Daniel J. Public Aid to Nonpublic
     Schools. Lexington, MA: D.C. Heath and
     Co. , 1974.

Primarily an economic and public policy analysis of the school aid issue. Examines the market conditions and the traditional arguments for public assistance to private schools and concludes that there is little empirical evidence or theoretical justification to support such assistance.

123.   U. S. Congress. Senate. Committee on Finance. Hearings on the Educational Opportunity and Equity Act of 1982 Relating to Tuition Tax Credits for Elementary and Secondary Education. 97th Cong. , 2nd sess. , 1982.

Hearings before the Senate Committee on Finance on a federal bill which would provide provisional tax credits for tuition paid to private, non-racially discriminatory elementary and secondary schools. Position papers and arguments presented by various interest groups on economic, societal, educational and constitutional grounds. Among the groups represented are the American Civil Liberties Union, the American Federation of Teachers, Americans United for Separation of Church and State, the Moral Majority, and the League of Women Voters.

124.   U. S. Congress. Senate. Subcommittee on Taxation and Debt Management of the Committee on Finance. Hearings on the Tuition Tax Relief Act of 1981. 97th Cong. , 1st sess. , 1981.

Hearings before the Senate Subcommittee on Taxation and Debt Management on a federal act which would provide tax credits for a portion of tuition and fees paid by parents of children attending private elementary and secondary schools. Numerous interest groups, including the Heritage Foundation, the American Civil

Liberties Union, the Catholic Conference,
Citizens for Educational Freedom, the National
Education Association, the American Interprise
Institute, the Moral Majority, the American
United for Separation of Church and State,
present position papers concerning the
economic, social, educational and
constitutional issues involved in the
legislation.

125. Weber, Paul J. and Dennis A. Gilbert. Private
Churches and Public Money: Church-
Government Fiscal Relations. Westport, CT:
Greenwood Press, 1981.

From a fiscal policy perspective, the
authors objectively and systematically
integrate constitutional law and the economic,
public policy considerations of the church-
state question. Advocating a policy of "fiscal
neutrality" which is faithful to the principles
of equal treatment endorsed by the religion
provisions of the First Amendment, the authors
examine their policy in terms of its
efficiency, effectiveness, responsiveness, and
equity.

126. West, E. G. Nonpublic School Aid: The Law,
Economics and Politics of American
Education. Lexington, MA: Lexington Books,
1976.

Informative exchange, through a series of
essays and rebuttals between West and experts
in the fields of law, economics and education,
on the issue of public aid to nonpublic
schools. West contends that private schools
play a valuable role in society, while public
monopolization of education tends to raise
costs while lowering quality and efficiency.
West proposes and argues the virtues of tuition

tax deductions, public school user's fees and
other plans to advance the cause of private
education. He also calls upon the courts to
return to the original purposes of the First
Amendment which were to prevent official
sanction of a single orthodoxy while
encouraging the free competition of ideas.

CHAPTER 4
STATE REGULATION OF RELIGIOUS SCHOOLS
James C. Carper

127. Arons, Stephen. Compelling Belief: The
Culture of American Schooling. New York:
McGraw-Hill Book Company, 1983.

Examines conflicts between families and
state authorities over school policies and
practices, including the clash between
fundamentalist Christians and state authorities
in Kentucky over regulation of their schools.

128. Bainton, Denise M. "State Regulation of
Private Religious Schools and the State's
Interest in Education." Arizona Law Review
25 (1983): 123-49.

Analyzes the three-part test for resolving
the conflict between state approval
requirements for private religious schools and
the right to the free exercise of religion.
Reviews cases involving parental choice and
state interest in education. Cautions that
standardized testing may result in more rather
than less regulation of religious schools.
Urges carefully tailored regulations when the
educational goals of the state burden free
exercise of religion.

129.   Baker, Michael D.   "Regulation of
       Fundamentalist Christian Schools: Free
       Exercise of Religion v. the State's Interest
       in Quality Education."   Kentucky Law Journal
       67 (1978-79): 415-29.

       Reviews the issues involved in Kentucky
       State Board for Elementary and Secondary
       Education v.   Radasill (1979), in which the
       Kentucky Supreme Court invalidated textbook
       approval, curriculum, and teacher certification
       standards.   Argues that state regulations did
       not significantly burden the fundamentalist
       schools involved in the case.

130.   Ball, William B.   Constitutional Protection of
       Christian Schools.   Whittier, CA:
       Association of Christian Schools
       International, 1981.

       Argues that the state may not control,
       dictate, or supervise the religious mission of
       a religious school.   Claims that the state may
       reasonably regulate in a limited number of
       areas, namely, health, safety, sanitation, and
       core curriculum.

131.   Ball, William B.   Preserving America's
       Educational Freedom.   Public Policy
       Education Fund, Inc., Special Report #27,
       September 1984.

       Reviews three critical dimensions of the
       controversy over state regulation of religious
       schools: "vagueness versus clarity in
       regulatory laws," "government prescriptions
       versus 'proof in the pudding,'" and "compelling
       state interest versus entanglement."   Asserts
       that state regulation must be kept at a minimum
       in order to protect religious and educational
       freedom.

132. Binder, Timothy J. "Douglas vs. Faith Baptist
     Church Under Constitutional Scrutiny."
     Nebraska Law Review 61 (Spring 1982): 74-97.

     Criticizes the Nebraska Supreme Court's
     decision in Douglas v. Faith Baptist Church,
     in which the court upheld the application of
     state licensing and teacher certification
     requirements to a fundamentalist school
     operated by Faith Baptist Church of Louisville,
     Nebraska. Reviews free exercise of religion
     issues and concludes that the court failed to
     give adequate weight to the fundamental right
     of parents to direct the education of their
     children.

133. Bird, Wendell R. "Freedom from Establishment
     and Unneutrality in Public School
     Instruction and Religious School
     Regulation." Harvard Journal of Law and
     Public Policy 2 (June 1979): 125-205.

     Analyzes the meaning of the establishment
     clause of the First Amendment. Argues that the
     free exercise and establishment clauses are
     violated by burdensome state regulation of
     religious schools.

134. Blaunstein, Phyllis L. "Public and Nonpublic
     Schools: Finding Ways to Work Together."
     Phi Delta Kappan 67 (January 1986): 368-372.

     Describes sources of conflict between public
     officials and private schools over the proper
     extent of state regulation. Discusses
     structures in four states for enhancing
     communication between public and private
     officials. Claims that these structures have
     led to productive dialogue and cooperative
     relationships.

135. Carper, James C. "The Whisner Decision: A
      Case Study in State Regulation of Christian
      Day Schools." Journal of Church and State
      24 (Spring 1982): 282-301.

      Examines the context of the Ohio Supreme
      Court decision State v. Whisner (1976), in
      which the court ruled that the state's
      regulatory system as applied to a Christian
      school violated free exercise of religion and
      parental rights. Reviews the issues involved
      in the case and asserts that future attempts by
      state agencies to regulate church ministries
      will likely lead to more litigation.

136. Carper, James C. , and Neal E. Devins.
      "Rendering Unto Caesar: State Regulation of
      Christian Day Schools." Journal of Thought
      20 (Winter 1985): 99-113.

      Describes the nature of the controversy
      between state officials and Christian school
      leaders. Provides examples of the
      "negotiation, legislation, and litigation"
      strategy used by Christian educators. Analyzes
      conflicting judicial approaches to the
      controversy (Ohio and Nebraska) and concludes
      that challenges to state regulation will
      continue as long as government officials remain
      committed to the values of standardization and
      centralization.

137. Carper, James C. , and Neal E. Devins. "The
      State and the Church School." In Religion
      and the State: Essays in Honor of Leo
      Pffefer, pp. 211-232. Edited by James E.
      Wood, Jr. , Waco: Baylor University Press,
      1985.

      Discusses the nature of the controversy
      between state education officials and Christian

educators. Examines the issues courts face
when deciding cases involving state regulation
of religious schools. Reviews conflicting
judicial resolutions of this controversy.
Concludes that court decisions will likely
remain at odds with one another until the U.S.
Supreme Court addresses the problem.

138. Daley, Richard C. "Public Regulation of
    Private Religious Schools." Ohio State Law
    Journal 37 (Fall 1976): 899-925.

    Discusses the scope and effect of the Ohio
    Supreme Court's decision in State v. Whisner
    (1976). Argues that the court was too
    deferential to the free exercise claims of
    Whisner and Tabernacle Christian School.
    Asserts that the state has an important
    interest in supervising private religious
    schools.

139. Devins, Neal E. "State Regulation of Christian
    Schools." Journal of Legislation 10 (Summer
    1983): 351-381.

    Analyzes the positions and policy arguments
    of Christian school leaders and state education
    officials. Argues that in light of conflicting
    decisions in state regulation cases, the courts
    should adopt a standard of review that will
    lead to predictable outcomes. Contends that
    courts should require the state to offer "clear
    and convincing proof" that its regulatory
    system is the least restrictive means available
    to satisfy its interest in providing all
    children an educational opportunity.

140. Diehl, Barbara R. "The Right to Regulate
    Nonpublic Education." Urban Lawyer 15
    (Winter 1983): 97-111.

Describes the general framework of state
regulation of private schools. Reviews
regulation of nonpublic schools in New York
that requires such schools to provide a
substantially equivalent education. Recommends
that the state department make the
determination of equivalency rather than the
courts or local agencies.

141. Drake, Jeffrey A. "Attempted State Control of
      the Religious School." Ohio Northern Law
      Review 7 (October 1980): 954-974.

      Approves of the Ohio Supreme Court's
      decision in State v. Whisner (1976), which
      effectively deregulated independent, religious
      schools. Argues that the state has a
      legitimate interest in the "products" of
      religious schools (students' reading, writing,
      and computing proficiency), but not in the
      "recipe" (teacher qualifications, textbook
      selection, and instructional methods).

142. Erickson, Donald A., ed. Public Controls for
      Nonpublic Schools. Chicago: University of
      Chicago Press, 1969.
      Contains materials from a national
      invitational conference on "State Regulation of
      Nonpublic Schools," sponsored by the Midwest
      Administration Center, University of Chicago,
      March 1967. Discusses conflicts between state
      agencies and the Amish, the rationale for state
      regulation, legal issues, racial equality in
      nonpublic schools, and the relationship between
      public funding and state control. Focuses on
      how nonpublic education can be both free and
      responsible.

143. Evenson, J. Eric II. "State Regulation of
      Private Religious Schools in North
      Carolina--A Model Approach." Wake Forest
      Law Review 16 (June 1980): 405-437.

Describes the 1979 North Carolina statute that exempts private religious schools from state regulation. Argues that it is a constitutionally acceptable approach to balancing state interests and parental and free exercise rights.

144. Higgins, Michael J. "State vs. Faith Baptist Church: State Regulation of Religious Education." Creighton Law Review 15 (1981): 183-195.

Discusses the free exercise and establishment clauses in the context of the Nebraska Supreme Court's ruling in Faith Baptist Church (1981). Maintains that Faith Baptist's case was weak and the court made a reasonable effort to accommodate the church's free exercise rights.

145. Johnson, Gene. "Fundamentalist Christians vs. Nebraska: The Conflict Over the Regulation of Private Schools, 1977-1984." Ed. D. dissertation. University of Kansas, 1985.

Describes the recent conflict in Nebraska between several fundamentalist churches, particularly Faith Baptist Church of Louisville, and state authorities over regulation of religious schools.

146. Kinder, Paul A. "The Regulation and Accreditation of Non-Public Schools in the United States." Ed. D. dissertation. University of Missouri-Columbia, 1982.

Examines laws and regulations that affect the operation of nonpublic schools in the United States. Surveys state departments of education, accrediting associations, and court cases dealing with accreditation of nonpublic schools.

147. Lines, Patricia M. "Private Education Alternatives and State Regulation." _Journal of Law and Education_ 12 (April 1983): 189-234.

Discusses the rapid growth of home schooling and Christian day schools. Reviews existing state regulation on nonpublic education and its constitutional and public policy implications. Recommends alterations of compulsory school attendance laws to accommodate nonpublic education options. Includes lists of basic compulsory school attendance requirements by state.

148. Lines, Patricia M. "State Regulation of Private Education." _Phi Delta Kappan_ 63 (October 1982): 119-123.

Reviews trends in state regulation of private education, recent court cases involving fundamentalist schools, and public policy issues. Urges cooperation among all parties concerned.

149. Mawdsley, Ralph D. and Steven P. Permuth. _Legal Problems of Religious and Private Schools._ Topeka: National Organization on Legal Problems of Education, 1983.

Examines legal problems facing nonpublic schools, including governmental regulation.

150. Mawdsley, Ralph D. and Steven P. Permuth. "State Regulation of Religious Schools." _NOLPE School Law Journal_ 11 (1983): 55-64.

Suggests that recent conflicts between religious schools and state authorities seeking to regulate them are the result of the failure of the United States Supreme Court to clarify free exercise and establishment clause guidelines as they apply to such conflicts.

151. McCoy, Deborah S. "State Regulation of Private Church Schools: An Examination of Vermont's Act 151." Vermont Law Review 8 (Spring 1983): 75-118.

Analyzes constitutional arguments employed by fundamentalists against state regulation of their schools. Discusses the Vermont legislature's response to the Vermont Supreme Court's ruling in State v. LaBarge (1976), which effectively undermined the laws on compulsory education and private school approval. Expresses concern that the legislature's response, Act 151, contains a loophole whereby private schools can escape regulation.

152. McLaughlin, Raymond. A History of State Legislation Affecting Private Elementary and Secondary Schools in the United States, 1870-1945. Washington, DC: Catholic University of America Press, 1946.

Traces the development of state legislation related to supervision of nonpublic schools.

153. Murren, Philip J. and Bob W. Brown. "Church Schools, State Regulation: Two Views." Church and State, May 1980, pp. 6-10.

Presents two perspectives on the extent to which state authorities may regulate private, especially church-related schools.

154. O'Reilly, Robert C., and Fellman, Beverly. The
      Clash Between Private Religious Schools and
      State Regulations. Arlington, VA: ERIC
      Document Reproduction Service, ED 221 921,
      1983.

      Reviews court decisions concerning state
      regulation of religious schools. Examines
      legislative attempts to resolve the recent
      controversy in Nebraska between Faith Baptist
      Church and state officials.

155. "The Report of the Governor's Christian School
      Issue Panel." By Robert M. Spire, Chairman.
      Lincoln, NE, January 26, 1984.

      Discusses the controversy in Nebraska
      concerning state regulation of Christian
      schools. Analyzes public policy and legal
      issues. Asserts that several state regulations
      are too restrictive when applied to Christian
      schools. Recommends exemption from state
      licensing and teacher certification
      requirements.

156. Saltsman, Robert. "State vs. Whisner: State
      Minimum Educational Standards and Non-Public
      Religious Schools." Ohio Northern
      University Law Review 4 (July 1977):
      710-719.

      Reviews the Ohio Supreme Court's decision in
      State v. Whisner. Claims that the court did
      not give adequate consideration to the state's
      compelling interest in maintaining minimum
      educational standards for private schools.

157. Shugrue, Richard E. "An Approach to Mutual
      Respect: The Christian Schools
      Controversy." Creighton Law Review 18
      (1985): 219-257.

Reviews the confusing background of free
exercise and establishment clause analysis in
order to construct a general framework for the
resolution of conflicts over state regulation
of religious schools. Discusses religious,
educational, and legal issues involved in the
recent confrontation between Nebraska
authorities and fundamentalist Christian
educators. Criticizes the Nebraska Supreme
Court for being overly deferential to state
interests. Urges legislative rather than
judicial solutions.

158. Van Geel, Tyll. "Religious and Nonreligious
    Private Schools: The Constitution and State
    Regulation." Paper presented at the annual
    meeting of the American Educational Research
    Association, Chicago, April 3, 1985.

    Suggests that one of the most immature areas
    of constitutional law is that which deals with
    state regulation of private schools. Explores
    the ambiguities of current judicial reasoning
    concerning this problem. Outlines in
    considerable detail an approach for resolving
    constitutional confrontations that "tilts" in
    favor of accepting risks associated with
    underregulation and against accepting the risks
    of overregulation.

159. West, Cynthia W. "The State and Sectarian
    Education: Regulation to Deregulation."
    Duke Law Journal (1980): 801-846.

    Examines the constitutional boundaries
    within which the state may regulate private
    schools. Uses cases from Ohio, Kentucky, and
    North Carolina as a basis for analysis.
    Expresses concerns about the results of
    deregulation of religious schools in North
    Carolina and elsewhere.

CHAPTER 5
AMISH SCHOOLS
Albert N. Keim

Part I: Historical

160. Arnold, Eberhard. Children's Education in
     Community. Rifton, NY: Plough Publishing
     House, 1976.

     Concise essay on Hutterian educational
     purpose as understood by a leader of the
     Society of Brothers.

161. Backgrounds of The Old Order Mennonite
     Parochial Schools of Pennsylvania.
     Gordonville, PA: 1969.

     Compilation of petitions to Pennsylvania
     School authorities regarding Amish Parochial
     School concerns from 1937 to 1969.

162. Beiler, Aaron E. Record of Principles
     Pertaining to the Old Order Amish Church
     Sect School Committee. Reaffirmed and
     approved through counsel of the committee,
     August 9, 1961. Gap, PA: School Committee,
     1961.

     Excellent formal statement of policy
     regarding Amish purposes in education. These
     standards govern nearly all Amish Schools.

163. <u>Blackboard</u> <u>Bulletin</u>. Pathway Publishers,
     Aylmer, Ontario, Canada.

     Monthly magazine for Amish and "plain"
     Mennonite teachers and parochial school
     patrons.

164. Buchanan, Frederick S. "The Old Path: A Study
     of Amish Response to Public Schooling in
     Ohio." Ph.D. dissertation. Ohio State
     University, 1967.

     A pioneering study of Amish objections and
     actions in response to pressure by public
     school officials to enforce compulsory
     attendance in public schools.

165. Byler, Uria R. <u>School</u> <u>Bells</u> <u>Ringing:</u> <u>A</u> <u>Manual</u>
     <u>for</u> <u>Amish</u> <u>Teachers</u> <u>and</u> <u>Parents</u>. Aylmer,
     Ontario: Pathway Publishing Corporation,
     1969.

     A practical teachers' handbook and resource
     book written for Amish teachers by an Amish
     teacher.

     Erickson, Donald A. <u>Public</u> <u>Controls</u> <u>for</u> <u>Non-</u>
     <u>Public</u> <u>Schools</u>. Chicago, IL: University of
     Chicago Press, 1969.

     * See item 143.

166. Hostetler, John A. <u>Anabaptist</u> <u>Conception</u> <u>of</u>
     <u>Child</u> <u>Nurture</u> <u>and</u> <u>Schooling:</u> <u>A</u> <u>Collection</u>
     <u>of</u> <u>Source</u> <u>Material</u> <u>Used</u> <u>by</u> <u>the</u> <u>Old</u> <u>Order</u>
     <u>Amish</u>. Philadelphia, PA: Temple
     University, 1968.

     This is a valuable source book of basic
     documents from Amish history beginning in the
     16th century. The most recent source document
     is 1966.

167. Hostetler, John A. Education and Marginality
      in the Communal Society of the Hutterites.
      University Park, PA: Pennsylvania State
      University, 1965.

      An investigation of how moral values are
      transmitted to children in a communal society.
      The research found four factors - overemphasis
      on the individual, breakdown in the balance of
      power between the family and the colony,
      leadership failure, and idiosyncrasy - which
      lead to the marginalizing of Hutterite members.

168. Hostetler, John A. "Education in Communitarian
      Societies; the Old Order Amish and the
      Hutterian Brethern." In Education and
      Cultural Process, pp. 119-135. Edited by
      George Spindler. New York: Holt, Rinehart
      and Winston, 1974.

      Amish and Huttterite societies differ
      greatly in organization and form, but their
      fundamental need to make education integral to
      their culture is shared by both. This essay
      analyses how each community organizes its
      educational efforts to achieve its purposes.

169. Hostetler, John A. and Gertrude Enders
      Huntington. Children in Amish Society:
      Socialization and Community Education. New
      York: Holt, Rinehart and Winston, 1971.

      Demonstrates the powerful effects of
      education when formal schooling is indigenous
      to its social and cultural context. The
      research represented by this monograph is a
      basic framework for all subsequent studies of
      Amish education.

170. Huntington, Abbie Gertrude Enders. "Dove At
     the Window: A Study of An Old Order Amish
     Community in Ohio." Ph.D. dissertation.
     Yale University, 1956.

     Comments of a detailed sociological study of
     an Amish community.

171. Loomis, Charles P. and Carl R. Jantzen.
     "Boundary Maintenance vs. Systemic Linkage
     in School Integration: The Case of the
     Amish in the United States." The Journal of
     the Pakistan Academy for Village Development
     3 (October 1962): 1-25.

     Provides a basic sociological framework for
     the study of the Amish school as a boundary
     maintenance mechanism. A convincing
     demonstration of the importance of Amish
     schools for Amish culture and society.

172. Miller, Wayne. "A Study of Amish Academic
     Achievement." Ph.D. dissertation.
     University of Michigan, 1969.

     Using standardized tests for intelligence
     and achievement, the researcher found that
     Amish schools in a variety of Amish communities
     in the midwest and Ontario perform their
     educational tasks at acceptable levels in
     preparing Amish youngsters for life in Amish
     society.

173. Minimum Standards for the Amish Parochial and
     Vocational Schools of the State of
     Pennsylvania. Adopted and approved by the
     Old Order Book Society, Old Order Amish
     School Committee and the Old Order Mennonite
     School Committee. Gordonville, PA: 1969.

Designed to govern the administration and
practice of Amish and Old Order Mennonite day
schools in Pennsylvania, and as a common
statement for presentation to school
authorities regarding standards to meet state
education laws.

174. Rideman, Peter. Account of Our Religion.
      London: Hodder and Stoughton, Ltd. , 1965.

      This confession is the cornerstone of
      Hutterian faith and practice. The education of
      children was a key concern for Rideman.

175. Stoll, Joseph. Child Training. Aylmer,
      Ontario: Pathway Publishing Corporation,
      1976.

      The Amish love their children and this book
      reflects the warm affection children experience
      in the Amish home, school and community.

176. Stoll, Joseph. The Challenge of the Child.
      Aylmer, Ontario: Pathway Publishing
      Corporation, 1967.

      Consists of a series of articles from the
      Blackboard Bulletin, a school journal published
      for Amish school teachers. The material spans
      the period 1957 - 1966 during a particularly
      robust period of Amish Day School growth.
      Selections are written by Amish teachers and
      preachers. Excellent source material.

177. Stoll, Joseph. Who Shall Educate Our Children.
      Aylmer, Ontario: Pathway Publishing
      Corporation, 1965.

      Summarizes the Amish argument against modern
      consolidated public schools for Amish children.

178. <u>Tips for Teachers</u>. <u>A</u> <u>Handbook for Amish</u>
     <u>Teachers</u>. Aylmer, Ontario: Pathway
     Publishing Corporation, 1970.

     Develops a pedagogical design for teachers
     in Amish schools, most of whom do not have
     formal teacher training.

179. Wittmer, Joe. "Amish Schools Today." <u>School</u>
     <u>Aid Society</u> 99 (April 1971): 227-230.

     Describes the Amish schools in Indiana as of
     1971. Reviews their pedagogy, philosophy of
     education and the specific relationships and
     understandings the Amish school leaders have
     established with the public school officials of
     Indiana.

Part II: Contemporary

180. <u>Complete Reading Program, Grades One to Eight</u>.
     Aylmer, Ontario: Pathway Publishing
     Corporation, 1968 - present.

     Comprehensive effort to provide reading
     instruction materials tailored to Amish pupil
     needs and Amish ideals.

181. <u>Guidelines in Regards to the Old Order Amish or</u>
     <u>Mennonite Parochial Schools</u>. Gordonville,
     PA: Old Order Amish Steering Committee,
     1978.

     The most recent statement for the regulation
     of Amish schools. This statement is used by
     nearly all Amish schools in the United States.

182. Hostetler, John A. <u>Amish Society</u>. Baltimore,
     MD: Johns Hopkins Press, 1980.

Describes the interplay of custom and change as the Amish community faces the challenge of modern society. The chapter on education focuses on the Amish school as an important aspect in the socialization of Amish children into the Amish society. This book is the basic work on the Amish.

183. Hostetler, John A. and Nancy L. Gaines. A Bibliography of the Old Order Amish: Sources Available in English. Philadelphia, PA: Temple University, 1984.

Exhaustive list of materials on all aspects of Amish life and society. This is a necessary tool for research in Amish matters.

184. Keim, Albert N. Compulsory Education and the Amish: The Right Not To Be Modern. Boston, MA: Beacon Press, 1975.

Analyses the implications, for church - state relations and Amish education, of the landmark Wisconsin v. Yoder 406 U.S. 205 (1972) Supreme Court decision freeing Amish children from compulsory schooling beyond the eighth grade. Contributors to the volume include Donald Erickson, John A. Hostetler, Leo Pfeffer and other distinguished legal experts and educators.

185. Wittmer, Joe. "Be Ye A Peculiar People." Contemporary Education 54 (March 1983): 179-183.

Description of an Amish youth's attendance in a public school during World War II. Persuasive argument for Amish private schooling.

CHAPTER 6
BAPTIST SCHOOLS
James C. Carper

Part I: Historical

186. Craft, Robert H. "An Analysis of Protestant
     Parochial Education in America and the
     Relationship to the Baptist Day School
     Movement." Th.M. thesis. Central Baptist
     Theological Seminary, 1957.

     Describes the characteristics and current
     status of the small number of day schools
     affiliated with American Baptist churches
     (seventeen in the Los Angeles area) and
     Southern Baptist churches. Claims that
     American and Southern Baptist Convention
     leaders are generally supportive of public
     education and cautious about Baptist weekday
     schools, excepting pre-school and kindergarten
     programs.

187. Craft, Robert H. "An Analysis of the Baptist
     Elementary Schools in Los Angeles." D.R.E.
     dissertation. Central Baptist Theological
     Seminary, 1959.

Analyzes the origins, organization,
personnel, curriculum, and financing of the
association of Los Angeles Baptist Elementary
Schools (nineteen in 1957, all affiliated with
American Baptist churches).

188. Curran, Francis X. The Churches and the
      Schools: American Protestantism and Popular
      Elementary Education. Chicago: Loyola
      University Press, 1954.

Argues that Baptists in the nineteenth
century, as well as most other Protestant
denominations, refused to defend the
traditional claim of the Christian church to
control elementary education. Asserts that
anti-Catholicism led them to eschew Baptist
primary schools and to embrace common schools,
which were quasi-Protestant institutions.

189. Daniel, W. Harrison. "Southern Baptists and
      Education, 1865-1900: A Case Study."
      Maryland Historical Magazine 64 (Fall 1969):
      218-247.

Describes Baptist educational efforts in
Virginia, including schools for the children of
disabled and deceased Confederate soldiers,
female institutes, and academies. Claims that
a majority of Virginia Baptists supported
public primary schooling.

190. Encyclopedia of Southern Baptists, 1982 index.
      S.v. "Academies, Bible Schools, and
      Institutes."

Indexes historical sketches of approximately
200 Baptist academies and similar institutions
that appear in the four volume Encyclopedia of
Southern Baptists.

191. Ford, Lester H. "A History of San Marcos
     Baptist Academy, 1907-1959." Ed. D.
     dissertation. University of Northern
     Colorado, 1960.

     Traces the development of one of the oldest
     remaining Baptist academies.

192. Gobbel, Luther L. Church-State Relationships
     in North Carolina Since 1776. Durham: Duke
     University Press, 1938.

     Notes that Baptists generally supported the
     state in efforts to establish free schools in
     the 1840s. Describes Baptist efforts to
     establish academies in the absence of public
     high schools in the late nineteenth century.
     Argues that by the 1920s Baptists began to rely
     more on public high schools.

193. Magruder, Edith C. A Historical Study of the
     Educational Agencies of the Southern Baptist
     Convention. New York: Teachers College,
     Columbia University, 1951.

     Analyzes the forces that shaped the
     development of Southern Baptist educational
     institutions. Notes that the number of
     Southern Baptist academies fell from forty-five
     in 1927 to seven in 1946, thus revealing the
     tendency to discourage denominational high
     schools. Contends that like most other
     Protestant bodies Baptists have traditionally
     supported public education and believed that
     public schools could teach morals without
     offending conscience.

194. Ognibene, Richard. "The Baptist Academy
     Movement in the Late Nineteenth Century."
     Foundations 22 (July-September 1979):
     246-260.

Describes the efforts of Northern Baptists
to establish academies between 1870 and 1900.
Argues that though there was much rhetoric, the
results were disappointing. Notes that only
approximately twenty-five academies were
operating in northern and midwestern states in
1900, and only five still exist. Attributes
the failure of the academies movement to
competition from public high schools, historic
Baptist ambivalence toward higher education,
Baptist polity, lack of support from pastors
and local churches, and Baptist opposition to
Catholic parochial schools.

195. Ognibene, Richard. "Catholic and Protestant
     Education in the Late Nineteenth Century."
     Religious Education 77 (January-February
     1982): 5-20.

     Analyzes Protestant and Catholic educational
     strategies in the late nineteenth century.
     Challenges the assertion that Protestants
     embraced the increasingly secular public school
     system because they had Sunday schools to teach
     significant religious truths. Uses Northern
     Baptists as a case in point.

196. Schultz, Joseph R. "A History of Protestant
     Christian Day Schools in the United States."
     Ph.D. dissertation. Southwestern Baptist
     Theological Seminary, 1954.

     Describes the small number (less than fifty)
     of elementary and secondary schools affiliated
     with American and Southern Baptist churches in
     the early 1950s. Claims that the Southern
     Baptist Convention was divided on the
     feasibility of day schools.

197. Slaught, Lawrence T. Multiplying the Witness:
     150 Years of American Baptist Educational

Baptist Schools 79

Ministries. Valley Forge, PA: Judson
Press, 1974.

Reviews the development of various American
Baptist educational efforts, including a small
number of secondary schools.

198. Vandever, William T. "An Educational History
of the English and American Baptists in the
Seventeenth and Eighteenth Centuries."
Ph.D. dissertation. University of
Pennsylvania, 1974.

Examines the educational theories and
achievements of the seventeenth and eighteenth
century Particular Baptists in England and
America.

199. Wilson, Carl B. The Baptist Manual Labor
School Movement in the United States. Waco:
Baylor University Press, 1937.

Describes the origin, development, and
significance of the antebellum Baptist manual
labor school movement. Argues that manual
labor schools represented a compromise between
those who opposed special training for
ministers and those who advocated academic
education for ministers. Points out that many
of these secondary schools were converted into
colleges.

200. Withoft, Mabel S. Oak and Laurel: A Study of
the Mountain Mission Schools of the Southern
Baptists. Nashville: Sunday School Board
of the Southern Baptist Convention, 1923.

Describes most of the academies and
institutes founded by Southern Baptists in the
early twentieth century to educate the children
of the southern Appalachian and Ozark
mountains.

Part II: Contemporary

201. Byrom, Jack E. "What's Happening in Baptist
      Academies." The Southern Baptist Educator,
      July-August 1973, pp. 15-16.

      Reports on the current status of the eight
      academies that are members of the Association
      of Southern Baptist Colleges and Schools.
      Differentiates between the academies, which are
      residential and supported by the convention,
      and Baptist day schools operated by local
      churches.

202. Encyclopedia of Southern Baptists, 1982 supp.
      S.v. "Baptist Private Schools Movement," by
      G. Thomas Halbrooks.

      Asserts that during the 1960s and 1970s the
      number of Baptist day schools operated by local
      churches grew rapidly, reaching a total of 416
      by 1980. Notes that despite this expansion,
      the Southern Baptist Convention passed a
      resolution in 1979 supporting public schools.

203. Encyclopedia of Southern Baptists, 1982 supp.
      S.v. "Southern Baptist Association of
      Christian Schools," by G. Thomas Halbrooks.

      Describes the formation of this
      organization, which has no official Southern
      Baptist Convention affiliation, in 1980 to
      enhance the image of Christian schools.

204. Hester, H.I. Partners in Purpose and Progress:
      A Brief History of the Education Commission
      of the Southern Baptist Convention.
      Nashville: The Education Commission of the
      Southern Baptist Convention, 1977.

Comments briefly on the current status of
the academies supported by the Southern Baptist
Convention.

205. Hester, H. I. Southern Baptists in Christian
      Education. Murfreesboro, NC: Chowan
      College School of Graphic Arts, 1968.

Contains 1966-1967 statistics on the seven
academies affiliated with the Southern Baptist
Convention.

206. Research Services Department, Sunday School
      Board of the Southern Baptist Convention.
      Southern Baptist Day Schools. Nashville:
      Sunday School Board of the Southern Baptist
      Convention, 1976.

Summarizes the characteristics of 189 day
schools sponsored by Southern Baptist churches.
Reports that only 14 percent of these
institutions were founded before 1965.

207. Southern Baptist Convention. Annual of the
      Southern Baptist Convention, 1984.
      Nashville: Executive Committee of the
      Southern Baptist Convention, 1984.

Contains statistical data on the nine
academies currently supported by the Southern
Baptist Convention.

208. Whitescarver, K. T. "The Role of the Baptist
      Academy in Today's Society." The Southern
      Baptist Educator, September-October 1977,
      pp. 15-16.

Argues that Baptist academies have an
unprecedented opportunity to contribute to the
moral reconstruction of American society.

CHAPTER 7
CATHOLIC SCHOOLS
Bruno V. Manno and Matthew R. Wilt

BIBLIOGRAPHIC SOURCES
There are two associations which serve as
references for information on Catholic schools.   They
are:
Catholic Library Association (CLA)
461 West Lancaster Ave.
Haverford, PA   19041
(215) 649-5250
National Catholic Educational Association (NCEA)
Suite 100, 1077 30th St. , N.W.
Washington, DC   20007
(202) 293-5954.

The CLA is responsible for producing three reference
tools.
   The Guide to Catholic Literature: an author-
   title-subject index in one straight alphabetical
   order, with biographical and critical notes and
   references, of books and pamphlets by Catholics or
   of particular Catholic interest, published
   originally or in revised edition, in any language
   and in any country, during the years 1888-1967.

   The Catholic Periodical Index: a cumulative
   author and subject index to a selected list of
   Catholic periodicals from 1930 to 1966.

In 1967 the Guide and Index were joined to form
The Catholic Periodical and Literature Index: a
cumulative author-subject index to a selective
list of over 200 Catholic periodicals, from the US
and abroad and an author-title-subject
bibliography of adult books by Catholics, with a
selection of Catholic interest books by other
authors from 1967 to the present.

Various volumes of these three publications are
available through the CLA. Out of print volumes are
available from University Microfilms. Write the CLA
for more information.

The NCEA publishes Catholic educational books,
pamphlets, other print and non-print material, and a
professional journal, Momentum. Every two years a
complete index of Momentum is issued. This
bibliography includes some references to NCEA
publications and articles from Momentum. For more
information on the complete list of publications,
write the NCEA Publications Office.

NCEA archives covering the years 1904 to 1966 are
in the possession of the library of The Catholic
University of America, Washington, DC. For more
information write

           The Catholic University of America
           John K. Mullen Memorial Library
           Washington, DC   20064
           (202) 635-5065.

COMPILING THIS BIBLIOGRAPHY

For this collection, the compilers conducted an
ERIC search from 1965 to 1985 as well as a review of
CLA and NCEA reference material from 1975 to 1985. A
more general review of earlier material was also
undertaken. Most of the references cited here were

published after 1975. The bibliography, therefore, has an intentional contemporary slant with a few references to important works appearing prior to 1975.

This approach was undertaken for two reasons. The first arises from the event referred to as the Second Vatican Council. Begun in 1960, it concluded its deliberations in 1965 and profoundly influenced all aspects of Catholicism, including United States Catholic elementary and secondary schools. The second reason is that there is an enormous literature on Catholic schools. Taking these two facts and the limits imposed by space into account, it seemed wise to present a review of the contemporary post-conciliar literature beginning with 1975, ten years after the closing of the Council.

The form used to present the bibliography departs from that used in other chapters. Rather than annotating each entry, references are listed under selected subject headings. This was done so that more entries could be included.

ADMINISTRATION: ADMINISTRATORS

Two factors unite to make this topic a fertile field for discussion and debate. First, because of the decentralized organization of Catholic schools, the preparation of administrators, especially principals, is a key element in creating an effective and thriving school culture. Recent research on effective public and private schools supports this stress on the importance of the principal.

In addition, increasing numbers of Catholic school principals are laypersons. The 1984 figure is slightly over 30 percent, up from the 1982 figure of about 26 percent. Many of these laypersons come to the principalship with little or no formal training in those areas of governance and administration unique to the Catholic school principalship. The publications which follow speak to various aspects of this question of how best to recruit, prepare, and evaluate present and potential Catholic school principals.

209. Bonaccorsi, Ralph. "The Recruitment, Selection, and Evaluation of the Principal." Momentum, February 1978, pp. 18-22.

210. Brock, Michael. "The Principal and Public Relations." Momentum, October 1982, pp. 15-17.

211. Brooks, Winston, and Robert Palestini. "The Formation of Principals: Two Views." Momentum, December 1982, pp. 28-29.

212. Drahmann, Theodore. The Catholic School Principal: An Outline for Action. Washington, DC: NCEA, 1981.

213. Drahmann, Theodore. Governance and Administration in the Catholic School. Washington, DC: NCEA, 1985.

214. Drahmann, Theodore. "Principal of the Future: Would God Do?" Momentum, September 1984, pp. 70-71.

215. Keefe, James. "Principals and Parents: Partners or Partisans?" Momentum, December 1976, pp. 21-23.

216. McDermott, Edwin. "The Principal as Religious Leader." Momentum, February 1985, p. 49.

217. Manno, Bruno V. "Training Catholic School Principals." Today's Catholic Teacher, September 1985, pp. 32-35.

218. Manno, Bruno V. Those Who Would Be Catholic
      School Principals: Their Recruitment,
      Preparation, and Evaluation. Washington,
      DC: NCEA, 1985.

219. Marcial, Gerald. "Priest/Principal: An
      Endangered Species." Priest, March 1981,
      pp. 6-7.

220. Newton, Robert. "Can Principaling Be Both
      Ministry and Professional?" Ministry
      Management, February 1981, pp. 1-3.

221. Rogus, Joseph. "A Tool for Teacher and
      Principal Self-Improvement." Today's
      Catholic Teacher, November/December 1982,
      pp. 33-35.

222. Traviss, Mary Peter. "The Principal, Moral
      Education, and Staff Development."
      Momentum, December 1975, pp. 16-20.

BILINGUAL EDUCATION

The bilingual education movement has been directed
toward approximately 3.6 million U.S. school-age
children with limited language ability. These
articles provide some information on what Catholic
schools are doing in bilingual language instruction.

223. Baca, Leonard and Jim Bransford. "Meeting the
      Needs of the Bilingual Handicapped Child."
      Momentum, May 1981, pp. 26-29.

224. Elford, George. "Catholic Schools and
      Bilingual Education." Momentum, February
      1983, pp. 35-37.

BOARDS OF EDUCATION; LAY INVOLVEMENT (See also
      Parental Involvement)

The renewed post-Vatican II emphasis on shared
responsibility coupled with parental and lay
involvement in Church life has affected the notion of
school governance. The governance of a Catholic
school takes place, though, within a larger parish,
diocesan, and/or religious order setting. These
publications examine conflicts and tensions brought
on by these two facts and offer various approaches to
resolving the conflicts when they exist.

225.   Brent, Daniel, and Carolyn Jurkowitz. School
       Board Study Programs: Board Members Manual,
       Series I and II Study Programs. Washington,
       DC: NCEA, 1983 and 1984.

226.   Harper, Mary-Angela. Ascent to Excellence in
       Catholic Education: A Guide to Effective
       Decision Making. Washington, DC: NCEA,
       1980.

227.   Harper, Mary-Angela. Developing Performance
       Excellence in Catholic Educational
       Policymaking: A Handbook of Training
       Programs. Washington, DC: NCEA, 1982.

228.   Manno, Bruno V. "Lay Involvement in Catholic
       Schools." America, October 27, 1984, pp.
       246-247.

229.   Murdick, Olin. "Who Runs Catholic Schools? A
       Model for Shared Responsibility." Notre
       Dame Journal of Education 6 (Summer 1975):
       105-190.

230.   Sheehan, Lourdes. "Catholic School Boards Must
       Recognize the Authority Structure."
       Momentum, February 1985, pp. 32-33.

CHURCH DOCUMENTS

Since Vatican Council II, several key documents
have been written and distributed by various official
international and national Catholic Church
assemblies, Congregations, and Conferences. The
following is a list of these key documents, beginning
with the document issued as a result of Vatican
Council II.

231. "Declaration on Christian Education." In The
     Documents of Vatican II, pp. 637-651.
     Edited by Walter Abbott. New York: America
     Press, 1966.

232. The Holy See. The International Year of
     Disabled Persons. Washington, DC: NCEA,
     1981.

233. National Committee on Human Sexuality
     Education: Education in Human Sexuality for
     Christians. Washington, DC: United States
     Catholic Conference Publications, 1981.

234. National Conference on Catholic Bishops. Basic
     Teachings for Catholic Religious Education.
     Washington, DC: United States Catholic
     Conference Publications, 1973.

235. National Conference on Catholic Bishops. "Let
     the Little Children Come to Me": A
     Statement on Early Childhood Care and
     Education. Washington, DC: United States
     Catholic Conference Publications, 1977.

236. National Conference on Catholic Bishops. To
     Teach As Jesus Did. Washington, DC: United
     States Catholic Conference Publications,
     1973.

237. Sacred Congregation for Catholic Education.
      The Catholic School. Washington, DC:
      United States Catholic Conference
      Publications Office, 1977.

238. Sacred Congregation for Catholic Education.
      Educational Guidance in Human Love:
      Outlines for Sex Education. Washington, DC:
      United States Catholic Conference
      Publications, 1983.

239. Sacred Congregation for Catholic Education.
      Lay Catholics in Schools: Witnesses to
      Faith. Boston: St. Paul, 1982.

240. Sacred Congregation for the Clergy. General
      Catechetical Directory. Washington, DC:
      United States Catholic Conference
      Publications, 1971.

241. Synod of Bishops. Catechetics In Our Time With
      Special Reference to Catechetics for
      Children and Young People. Washington, DC:
      United States Catholic Conference
      Publications, 1976.

COMPUTERS; TECHNOLOGY

    Like all schools, Catholic schools are trying to
come to terms with the new technology made available
through the use of computers. In fact, since 1983,
the NCEA annual convention has included a
Technologies Conference. These articles discuss
various aspects of the new technology as it relates
to the Catholic school situation.

242. Barton, Jean. "Catholic Schools and the
      Revolution." Momentum, September 1983, pp.
      9-12.

243. Baumgaertner, William. "Communications and
     Pastoral Studies." Momentum, February 1982,
     pp. 18-19.

244. Furlong, Mary. "Strengthening the Classroom
     Teacher Through Microcomputing Technology."
     Momentum, September 1983, pp. 12-14.

245. Furlong, Mary, and Yolanda George. "Technology
     in Catholic Schools: What Principals Need
     to Know." Today's Catholic Teacher,
     November/December 1984, pp. 38-39.

246. Maloy, Robert. "The Computer Challenge to
     Education." Momentum, December 1982, pp.
     14-16.

247. Novy, Helen. "A Student Centered Approach to
     the Computer." Momentum, May 1983, pp.
     35-37.

248. Pickert, Sarah, and Beverly Hunter.
     "Redefining 'Literacy'" Momentum, September
     1983, pp. 7-9.

CURRICULUM

A major way of supporting the Catholic dimension
of the school and teaching the vision and values
associated with Catholicism is through the school
curriculum. What gospel values should be integrated
into the curriculum and how can this be done are the
two main questions addressed in these publications.

249. Coreil, Judith. "A Different Kind of
     Excellence." Momentum, December 1984, pp.
     46-47.

250. DiSibio, Robert, and Fred Savitz. "A
     Curriculum Center for Grade Schools."
     Momentum, October 1982, pp. 46-47.

251. Fisher, Eugene. "Toward a High School
      Curriculum for Teaching About Jews and
      Judaism." SIDIC 3 (1983): 31-40.

252. Fortman, Angela Marie. "A Time of Sharing and
      Teaching Values." Today's Catholic Teacher,
      February 1985, p. 33.

253. Hackett, Peter. "Curriculum Matters: Catholic
      and Secondary Considerations." Month, June
      1981, pp. 190-194.

254. Jackson, D. A. "A Catholic Curriculum."
      Tablet, May 30, 1981, pp. 528-530.

255. Kealey, Robert. Curriculum in the Catholic
      School. Washington, DC: NCEA, 1985.

256. Keilocker, Francine. "Curriculum: The
      Question of Quality." Momentum, December
      1978, pp. 39-40.

257. McClelland, Vincent. "Curriculum Development."
      Tablet, November 1981, pp. 1176-1177.

258. Pilarczyk, Daniel. "What They Teach in Our
      Schools." Our Sunday Visitor Magazine,
      April 18, 1976, p. 1.

259. Reck, Carleen. "Integrating Gospel Values."
      Today's Catholic Teacher, January 1984, pp.
      26-27.

260. Reck, Carleen. "What's Catholic About Catholic
      Schools?" Momentum, October 1979, pp.
      45-49.

261. Stamschror, Robert. "Catholic High School
      Curriculum: What? When?" Ministry
      Management, April 1983, pp. 1-6.

262. <u>Vision</u> <u>and</u> <u>Values</u> <u>in</u> <u>the</u> <u>Catholic</u> <u>School:</u> <u>A</u>
     <u>Curriculum</u> <u>Process</u>. Washington, DC: NCEA,
     1981.

263. Young, Jerry. "Curriculum in the Elementary
     School." <u>Today's</u> <u>Catholic</u> <u>Teacher,</u> January
     1985, p. 56.

DEVELOPMENT (See also Finances; Planning)

The institutional enhancement or development of
Catholic schools has become a major topic of interest
to Catholic educators. This is due to several
factors, especially those associated with financing
Catholic schools. This enhancement has many related
dimensions--e. g., developing a case statement, good
public relations, annual fund and estate planning,
establishing an endowment, etc. These publications
review several aspects of the broad-based approach to
institutional enhancement called development.

264. Burke, Richard. <u>Catholic</u> <u>School</u> <u>Management</u>
     <u>Newsletter</u>. Published four times a year on
     various topics by Burke and Associates, 24
     Cornfield Lane, Madison, CT 06443.

265. Campbell, Cathy. "Some 'How-Tos' for Publicity
     Seekers." <u>Momentum,</u> May 1983, pp. 45-46.

266. Development "How To" Series Books on <u>Annual</u>
     <u>Fund/Estate</u> <u>Planning,</u> <u>The</u> <u>Case</u> <u>Statement,</u>
     <u>Public</u> <u>Relations,</u> <u>Understanding</u> <u>and</u>
     <u>Implementing</u> <u>Development,</u> and <u>Seeking</u>
     <u>Foundation</u> <u>Grants</u>. Washington, DC: NCEA,
     1984/1985.

267. "Development in Total Catholic Education."
     <u>Momentum,</u> September 1985 (theme issue).

268. Ensman, Richard. "Development, Marketing, and
     You." <u>Today's</u> <u>Catholic</u> <u>Teacher,</u> February
     1984, pp. 34-36.

269. Flynn, John. "Nine Deadly Development
       Trappers. " Today's Catholic Teacher, April
       1984, pp. 88-89.

270. Flynn, John. "Team Work and Development. "
       Today's Catholic Teacher, October 1984, pp.
       56-57.

271. Flynn, John, and Sam Kennedy. "Catholic School
       Development: Two Perspectives. " Momentum,
       February 1982, pp. 23-27.

272. Fuller, Donald. "Taking the Mystery Out of
       Marketing. " Momentum, February 1982, pp.
       31-33.

273. Jarc, Jerry. "An Endowment Fund Program for
       Secondary Schools. " Today's Catholic
       Teacher, April 1981, pp. 16-18.

274. Jarc, Jerry. "An Endowment Program at Work. "
       Today's Catholic Teacher, April 1984, p. 50.

275. Manno, Bruno V. "A Development Program for
       Your School. " Today's Catholic Teacher,
       November/December 1982, pp. 30-32.

276. Virgadamo, Steven. "Development a la Richard
       the Lion-Hearted. " Momentum, September
       1984, pp. 23-24.

EVALUATION

The critical assessment of the educational
endeavors of the Catholic school is a many faceted
effort. It begins with a clear policy presenting the
rationale for the evaluation and principals which
guide it. It then moves to the design of a plan
delineating the process to be used. These
publications discuss questions like: what is to be

evaluated; for what purpose; when should evaluations occur; when is the criteria used in an evaluation established; who establishes it; from what sources will information be sought; what procedures are used to gather it; to whom will it be presented and for what action; in what form will the results appear?

277. Butler, Loretta. "Evaluation and Future Planning: An In-Service Faculty Workshop. Today's Catholic Teacher, May 1980, p. 83.

278. Elford, George. "The Evaluation of the Catholic School: A Proposed Approach to the Design and Method." Today's Catholic Teacher, September 1975, pp. 22-29.

279. Kelly, Francis. "Evaluating our Catechetical Efforts." Momentum, May 1983, pp. 13-14.

280. Newton, Robert. Evaluation of Religious Formation Programs. Washington, DC: NCEA, 1979.

281. Reck, Carleen, and Judith Coreil. School Evaluation for the Catholic Elementary School. Washington, DC: NCEA, 1983.

282. Reck, Carleen, and Judith Coreil. Verifying the Vision: A Self-Evaluation Instrument for the Catholic School. Washington, DC: NCEA, 1984.

283. Sparks, Gary. "Teacher Evaluation as Christian Partnership." Today's Catholic Teacher, May/June 1985, pp. 32-33.

284. Traviss, Mary Peter. "A Western Approach to Evaluation: The Elementary Commission of the Western Catholic Education Association." Today's Catholic Teacher, September 1975, p. 39.

FAMILY

A key element of Catholic educational philosophy is that the parent is the primary educator of the child. For this reason, a special relationship must exist between the school, the parents, and the family. These articles examine various dimensions of this school and family relationship.

285. Brungs, Robert A. "Catholic Education and the Family." Communio 4 (Fall 1977): 284-288.

286. Corrado, Richard. "A Strategy for School-Family Relationships: The RFV Quotient." Momentum, February 1979, pp. 4-7.

287. Thomas, David. "Christian Socialization: A Shared Ministry of Family and School." Momentum, December 1980, pp. 23-27.

FINANCES

There are growing financial pressures on Catholic elementary and secondary schools. These are due to several factors among which four predominate. These are: the declining subsidy from donated services; increasing physical plant costs due to deferred maintenance; the need for improvement in faculty salaries; the need to increase expenditures in response to a concern about improving the quality of schools. These publications examine the different types of revenue which compose the financial base of Catholic schools, as well as how to expand that base.

288. Burke, Richard. "Effective Cash Management of Schools: The Budget as a Control Document." Momentum, December 1978, pp. 16-19.

289. Elementary School Financial Manual. Washington, DC: NCEA, 1984.

290. Fine, Leonard. "Financial Stability Through Pre-Paid Tuition." Momentum, October 1982, pp. 43-44.

291. Flynn, John. "Faith and Finance." Today's Catholic Teacher, May 1978, pp. 34-35.

292. Greeley, Andrew M. "A Preliminary Investigation on the Profitability of Catholic Schools." Momentum, December 1977, pp. 43-49.

293. Olley, Edmund W. "Negotiated Tuition: A Bird's Eye View." Today's Catholic Teacher, April 1979, p. 10.

NCEA Issues a biennial report on Catholic elementary and secondary school finances. Write to the NCEA Publications Office for more information.

GIFTED AND TALENTED; HANDICAPPED; SPECIAL EDUCATION

Passage of Public Law 94-142, the Education of all Handicapped Children Act, has affected Catholic schools. These publications discuss many of the theoretical and practical issues related to implementing PL 94-142.

294. Brooks, Benjamin, and Rochelle Simms. "Are Handicapped Children Welcome in Catholic Schools?" Momentum, February 1984, pp. 44-46.

295. Cook, Ellen. "Sensitizing the 'Able' Student to the Disabled." Momentum, May 1981, pp. 13-15.

296. Hall, Suzanne. "Catholic Education Becomes Special." Momentum, October 1979, pp. 18-23.

297. Hall, Suzanne. Challenging Gifted Students in
     the Catholic School. Washington, DC: NCEA,
     1985.

298. Hall, Suzanne, ed. Into the Religious
     Community: Religious Education With
     Disabled Persons. Washington, DC: NCEA,
     1982.

299. Hall, Suzanne. "The Parish School as Least
     Restrictive Environment." Momentum, May
     1981, pp. 40-41.

300. Harrison, Gerald. "Education of the Blind or
     Visually Impaired: The Need for Vision."
     Momentum, October 1981, pp. 14-16.

301. Jennings, Kathryn. Beginning Special Religious
     Education Programs. Washington, DC: NCEA,
     1980.

302. Kahn, Michael. "Preparing Non-exceptional
     Students for the Main-Streamed Classroom."
     Momentum, May 1981 (theme issue).

303. Katulak, Robert. "Ministry to the Gifted."
     Today's Catholic Teacher, October 1984, pp.
     47-48.

304. Mainstreaming: Responding to the Individual
     Needs of Children Within the Regular
     Classroom. Washington, DC: NCEA, 1983;
     video program.

305. Rolando, Mary. Recognizing and Helping the
     Learning Disabled Child in Your Classroom.
     Washington, DC: NCEA, 1978.

306. "Special Education." Momentum, May 1981 (theme
     issue).

HISTORY

Though Catholic schools existed in the U.S.
before, the Council of Baltimore held in 1885 is
generally considered to be the official foundation of
these schools. It was then that the American
Catholic bishops declared "... that near every Church
a parish school... is to be built and maintained in
perpetuum. ..." The move from principle to practice
was never fully accomplished.

During the long history of Catholic schooling in
the U.S. and prior to that in the new world, much has
been done. The schools have functioned and continue
to function in various ways. These publications
overview this long history and discuss various
aspects of it.

307. Buetow, Harold A. "Historical Overview of
        Catholic Teacher Education." School and
        Society 100 (March 1972): 165-172.

308. Buetow, Harold A. A History of Catholic
        Schooling in the United States. Washington,
        DC: NCEA, 1985.

309. Buetow, Harold A. Of Singular Benefit: The
        Story of Catholic Education in the U.S. New
        York: Macmillan, 1970.

310. Gleason, Philip. "In Search of Unity:
        American Catholic Thought, 1920-1960."
        Catholic Historical Review 65 (April 1979):
        185-205.

311. Hennessey, James. American Catholics. New
        York: Oxford, 1982; numerous references to
        the history of Catholic schools.

312. Horrigan, Donald. The Shaping of NCEA.
        Washington, DC: NCEA, 1979.

313. Hunt, Thomas C. , and Norlene Kunkel. "Catholic
      Schools: The Nation's Largest Alternative
      School System." In Religious Schooling in
      America, pp. 1-34. Edited by James C.
      Carper and Thomas C. Hunt. Birmingham, AL:
      Religious Education Press, 1984.

      Lannie, Vincent P. "Church and School
      Triumphant: The Sources of American
      Catholic Educational Historiography."
      History of Education Quarterly 16 (Summer
      1976): 131-145.

      *See item 1166.

314. Lockwood, Robert A. "The Catholic School in
      America: Then and Now." Our Sunday Visitor
      Magazine, April 18, 1976, pp. 4-5.

315. Maycock, Louise, and Allen Glatthorn. "NCEA
      and the Development of the Post-Conciliar
      Catholic School." Momentum, December 1980,
      pp. 7-9.

316. McClusky, Neil G. , ed. Catholic Education in
      America. New York: Columbia University -
      Teachers College, 1964.

      Ryan, Mary Perkins. Are Parochial Schools the
      Answer? New York: Holt, 1963.

      * See item 1102.

JUSTICE AND PEACE

     There has been a major emphasis on education for
justice and peace in the theological writing done
after Vatican Council II. With its clear focus on
educating to gospel values, the Catholic school is
seen as a primary forum for articulating the need for
this education and forming

those who are associated with it to the demands of
justice and peace. These publications examine the
many issues related to education for justice and
peace and those approaches which may be appropriate
for the Catholic schools.

317. Carey, Loretta. <u>Directions for Justice and
      Peach Education in the Catholic Elementary
      School</u>. Washington, DC: NCEA, 1985.

318. Carey, Loretta. "Peace and Justice Education:
      Adopting the Infusion Method." <u>Momentum</u>,
      October 1982, pp. 40-42.

319. Carey, Loretta. "Redefining the Ministry of
      Teaching: Service to the Global Community."
      <u>Momentum</u>, October 1977, pp. 17-20.

320. Christensen, Richard. "Social Justice - the
      Missing Educational Objective." <u>Momentum</u>,
      February 1984, pp. 54-55.

321. Elias, John, and Dorothy Schuette. "What Will
      Parents Say About Teaching the War and Peace
      Pastoral?" <u>Momentum</u>, December 1983, pp.
      34-36.

322. Gerrity, Thomas, and Robert Clarke. "Holocaust
      Studies: An Approach to Peace." <u>Momentum</u>,
      December 1983, pp. 36-37.

323. Kealey, Robert. <u>Everyday Issues Related to
      Justice and Other Gospel Values</u>.
      Washington, DC: NCEA, 1984.

324. Kleinstuber, Joseph. "Can a Catholic Military
      School Promote Justice and Peace?"
      <u>Momentum</u>, December 1983, pp. 43-44.

325. Lesley, Roberta. "Educating for Justice: One
      Model." <u>Momentum</u>, February 1981, pp. 32-34.

326. Markham, Stephen. "The Bishop's Pastoral, 'The Challenge of Peace': A Direction for Peace and Justice Education." Ministry Management, April 1984, pp. 1-4.

327. O'Hare, Padraic, ed. Education for Peace and Justice. New York: Harper and Row, 1983.

328. Sheldon, Charles. "The Adolescent, Social Justice, and the Catholic School: A Psychological Perspective." Living Light 17 (Fall 1980): 223-233.

329. Van Merrienboer, Edward, Veronica Grover, and William Cunningham. Seeking a Just Society: A K-12 Curriculum Design. Washington, DC: NCEA, 1978.

330. Vanier, Jean. The Challenge and Response to Peace for Catholic Educators. Washington, DC: NCEA, 1984; video program.

331. Warren, Michael. "High Schools with A Difference." Living Light 19 (September 1982): 56-64.

LAW

School law is a topic on which all school personnel need to be well versed. The needs of Catholic school administrators are different, though, than public school educators. These publications summarize some of the major issues relative to school law as it relates to Catholic schools.

332. Harshman, Daniel. "Lay Teachers in Church Operated Schools." Duquesne Law Review 18 (Fall 1979): 135-150.

333. Permuth, Steve P., Ralph Mawdsley, and Joseph Daly. The Law, the Student, and the

Catholic School. Washington, DC: NCEA, 1981.

334. Yeager, Robert. "Legal Needs of Catholic
     School Administrators." Catholic Lawyer 27
     (Summer 1982): 255-257.

MANAGEMENT; PLANNING (See also Development)

Effective management of resources is a primary
concern of all educators, especially administrators.
From a Christian perspective, it is an aspect of good
stewardship. These publications discuss some of the
practical implications of adhering to a policy of
sound management.

335. Burke, Richard. "Good Management is Vital for
     Success." Momentum, December 1984, pp.
     22-24.

336. DeRoche, Edward, Robert Infantino, and Joseph
     Rost. "Should We Open a New School?"
     Momentum, February 1982, pp. 34-36.

337. Jarc, Jerry. "Beyond the Five-Year Plan."
     Today's Catholic Teacher, April 1985, p. 56.

338. Strommen, Merton. Five Shaping Forces - Using
     Organizational Dynamics to do More With
     Less. Washington, DC: NCEA, 1982.

MINORITIES (See also Multi-Cultural Education; Non-
     Catholics)

Catholic and non-Catholic minorities are enrolling
in Catholic schools in increasing numbers. In
1969-70, non-caucasian minorities accounted for 9.5
percent of total Catholic school enrollment. In
1983-84, they were slightly over 20 percent of total
enrollment. This was an increase of around 175,300
students, or about 41 percent. This occurred during

a general period of Catholic school enrollment
decline that witnessed the loss of about 36 percent
of the total student population.

These and other data document how Catholic schools
during the last 20 years have deepened their
longstanding educational involvement with non-
caucasian minority education, especially in the inner
cities of our major urban centers. The articles
which follow examine some of the issues raised by
this involvement in the urban education of
minorities.

339. Buetow, Harold A. "The Underprivileged and
      Roman Catholic Education." Journal of Negro
      Education 40 (Fall 1971): 373-389.

340. Bui, Thu. "Meeting the Needs of Indochinese
      Students." Momentum, February 1983, pp.
      20-22.

341. Ford, Elinor. "The Saga of America's Catholic
      Inner City Schools." Momentum, October
      1979, pp. 53-54.

342. Greeley, Andrew M. "Catholic High Schools: An
      Effective Inner City Ministry." National
      Catholic Reporter, December 31, 1982, pp.
      11-12.

343. Kearney, James. "The Urban Catholic School: A
      Valuable Part of American Education." NASSP
      Bulletin 66 (March 1982): 38-45.

344. Keys, Christopher. "Renewal Processes in Urban
      Parochial Schools." Theory into Practice 18
      (April 1979): 97-105.

345. King, Edith. "Promising Practices in Teaching
      Ethically Diverse Children." Momentum,
      February 1983, pp. 38-40.

346. Marion, Robert. "Strategies for Communicating
      with Parents of Black Exceptional Children."
      Momentum, May 1981, pp. 13-15.

347. National Office for Black Catholics (NOBC).
      "The Crisis of Black Education in the Black
      Community." City of God 2 (Summer 1980):
      39-46.

348. O'Brien, Timothy, and Donald Zewe. "Hope in
      the Inner City." Momentum, February 1981,
      pp. 11-13.

349. Wallis, Patricia. "Holistic Learning - A Must
      with American Indian Students." Momentum,
      February 1983, pp. 40-42.

MULTICULTURAL EDUCATION (See also Minorities; Non-
      Catholics)

     A major impetus behind the endeavor began in 1865
to inaugurate a national policy on schooling for
Catholics was a multicultural issue. How can one
best educate a growing number of Catholic immigrants,
many of whom were from different cultural and
linguistic backgrounds? This issue continues to be
with Catholic schools today, though some aspects of
it have changed. These schools were once filled with
students from poor, ethnic, Catholic families, mostly
of Eastern and Western European descent. Today,
those poor have been replaced by the new urban poor -
primarily blacks, Hispanics, and Asians. These
publications discuss some of the new questions
arising out of this new situation.

350. Muller, Robert. "Catholic Education: A World
      of Difference." Catholic Library World,
      July/August 1981, pp. 32-37.

351. "Multicultural Education." Momentum, February
      1983 (theme issue).

352. "Multicultural Pluralism." Momentum, October
     1975 (theme issue).

NON-CATHOLICS (See also Minorities; Multicultural
     Education)

In 1969-70, non-Catholic enrollment in Catholic
schools stood at 2.7 percent of total enrollment. In
1983-84, that figure was 11.6 percent. This
reflected an increase of 217,500 students or 173
percent. This dramatic increase in enrollment has
been an opportunity for Catholic educators to examine
several issues, especially those related to the
religious education of non-Catholics. These
publications examine some of the theoretical and
practical considerations.

353. Foley, Annmarie, Dolores Follock, and Teresa
     Walker. "Meeting the Religious Needs of
     Non-Catholics in Catholic Schools."
     Momentum, February 1981, pp. 22-23.

354. Hawker, James. "Arousing the Beginnings of
     Faith." Momentum, February 1982, pp. 28-30.

355. Hawker, James. The Non-Catholic in the
     Catholic School. Washington, DC: NCEA,
     1984.

PARENTAL INVOLVEMENT (See also Boards of Education;
     Lay Involvement)

According to Vatican II, "...the family is the
first school." For many years, Catholic schools have
involved parents in the schools in an ancillary
manner focused on raising funds and supplying
volunteers. Vatican II, though, placed a strong
emphasis on "...the family (as) the first school."
Flowing from this emphasis has been an attempt to
stress partnership and collaboration in the
educational process. Practically, for example, this

had led to parental involvement in sacramental preparation programs. These publications discuss various aspects of this topic.

356. Amendolara, Loraine. "Are Parents a Part of Your Educating Community?" Momentum, December 1984, pp. 56-57.

357. Barnds, Mary Lynch. "Parents Involved in What-Why?" Momentum, September 1983, pp. 38-39.

358. Burke, Thomas R. "A Catholic Parent Looks at the Catholic School." Today's Catholic Teacher, March 1978, pp. 60-61.

359. Ford, Elinor. "Why a National Forum of Catholic Parent Organizations?" Momentum, December 1976, pp. 27-29.

360. Gallagher, John. "Parents' Right to Educate: A Right Inalienable." Homiletic and Pastoral Review 76 (December 1975): 29-32.

361. Gallagher, William. "Parents as Partners in the Catholic School Apostolate." Momentum, December 1976, pp. 25-26.

362. Growing Together: Young Adolescents and Their Parents. Washington, DC: NCEA, 1985.

363. Harper, Mary Angela. "The Sleeping Giant: Parent Power in Catholic Education." Today's Catholic Teacher, April 1976, pp. 33-34.

364. Reichert, Richard, and Sara Reichert. "Partners in Education: What's Realistic?" Momentum, May 1980, pp. 8-9.

365. Schillo, Genevieve. "The Parents' Organization and Catholic Schools." Today's Catholic Teacher, October 1981, p. 36.

366. Sheridan, Gerry. "Parents: The Primary
      Educators of Children." Catechist,
      September 1982, pp. 40-42.

367. Weiss, Edward. The Parent, the Parish, and the
      Catholic School. Washington, DC: NCEA,
      1985.

PASTOR; PRIEST

The pastor is a key member of the several groups
of persons involved in the educational ministry of
the Catholic school. Within this educational
community of shared ministry and decision making,
what is the role of the pastor in relating to the
principal, the board, parental groups, financial
issues, etc.? These publications look at these
questions.

368. Bernardin, Joseph. "The Role of the Religious
      Leader in the Development of Public Policy."
      Priest, January 1985, pp. 32-37.

369. Gilbert, John. Pastor as Shepherd of the
      School Community. Washington, DC: NCEA,
      1983.

370. Grecco, Richard. "The Role of the Priest in
      Our Catholic Schools." Priest, September
      1983, pp. 34-38.

371. Marcial, Gerald. "Priest/Principal: An
      Endangered Species." Priest, March 1981,
      pp. 6-7.

372. Sullivan, Eugene, and Carl Schipper. "Parish
      Priests and Parish Schools." Church,
      September 1985, pp. 40-41.

PERSONNEL RELATIONS; STAFFING; TEACHERS

When the Vatican Council was convened in 1960,
almost 75 percent of those staffing Catholic schools
were priests or religious. Today, in 1986, almost 80
percent of the staff is composed of laypersons. If
this rate continues, projections are that by 1995
priests and religious will account for only 2 percent
of total staff.

This transformation from predominantly religious
to lay staffing involves both continuity and change.
Strong consensus exists within the faculties about
the academic purposes of the school, the organization
and methods of instruction employed to address these
purposes, and conceptions of the staff's role in
Catholic education. This is a story of continuity.

Differences between faculty exist when analyzing
religious practices and opinions on moral issues.
These mirror the conflicting perspectives with
American Catholicism in general. This is much more a
story of change.

These publications provide a selective overview of
those major theoretical and practical issues arising
from this change in staffing patterns.

373. Bleich, Russell. "Teachers and Teaching: What
      Makes Catholic Schools Different."
      Momentum, September 1984, p. 34.

374. Code of Ethics for the Catholic School Teacher.
      Washington, DC: NCEA, 1982.

375. Donahue, John. "A Vatican Salute to Catholic
      Lay Teachers." America, October 30, 1982,
      pp. 251-252.

376. Draina, Lois. "Master Teacher Plan is Feasible
      for Catholic Schools." Momentum, September
      1984, pp. 46-47.

377. Egan, Katherine. Beginnings: The Orientation
     of New Teachers. Washington, DC: NCEA,
     1981.

378. Go, Jenny. "Religious and Lay Collaboration in
     School." Seminarium, January/March, 1982,
     pp. 240-253.

379. Mahany, Barbara. "The Rugged Devotion of
     Teachers in Catholic Schools." US Catholic,
     September 1984, pp. 30-35.

380. McBride, Alfred. The Christian Formation of
     Catholic Educators. Washington, DC: NCEA,
     1981; also available on video.

381. McBride, Alfred. Creative Teaching in
     Christian Education. Boston: Allyn and
     Bacon, 1978.

382. McBride, Alfred. The Christian Formation of
     Catholic Educators. Washington, DC: NCEA,
     1981; also available on video.

383. McNearney, James. "Theological Reflection of
     Teachers." Today's Catholic Teacher,
     September 1984, p. 86.

384. The Pre-Service Formation of Teachers for
     Catholic Schools. Washington, DC: NCEA,
     1982.

385. Raftery, Francis. The Teacher in the Catholic
     School. Washington, DC: NCEA, 1985.

386. Rector, Theresa. "Black Nuns as Educators."
     Journal of Negro Education 51 (Summer 1982):
     238-253.

387. Rossiter, Graham. "The Place of the Teacher's
      Own Personal Commitments in Classroom
      Religious Education." Ministry Management,
      February 1984, pp. 1-3.

388. Sauve, James. "The Collaboration of Religious
      and Lay Educators in the Ministry of
      Teaching." Seminarium, January/March 1982,
      pp. 254-267.

389. "Thoughts Regarding Religious in Catholic
      Schools Today." Consecrated Life 3 (1978):
      169-196.

390. Vasiloff, Barbara. "The Teacher's Vital Role
      in Developing Student Discipline."
      Momentum, December 1982, pp. 23-26.

391. Vojcicki, Ted, and Kevin Convey. Teachers,
      Catholic Schools, and Faith Community: A
      Program of Spirituality. New York: Le
      Jacq, 1982.

392. Voss, Betty. "The Teacher as Artist and
      Spiritual Voyager." Momentum, December
      1984, pp. 6-8.

PHILOSOPHY

The Catholic school is an educational setting
within which a critical synthesis occurs between
culture and the Catholic religious vision. In
claiming to be Catholic, then, the school commits
itself to pursuing the meaning, value, and truth of
specific Catholic values and symbols without
compromising academic standards. Without this unique
mission, these schools have no Catholic reason for
existing.

In a descriptive sense, the Catholic tradition
uniquely configures a religious vision that

emphasizes the sacramental or incarnational, a drive toward rationality, an emphasis on tradition, a strong sense of authority, and a cultivation of the spiritual and aesthetic. At its base, the philosophy undergirding this configuration views reality as coherent and ultimately intelligible. Knowledge, then, is unifiable. The Christian faith as proclaimed and lived from within the Roman Catholic tradition is the key to this coherence, intelligibility, and oneness.

The American Catholic Bishops in their pastoral letter To Teach As Jesus Did say the philosophy of Catholic education has three aims. These are to teach the gospel message of Christ and authentic Catholic doctrine, to build an active and living school community of faith, and to help people grow in service to others. These are to be accomplished in an active manner working with the parents, the primary and first educators of children.

This collection of publications further specifies the many theoretical and practical aspects of this distinctive philosophy.

393.   Carmody, Brendon. "A Context for the Catholic Philosophy of Education." Lumen Vitae 36 (1981): 45-61.

394.   DeRosa, G. "The Catholic School and Scholastic Pluralism." L'Osservatore Romano (English version), May 11, 1978, p. 528.

395.   Dolan, Jay P. "Catholic Education - Why Bother?" Momentum, February 1979, pp. 28-29.

396.   Donohue, John. "A Vatican Statement on Education." America, August 13/20, 1977, pp. 67-70.

397. Elford, George. "Toward a Catholic School Philosophy." Today's Catholic Teacher, February 1975, pp. 20-21.

398. Garone, Gabriel M. "The Catholic School: Commentary." L'Osservatore Romano (English version), July 28, 1977, p. 487.

399. Hellwig, Monika. "What Makes Catholic Schools Catholic?" Ministry Management, October 1984, pp. 1-4.

400. Hunt, Thomas C. "Catholic Schools Today: Redirection and Redefinition." Living Light 17 (Fall 1980): 203-210.

401. McBride, Alfred. "Why Go to a Catholic School?" Catholic Light, February 19, 1985, pp. 105-109.

402. McBrien, Richard. "A Case for Catholic Education." Commonweal, January 21, 1977, pp. 41-44.

403. McCarthy, Abigail. "Parochial Schools, Still: A Focal Point for Catholic Identity." Commonweal, April 22, 1983, pp. 232-233.

404. McCormick, Michael W. "'To Teach As Jesus Did': Accountability in Perspective." Today's Catholic Teacher, January 1979, pp. 22-23.

405. McDermott, Edwin. Distinctive Qualities of the Catholic School. Washington, DC: NCEA, 1985.

406. Murdick, Olin. "Toward a Philosophy of Catholic Education." Today's Catholic Teacher, February 1984, p. 38.

407. O'Neill, Michael. New Schools in a New Church:
      Toward a Modern Philosophy of Catholic
      Education. Collegeville, MN: St. John's
      University Press, 1971.

408. O'Neill, Michael. "Toward a Modern Concept of
      'Permeation.'" Momentum, May 1979, pp.
      48-50.

409. O'Neill, Michael. "Toward a Profession of
      Catholic Education." Today's Catholic
      Teacher, January 1979, pp. 59-60.

410. Pennock, Michael. "The Heart of the Catholic
      School." Momentum, May 1980, pp. 24-27.

411. Pilarczyk, Daniel. "What Makes a Catholic
      School Catholic,?" pp. 16-22. In Seminar
      on Catholic Secondary Education: Now and In
      the Future. Washington, DC: NCEA, 1982.

PUBLIC POLICY

A false assumption behind much of the hostility to
private schools in general and Catholic schools in
particular is that only public schools can serve a
public interest. Catholic schools do contribute to
the public interest and serve a public purpose. They
do this by serving a public composed of different
religious, racial, ethnic, economic, and academic
groups. They also do this by providing social,
financial, and cultural benefits to local communities
and the nation as a whole. Because of this, public
policy should support them as a natural means of
human-capital development. These publications
discuss various ways in which public policy on
education should be reformed to support these
schools.

412. Bernardin, Joseph. "The Role of the Religious
      Leader in the Development of Public Policy."
      Priest, January 1985, pp. 32-37.

413. "Broadening Tuition Tax Credit Proposals:
      United States Catholic Conference
      Administrative Board," Origins, October 13,
      1983, pp. 309-310.

414. Byron, William. "Does the Church Have Anything
      to Say to American Education?" Living Light
      20 (June 1984): 295-304.

415. Catholic Bishops of New York State. "Tuition
      Tax Credits: A Statement." Catholic Mind,
      February 1982, pp. 10-12.

416. Esty, John. "The Public Purpose of Nonpublic
      Education." Momentum, September 1984, pp.
      48-50, 52.

417. Finn, Chester E., Jr. "Catholic and Public
      School Cooperation: It's Imperative."
      Momentum, May 1983, pp. 7-9.

      Gaffney, Edward, ed. Private Schools and the
      Public Good. Notre Dame, IN: University of
      Notre Dame Press, 1981.

      * See item 11.

418. Hurley, Mark. "Educational Rights Lost in the
      Shuffle." America, December 31, 1985, pp.
      431-433.

419. Krol, John. "Catholic Education and the Common
      Good of Our Nation." Dimension 9 (September
      1977): 77-83.

420. Lyke, James. "Tuition Tax Credits and the
      Poor." Origins, June 18, 1981, pp. 79-80.

421. McCormick, Michael W. "Catholic Schools and
      Educational Reform." Today's Catholic
      Teacher, September 1983, pp. 34-35.

422. McDermott, Edwin. "Family Choice in
      Education." _America,_ November 3, 1979, pp.
      205-253.

423. McElligott, Joseph. "The Voucher System."
      Momentum, May 1979, pp. 24-27.

424. McGarry, Daniel D. "The Advantages of Tuition
      Tax Credits." _Social_ _Justice_ 74
      (July/August 1983): 99-105.

425. Moynihan, Daniel P. "Government and the Ruin
      of Private Education." _Harpers,_ April 1978,
      pp. 23-28.

426. Moynihan, Daniel P. "A Matter of Justice."
      Catholic _Mind,_ December 1981, pp. 22-32.

427. Reagan, Ronald W. "Tuition Tax Credits."
      Origins, April 29, 1982, pp. 725-727.

428. Schwartz, Michael. "Educational Freedom:
      Right or Privilege?" _Liguorian,_ July 1982,
      pp. 9-12.

429. Schwartz, Michael. "A New Direction for the
      Courts on the School Question." _America,_
      October 29, 1983, pp. 251-254.

430. Valenti, Ronald. "Freedom in Education: The
      Case for Tuition Tax Credits." _Liguorian,_
      August 1983, pp. 34-38.

431. Young, David, and Steven Tigges. _Federal_
      Tuition _Tax_ _Credits_ _and_ _the_ _Establishment_
      Clause. Washington, DC: NCEA, 1982.

432. Young, David, and Steven Tigges. "Federal
      Tuition Tax Analysis." _Catholic_ _Lawyer_ 29
      (Winter 1983): 35-71.

RESEARCH

Many of the opinions and attitudes held by persons
hostile to Catholic schools are based on stereotypes
and false assumptions. These often link Catholic
school attendance to a single race, ethnic groups,
economic status, or intellectual level. The evidence
gathered from research on these schools refutes these
stereotypes. These schools are not havens for whites
fleeing public education or for an elite avoiding
social responsibility. In fact, they have less
racial and economic segregation than do public
schools. Furthermore, they embody two notions that
form the basis for the American tradition of common,
public schools: a natural mixing of diverse groups
of students and a closeness to the families and
communities they serve. These publications provide
evidence documenting these findings.

433. Bauch, Patricia. "Implications for Catholic
      Education from Goodlad's 'A Study of
      Schooling'." Momentum, September 1983, pp.
      15-18.

434. Benson, Peter, Robert Yeager, Michael Guerra,
      and Bruno V. Manno. The Catholic High
      School: A National Portrait. Washington,
      DC: NCEA, 1985.

435. Benson, Peter, Robert Yeager, Michael Guerra,
      Bruno V. Manno, and Philip Wood. Catholic
      High Schools: Their Impact on Low-Income
      Students. Washington, DC: NCEA, 1986.

436. Benson, Peter, and Michael Guerra. Sharing the
      Faith: The Beliefs and Values of Catholic
      High School Teachers. Washington, DC:
      NCEA, 1985.

437. Benson, Peter, Dorothy Williams, and Robert
      Yeager. "Study Assesses Quality of

Catholic High Schools." _Momentum,_
September 1984, pp. 4-6.

438. Benson, Peter, Carolyn Eklin, and Michael
      Guerra. "What Are the Religious Beliefs of
      Teachers in Catholic High Schools?"
      Momentum, February 1985, pp. 24-29.

439. Berrian, George. "NCEA Elementary Department
      Identifies Excellence." _Momentum,_ September
      1984, pp. 66-67.

440. Bryk, Anthony, Peter Holland, Valerie Lee, and
      Ruben Carriedo. _Effective Catholic Schools:
      An Exploration._ Washington, DC: NCEA,
      1984.

441. Bryk, Anthony. "Exploring Effective Catholic
      Schools." _Harvard Graduate School of
      Education Bulletin,_ Fall 1984, pp. 22-25.

442. Bryk, Anthony, and Peter Holland. "The
      Implications of Greeley's Latest Research."
      Momentum, October 1981, pp. 8-11.

443. Bryk, Anthony, and Peter Holland. "Research
      Provides Perspectives on Effective Catholic
      Schools." _Momentum,_ September 1984, pp.
      12-14.

444. _Catholic Schools in Action: The Notre Dame
      Study of Catholic Elementary and Secondary
      Schools._ Notre Dame, IN: University of
      Notre Dame Press, 1966.

445. Cibulka, James, Timothy O'Brien, and Donald
      Zewe. _Inner-City Private Elementary
      Schools._ Milwaukee: Marquette University
      Press, 1982.

446. Coleman, James S. , Thomas Hoffer, Sally
     Kilgore. High School Achievement: Public,
     Catholic, and Private Schools Compared. New
     York: Basic Books, 1982.

447. Convey, John. "Encouraging Findings About
     Student's Religious Values." Momentum, May
     1984, pp. 47-49.

448. Cooper, Bruce S. , Donald McLaughlin, and Bruno
     V. Manno. "The Latest Word on Private
     School Growth." Teachers College Record 85
     (Fall 1983): 88-98.

449. Delaney, Elaine, Jane Richards, and Marlene
     Strathe. "A Study of the Single Parent in
     the Catholic School." Momentum, December
     1984, pp. 41-43.

450. Doyle, Denis P. , and Marsha Levine. "Private
     Meets Public: An Examination of
     Contemporary Education." In Meeting Human
     Needs. Washington, DC: American Enterprise
     Institute, 1982.

451. Elford, George, and Patricia Feistritzer.
     "Report on the Contemporary Youth Concerns
     Survey." Momentum, May 1982, pp. 4-7.

452. FADICA, Toward More Effective Research in the
     Church. Washington, DC: FADICA, 1981.

     Fichter, Joseph H. Parochial Schools: A
     Sociological Study. Notre Dame, IN:
     University of Notre Dame Press, 1958.

     * See item 1120.

453. Greeley, Andrew M. Catholic High Schools and
     Minority Students. New Brunswick, NJ:
     Transaction Books, 1982.

454.   Greeley, Andrew M.   "The Catholic Schools," pp.
        129-149. In American Catholics Since the
        Council: An Unauthorized Report. Chicago:
        Thomas More, 1985.

455.   Greeley, Andrew M.   Catholic Schools in a
        Declining Church. New York: Sheed and
        Ward, 1976.

456.   Greeley, Andrew M.   "Schooling in the USA."
        Tablet, May 9, 1981, pp. 448-450.

457.   Greeley, Andrew M. , and Peter Rossi.   The
        Education of American Catholics. Chicago:
        Aldine Publishing, 1966.

458.   Hogan, Padraig.   "The Question of Ethos in
        Schools." Furrow, November 1984, pp.
        693-703.

459.   Kelly, James R.   "Catholic Schools in a
        Declining Church: A Review Article."
        America, May 15, 1976, pp. 424-426.

460.   Manno, Bruno V.   "An Update on the Coleman
        Study: An Interview with Sally Kilgore and
        Thomas Hoffer." Momentum, October 1982, pp.
        4-8.

461.   Manno, Bruno V.   "Catholic Elementary and
        Secondary Schools." Catholicism in Crisis,
        May 1983, pp. 9-11.

462.   Manno, Bruno V.   "The Catholic Family, the
        School, and the Religious Imagination: An
        Interview with Andrew Greeley." Momentum,
        February 1981, pp. 14-17.

463.   Manno, Bruno V.   "Young Catholics:
        Continuities and Changes - An Interview with
        William McCready." Momentum, October 1981,
        pp. 18-20.

464. Marmion, John P. "Catholic Education: The
        Changing Scene in America: The Education of
        Catholic Americans and the Study Catholic
        Schools in a Declining Church." Clergy
        Review 62 (July 1977): 285-288.

465. Murnane, Richard. "A Review Essay - A
        Comparison of Public and Private Schools:
        Lessons from the Uproar." Journal of Human
        Resources 19 (Spring 1984): 263-277.

466. Smith, Robert L. "Quality Private and Public
        Schools Compared." Momentum, May 1985, pp.
        36-39.

467. Strommen, Merton. "Eight Factors in School
        Vitality." Momentum, February 1980, pp.
        32-35.

468. Symposium: "The Catholic High School: A
        National Portrait." Momentum, May 1985, pp.
        8-23.

469. Symposium: "The Catholic School." New
        Catholic World, March/April 1981, pp. 52-91.

470. Symposium: see especially, Greeley, Andrew M.
        "A School Report." Tablet, March 27, 1976,
        pp. 313-319.

471. Symposium: "Greeley's Study on Catholic
        Schools." St. Anthony Messenger, August
        1976, pp. 20-26.

472. Symposium: see especially, Hornsby-Smith,
        Michael P., "Catholic Research Priorities";
        Wicker, Brian, "Adult Education"; Forrester,
        D., "Youth in the Church." Tablet, February
        24, 1979, pp. 183-189.

473. Symposium: see especially, McCready, William,
          "Generation Gap"; Gain, Michael, "Catholic
          Research." Tablet, November 29, 1975, pp.
          1163-1173.

474. Symposium: "Reflections on the 1981 Coleman
          Study." Momentum, October 1981, pp. 4-12.

475. Symposium: "A Research Report on Young
          Adolescents and Their Parents." Momentum,
          February 1984, pp. 8-16.

476. Symposium: "Toward the Tricentennial."
          Momentum, October 1976, pp. 2-56.

477. Thompson, Andrew. That They May Know You.
          Washington, DC: NCEA, 1982; a national
          analysis of the data from the NCEA religious
          education inventories.

478. Vitullo-Martin, Thomas. Catholic Inner-City
          Schools. Washington, DC: United States
          Catholic Conference Publications, 1979.

NCEA issues an annual report on Catholic elementary
          and secondary schools, that discusses
          enrollment, staffing, and school trends.
          Write to the NCEA Publications Office for
          more information.

SERVICE PROGRAMS

    Much of the recent literature on the reform of
public education calls for adding a mandatory
community service component to student curriculum
requirements. There is some irony in this call. As
long ago as 1972, the US National Conference of
Catholic Bishops stated that one of the aims of
Catholic schools is to help students grow in service
to others. Catholic educators saw that this could
best be accomplished by making community service

programs an integral component of a student's
Catholic school experience. The commentary prior to
the entries found in the Philosophy section provides
more information on this notion. These articles
provide a rationale for service programs and provide
practical suggestions on how best to foster them.

479. Buerman, Fred, and Ken Roling. "Student
        Service Programs are a Basic of Education."
        Momentum, December 1984, pp. 20-21.

480. Duffy, Joseph. "Service Programs: Do They
        Make a Difference?" Momentum, October 1982,
        pp. 33-35.

481. Murphy, Richard. "Establishing a Christian
        Service Program in the Catholic High
        School." Ministry Management, October 1985,
        pp. 1-4.

THEOLOGY; RELIGIOUS EDUCATION

All that is said in the Philosophy section serves
as useful commentary to the entries which follow. In
addition, though, it is helpful to stress one notion.
At base, Catholic schools have a theological reason
for existing. This is found in the person, message,
and life of Jesus Christ. This theological base of
education must influence the entire school. The
publications which follow examine the theoretical and
practical issues connected with this theological base
and how this conditions all which occurs within the
Catholic school.

482. A Vision for the Catechetical Ministry: An
        Instrument for Diocesan and Parish Planning.
        Washington, DC: NCEA, 1985.

483. Attridge, Terrence. "The Role of a Pastoral
        Office in a High School." Living Light 16
        (Winter 1979): 506-515.

484. Baum, William. "Vatican Report on Catholic
      Education: The 1983 Synod of Bishops."
      Origins, November 17, 1983, pp. 391-395.

485. Brown, Raymond. "The Dilemma of the
      Magisterium vs. the Theologians: Debunking
      Some Fictions." Chicago Studies 17 (Summer
      1978): 290-307.

486. Chittister, Joan. "No Time for Nicodemus: The
      Prophetic Role of Catholic Education."
      Origins, June 7, 1984, pp. 49-51.

487. Dulles, Avery. The Communication of the Faith
      and Its Content. Washington, DC: NCEA,
      1985.

488. Eckersley, Peter. "The Development of
      Chaplaincies in Catholic Schools."
      Momentum, September 1984, pp. 46-47.

489. Flynn, John. "The Teaching Ministry." Today's
      Catholic Teacher, February 1979, pp. 42-43.

490. Greenleaf, Richard. "The Leadership Crisis:
      What It Is and What To Do About It."
      Humanities 14 (November 1978): 297-308.

491. Groome, Thomas. Christian Religious Education:
      Sharing Our Story and Vision. New York:
      Harper, 1980.

492. Hawker, James. Catechesis in the Catholic
      School. Washington, DC: NCEA, 1985.

493. Hellwig, Monica. Tradition: The Catholic
      Story. New York: Pflaum, 1974.

494. Kearney, James. "The Ministry of the Teacher."
      Today's Catholic Teacher, January 1984, pp.
      48-49.

495. Marthaler, Berard, and Marianne Sawicke.
     Catechesis: Realities and Visions.
     Washington, DC: United States Catholic
     Conference Publications, 1977.

496. McBride, Alfred. "Catholic Schools: An
     Experience in Faith." Our Sunday Visitor
     Magazine, April 18, 1976, pp. 1-2.

497. Nicholas, K. "Toward a Theology of Education."
     Tablet, August 4, 1979, pp. 751-754.

498. Nunes, Stephen. "The Distinctive Roles of
     Catechist and Youth Minister in the Catholic
     High School." Living Light 17 (Summer
     1980): 144-149.

499. Reck, Carleen and Donald. "Catholic Education
     as a Ministry." Today's Catholic Teacher,
     September 1977, pp. 12-13.

500. Reynolds, Brian. "Peer Ministry in the
     Catholic High School." Ministry Management,
     October 1983, pp. 1-4.

501. Sork, David. The Catechist Formation Book.
     Ramsey, NJ: Paulist, 1981.

502. Stoever, Jane. "Schools as Faith Communities."
     National Catholic Reporter, October 22,
     1976, pp. 708-709.

503. Symposium: "Education in Values for the
     Catholic School." Lumen Vitae 37 (1982):
     249-294.

504. Symposium: "The Ministry of Teaching."
     Momentum, October 1977, pp. 4-52.

505. Traviss, Mary Peter. "The Ecclesial Mission of
     the School." Today's Catholic Teacher,
     September 1976, pp. 8-10.

506. Vision: A Christian Reality. Washington, DC:
      NCEA, 1982.

507. Warren, Michael. "Youth Ministry: The
      Dimensions of Care." Origins, January 28,
      1982, pp. 520-524.

508. Warrick, Keith. "Campus Ministry: What?
      How?" Ministry Management, December 1980,
      pp. 1-4.

509. Zanzig, Thomas. "Evangelization, Christian
      Religious Education, and Catechesis: Does
      Their Difference Make a Difference?"
      Ministry Management, April 1982, pp. 1-3.

UNIONS

Labor or employer-employee relations have
increasingly become an issue being faced by many of
those who are part of the Catholic school community.
Since this just desire to organize and bargain
collectively takes place within a school community of
faith, it should be done in a collaborative manner.
These publications examine various perspectives on
employer-employee relations within the Catholic
school.

510. Augenstein, John. A Collaborative Approach to
      Personnel Relations. Washington, DC: NCEA,
      1980.

511. Clifford, Peter. "Contracts, Unions, and
      Collective Bargaining." Momentum, April
      1971, pp. 32-37.

512. Grover, Veronica. "Justice for Teachers."
      Momentum, October 1979, pp. 14-16.

513. Fullerman, Joan, Julie Isert, and Patrick
     Reddington. "Justice for Teachers."
     Momentum, May 1978, pp. 29-32.

514. Leary, Mary Ellen. "Educators' Unions? Try
     Alternatives." National Catholic Reporter,
     June 18, 1976, p. 2.

MISCELLANEOUS

515. Berry, Dennis. "The Role of Athletics in
     Catholic Schools." Momentum, May 1982, pp.
     36-37.

516. Carr, Timothy. "Drug Abuse: Catholic Schools
     Are Not Immune." Momentum, May 1982, pp.
     11-14.

517. Contemporary Issues in Catholic High Schools.
     Washington, DC: NCEA, 1981.

518. Delaney, Elaine, Jane Richards and Marlene
     Strathe. "A Study of the Single Parent
     Child in Catholic Schools." Momentum,
     December 1984, pp. 41-43.

519. "Excellence in Catholic Education." Momentum,
     September 1984 (theme issue).

520. Flosi, James. "Children of Divorce."
     Momentum, October 1980, pp. 30-33.

521. Foster, Dorothy. "Saving Our Children From
     Alcoholism." Momentum, May 1982, pp. 15-17.

522. Fostering Discipline and Discipleship Within
     the Catholic Educational Community.
     Washington, DC: NCEA, 1985.

523. Gallagher, Vera. "The Dropout: A New
     Challenge to Catholic Education." Momentum,
     May 1985, pp. 40-41.

524. Garanzini, Michael. "Recognizing and
      Responding to the Child of Divorce."
      Momentum, May 1984, pp. 8-11.

525. McBride, Alfred. "Major Challenges Facing
      Catholic Education in the 1980s." Momentum,
      December 1982, pp. 9-11.

526. The Media Mirror: A Study Guide on Christian
      Values and Television. Washington, DC:
      NCEA, 1984.

527. O'Brien, J. Stephen, ed. Gathering God's
      People: Signs of a Successful Parish.
      Washington, DC: NCEA, 1982.

528. O'Laughlin, Jeanne. "The Future of Catholic
      Schools: A Perception." Education 102
      (Summary 1982): 322-325.

529. O'Neill, Michael. "Relationships and
      Schooling." Today's Catholic Teacher,
      February 1980, pp. 11-12.

530. Olsen, John, and Joseph Umphries. "Competency-
      Basecd Requirements: They Do Affect
      Catholic Schools." Momentum, February 1979,
      pp. 18-21.

531. Reitz, Donald J. "Coping With Student
      Pregnancy in the Christian Community."
      Momentum, December 1984, pp. 26-28.

532. Stafford, James. "Reflections on Catholic
      Education." Origins, June 2, 1983, pp.
      63-64.

533. Swenceski, Connie. "A New 'Parenting' Role for
      Schools." Momentum, February 1984, pp.
      24-26.

534. Traviss, Mary Peter.   Student Moral Development
         in the Catholic School.   Washington, DC:
         NCEA, 1985.

535. Vasiloff, Barbara.   "Discipline: The Challenge
         of the 80's."   Today's Catholic Teacher,
         October 1983, pp. 32-34.

536. Yeager, Robert, ed.   Catholic Secondary
         Education: Now and In the Future.
         Washington, DC: NCEA, 1982.

537. Zaffran, Ronald.   "Developmental Guidance in
         Catholic Elementary Schools."   Journal of
         Humanistic Education and Development 22
         (June 1984):   170-177.

538. Zaffran, Ronald.   "Developmental Guidance in
         Catholic Secondary Schools."   Journal of
         Humanistic Education and Development 23
         (March 1985):   134-144.

CHAPTER 8
CHURCH OF THE BRETHREN SCHOOLS
Murray L. Wagner

539. Bowman, Paul Haynes. Brethren Education in the
      Southeast. Bridgewater, VA: Bridgewater
      College, 1956.

      Traces the efforts of Brethren to found
      various preparatory schools from Maryland to
      Alabama, and shows how those efforts culminated
      in the establishment of Bridgewater College.
      Discusses attempts at providing secondary
      education beginning in 1958 at Cedar Grove
      Academy in Broadway, Virginia and ending with
      the closing of Daleville Academy in Daleville,
      Virginia in 1933.

540. Boyers, Auburn A. "Changing Conceptions of
      Education in the Church of the Brethren."
      Ph.D. dissertation. University of
      Pittsburgh, 1968.

      Summarizes the controversy over education
      that has been an integral part of Brethren
      history. Discusses how the historical Brethren
      attitudes toward education affected efforts to
      establish schools.

541. Flory, John S. "A History of Education in the
      Church of the Brethren." In Educational
      Blue Book and Directory, pp. 21-104. Edited
      by W. Arthur Cable and Homer F. Sanger.
      Elgin, IL: The General Education Board of
      the Church of the Brethren, 1923.

      Discusses the course of Brethren education
      beginning with ardent support of schools in the
      1700's, followed by a period of opposition to
      education, then a revival of interest in
      education in the late 1800's. Describes the
      academies (high school level) that were
      established beginning in 1852 which paved the
      way for Brethren colleges.

542. Hanle, Robert V. "A History of Higher
      Education in the Church of the Brethren."
      Ph.D. dissertation. University of
      Pennsylvania, 1974.

      Traces Brethren efforts to provide education
      at elementary, secondary and higher levels from
      1708-1908. Focuses on the effect that Brethren
      attitudes toward education had on educational
      endeavors.

543. Legman, James H. Beyond Anything Foreseen: A
      Study of the History of Higher Education in
      the Church and the Brethren. Prepared for
      the Conference on Higher Education and the
      Church of the Brethren at Earlham College.
      Richmond, IN: 1976.

      Focuses mainly on the development of
      Brethren colleges, mentioning the earlier
      schools of academy (high school) level that
      helped to prepare the way.

544. Noffsinger, John S. A Program for Higher
      Education in the Church of the Brethren.
      New York: Columbia University, 1925.

Gives a brief history of the three eras of
Brethren educational activities: 1) Colonial
(1708-1778); 2) Wilderness (1778-1850); and 3)
Liberalization (1850-present); then focuses
primarily on the establishment of colleges.

545.   Sharp, S. Z.   The Educational History of the
       Church of the Brethren.   Elgin, IL:
       Brethren Publishing House, 1923.

Begins with a history of Brethren education
from 1708-1960; then gives a short sketch of
each of the Brethren educational institutions
established between 1860 and 1923, including
both secondary and college levels.

Repositories

Relatively complete collections of Brethren
documents, literature, and periodicals may be found
in repositories as follows:

Ashland Theological Seminary Library, Ashland, Ohio
    44805

Bethany Theological Seminary Library, Meyers and
    Butterfield Roads, Oak Brook, Illinois   60521

Brethren Historical Library and Archives, Church of
    the Brethren General Offices, 1451 Dundee Avenue,
    Elgin, Illinois   60120

Bridgewater College Library, Bridgewater, Virginia
    22812

Elizabethtown College Library, Elizabethtown,
    Pennsylvania   17022

Grace Theological Seminary Library, Winona Lake,
    Indiana   46590

Juniata College Library, Huntingdon, Pennsylvania
16652

Manchester College Library, North Manchester, Indiana
46962

McPherson College Library, McPherson, Kansas   67460

University of La Verne Library, La Verne, California
91750

CHAPTER 9
EPISCOPAL SCHOOLS
John Paul Carter

Part I: Historical

COLONIAL BEGINNINGS

Because the Church of England was established, the roots and early history of Episcopal Church education must be found from sources which specialize on the colonial beginnings. The major collections of manuscripts and public records are to be found at Princeton University, in the combined resources of Colonial Williamsburg and the Swem Library at the College of William & Mary, at Columbia University (which was an Anglican foundation), and perhaps surprisingly in the microfilm collections of the University of Texas and the University of California at Berkeley. The Episcopal School in longest continuous existence is Trinity School, 139 W. 91st St., New York, NY 10024. Its earliest records are in the archives of Trinity Parish, 74 Trinity Place, New York, NY 10006, which is the mother church for all of the colony of New York.

In London, the Society for the Promotion of
Christian Knowledge was founded in 1699 to furnish
libraries, pamphlets and other Christian literature
under Anglican auspices. This was followed in 1701
with the founding of the Society for the Propagation
of the Gospel in Foreign Parts (SPG), purposed to
recruit and support missionaries and teachers
overseas. Both organizations continue to this day.

A complete set of the microfilms of the
proceedings, missionary correspondence, financial
reports, and political representations in England
before the various commissions of the government are
to be found in the library of the University of
Texas. An eastern source of microfilmed material of
the SPG is the Missionary Research Library at Union
Theological Seminary, New York City. Two journals of
long standing with many articles relating to the
earliest Anglican education are The Historical
Magazine of the Episcopal Church, Box 2247, Austin,
TX 76748; and The William & Mary Quarterly,
Williamsburg, VA 23185 -- collections of the former
will be found in the library of every seminary of the
Episcopal Church, and of the latter at every major
university library.

Works which provide adequate resources for survey,
basic background, and specific educational activities
of the Episcopal Church are listed in the section
below.

546.   Bailyn, Bernard. Education in the Forming of
       American Society. Chapel Hill: University
       of North Carolina Press, 1960.

547.   Ballou, Richard Boyd. "The Grammar Schools in
       Seventeenth Century Colonial America."
       Ph.D. dissertation. Harvard University,
       1940.

548. Bell, Sadie. The Church, State, and Education in Virginia. Philadelphia: The Science Press, 1930.

549. Bruce, Philip Alexander. Institutional History of Virginia in the Seventeenth Century, 2 vols. New York: G. P. Putnam's Sons, 1910.

550. Brydon, George Maclaren. Virginia's Mother Church and the Political Conditions Under Which It Grew. Vol. 1. Richmond: Virginia Historical Society, 1947, and Vol. 2. Philadelphia: Church History Society, 1952.

551. Calam, John. "Parsons and Pedagogues: The S. P. G. Adventure in American Education." Ph. D. dissertation. Columbia University, 1969.

552. Eggleston, Edward. The Transit of Civilization from England to America in the Seventeenth Century. New York: D. Appleton & Co., 1900.

553. Morison, Samuel Eliot. The Pilgrim Pronaos: Studies in the Intellectual Life of New England. New York: New York University Press, 1936.

554. Morton, Richard L. Colonial Virginia, 2 vols. Chapel Hill: The University of North Carolina Press, 1960.

555. Vassar, Rena Lee. "Elementary and Latin Grammar School Education in the American Colonies, 1607-1700." Ph. D. dissertation. University of California, Berkeley, 1958.

556. Webb, William Kemp. The Support of Schools in Colonial New York by the Society for the Propagation of the Gospel in Foreign Parts. New York: Teachers College, Columbia University, 1913.

557. Wells, Guy Fred. Parish Education in Colonial
     Virginia. New York: Teachers College,
     Columbia University, 1923.

POST-REVOLUTION

After the Revolution, the disestablishment left
the successor church, The Protestant Episcopal Church
in the United States of America, reeling, broken, and
virtually destitute. Before the War, with neither
seminaries nor bishops in the colonies, the supply of
clergy had always been meager, but now with many of
the clergy gone as Tories, the ranks were decimated.
In some cases church buildings were expropriated.
Tax support and glebe lands were removed. The
picture in 1800 was one of ruin; but by 1900, the
Episcopal Church was strong and vigorous, an
accelerating force that rode the crest of the social
and economic advances of the age. The establishment
of Episcopal boarding schools during the 19th century
placed the Church at the very leadership of American
private education and this growth continued until the
Depression. The Episcopal High School, Groton, St.
Paul's School, St. Mark's School, St. James', and
many others exercised powerful influence. Several
key works which deal with the boarding school
movement follow.

558. Auburn, Davis Ashburn. Peabody of Groton. New
     York: Coward McCann, 1944.

     Provides an excellent biography of Peabody
     and Groton.

559. McLachlan, James. American Boarding School.
     New York: Charles Scribner's Sons, 1970.
     (See especially Chapter 9.)

     Presents an accurate overview of life in
     Episcopal boarding schools.

560. Skardon, Alvin Wilson. <u>Church</u> <u>Leader</u> <u>in</u> <u>the</u>
      <u>Cities</u>. Philadelphia: University of
      Pennsylvania Press, 1971.

      Describes the life of William Augustus
      Muhlenberg, and portrays the development of
      Episcopal education in the cities.

PARISH DAY SCHOOLS

   With the rise of the Sunday School movement, some
      of the more affluent and socially conscious
      parishes became concerned with the educational
      needs of the industrial and urban poor. Many
      of the clergy and lay leaders who had taken
      responsibility in the development of public
      schools now turned their attention toward
      parish day schools. Impetus was added with the
      social gospel concerns that marked the years
      following the Civil War. These parish day
      schools were not at first closely allied to the
      boarding schools, nor were they well-organized
      as were the boarding schools. Albright's work,
      with its careful index, is a most helpful
      source for this period.

561. Albright, Raymond W. <u>A</u> <u>History</u> <u>of</u> <u>the</u>
      <u>Protestant</u> <u>Episcopal</u> <u>Church</u>. New York:
      Macmillan Co. , 1964.

562. Cremin, Lawrence A. <u>American</u> <u>Education:</u> <u>The</u>
      <u>National</u> <u>Experience,</u> <u>1783-1876</u>. Vol. 2.
      New York: Harper & Row, 1980.

FROM THE CIVIL WAR TO THE DEPRESSION

   From the Civil War to the Depression, both the
boarding schools and the parish day schools
maintained a steady and evolutionary growth. The
period of great advance came during and after World
War II. The headmasters of the most prestigious

schools had long been allied in the Headmaster's
Association, and many of them led Episcopal schools.
When the Church began to concentrate on Christian
Education shortly after the close of the war, the
headmasters of Groton, Kent, Wooster, and other
leading schools were enlisted to work with the parish
day schools, then organized as the Episcopal School
Association. The result was the formation of the
National Association of Episcopal Schools, with
generous assistance from the Department of Christian
Education of the Episcopal Church. Under a
succession of leaders, this organization continues
and is housed in the headquarters of the Church at
815 Second Avenue, New York, NY 10017. Under its
stimulus, subdivisions have been made for pre-
schools, lower schools, and upper schools, and all
have available publications and conference reports.
Large and influential conferences have been held at
three-year intervals since 1957. Representative
works from this period are identified below.

563. Baldwin, A. Graham and Earl G. Harrison, Jr.
     Commitment and the School Community.
     Greenwich: Seabury, 1960.

564. Church Ideals in Education. New York, 1916.
     (A description of the aims and work of the
     General Board of Religious Education of the
     Protestant Episcopal Church.)

565. Evaluative Criteria for the Schools Associated
     with the Episcopal Church. Published first
     in 1962 by the Committee on Standards and
     Criteria of the Episcopal School
     Association, and revised periodically, is
     available through the office of the National
     Association of Episcopal Schools, 815 Second
     Avenue, New York, NY 10007.

566. Gaebelein, Frank E., Earl G. Harrison, Jr., and
     William L. Swing. Education for Decision.
     Seabury: Greenwich, 1963.

567. Parish Day School Report. New York:
     Department of the Protestant Episcopal
     Church. Issued in 1953, 1957 et. seq.

568. Strachan, Malcolm and Alvord Beardslee. The
     Christian Faith and Youth Today. Greenwich,
     CT: Seabury Press, 1957.

569. The Constitution for the Episcopal School
     Association. New York: 1956. (Available
     from the office of the National Episcopal
     Schools.)

570. The Constitution of the National Association of
     Episcopal Schools. rev. (Available from the
     office of the National Episcopal Schools.)

MID-CENTURY EDUCATIONAL EFFORTS

571. Agee, James. The Morning Watch. New York:
     Houghton Mifflin, 1961.

     Deals with life at a boarding school for
     mountain boys on the Cumberland Plateau of
     Tennessee.

572. Auchinclos, Louis. The Rector of Justin. New
     York: Houghton Mifflin, 1964.

     Describes life at a famous Massachusetts
     boarding school for sons of the elite.

573. Brickman, Clarence W. ed. The Church's
     Ministry of Reconciliation in the Field of
     Education. New York: Department of
     Christian Education of the National Council
     of the Protestant Episcopal Church, 1964.

574. Brickman, Clarence W., ed. The Church's
     Schools in a Changing World. Greenwich, CT:
     Seabury Press, 1961.

575. Fuller, Edmund, ed. The Christian Idea of
      Education. New Haven: Yale University
      Press, 1957.

576. Fuller, Edmund, ed. Schools and Scholarship.
      New Haven: Yale University Press, 1962.

      Provides, with The Christian Idea of
      Education, an excellence insight into the level
      of intellection that underlies the creative
      level of the Episcopal Schools movement. These
      two volumes (numbers 575 and 576) are the
      result of two conferences which celebrated the
      fiftieth anniversary of Kent School. These
      conferences were highlighted by the
      presentations of major Christian intellectuals
      as speakers/reflectors upon Christian
      education, e. g. , Jacques Maritain, George
      Florovsky, Reinhold Niebuhr, John Courtney
      Murray, Henri Peyre, Albert Mollegen, Anne
      Freemantle, William G. Pollard, and Edward
      Teller.

577. Reischauer, Edwin O. Education Toward the
      Twenty-first Century. New York: Knopf,
      distributed by Random House, 1973.

      Contains his central ideas on education
      which were delivered at the Triennial
      Conference of the National Association of
      Episcopal Schools.

CHAPTER 10
EVANGELICAL REFORMED CHURCH SCHOOLS
Charles R. Kniker

578. Banzhaf, Richard F. "The Eight Colleges of the
      Evangelical and Reformed Church: A Study in
      Changing Religious Character." Ed. D.
      dissertation. Teachers College, Columbia
      University, 1973.

      Discusses the mingling of diverse
      denominational traditions from 1837 to 1972
      within the educational institutions of the
      Evangelical and Reformed Church, including the
      impact made by the parochial schools, pp.
      23-84.

579. Bek, William G. "The Followers of Duden: The
      First German Public School West of the
      Mississippi." Missouri Historical Review 16
      (October 1921): 119-45.

      Describes the beginnings of German parochial
      schools in the frontier St. Louis area.

580. Brueggeman, Walter. The Evangelical Catechism
      Revisited. St. Louis: Eden Publishing
      House, 1986.

Analyzes the Evangelical Catechism, a major tool used by German Evengelicals in America for confirmation of students following their training in parochial schools.

Curran, Francis X.   The Churches and the Schools: American Protestantism and Popular Elementary Education.   Chicago: Loyola University Press, 1954.

* See item 188.

581.   Dubbs, Joseph Henry.   Historic Manual of the Reformed Church.   Lancaster, PA: Inquirer Printing Co. , 1885.

Provides a summary of parochial and Sunday schools within the German Reformed Church, pp. 340-343.

582.   Koenig, Robert E.   "Our Educational Heritage Through the Evangelical Tradition."   Church School Worker 7 (December 1966): 19-23.

Includes a brief survey of Evangelical parochial schools (with statistical data) from the 1860s to World War I.

583.   Livingood, Frank G.   Eighteenth Century Reformed Church Schools.   Norristown, PA: Norristown Press, 1930.

Reports the results of a survey of 124 church schools in 188 German Reformed Churches during the eighteenth century, including lists of more than one hundred parish school teachers.

584.   Pedagogical Journal (in German).

Addresses parochial school teachers, conveying to them ideas of Froebel and Pestalozzi. Published monthly, from 1983 to 1898, by the German Evangelical Synod of North America.

585. Schaff, Philip. _America: A Sketch of Its Political, Social, and Religious Character_. Cambridge, MA: Harvard University Press, 1961.

Describes the German Reformed and the German Evangelical Churches in America, in a reprint of a classic 1854 account, pp. 159-166.

586. Schneider, Carl E. _The German Church on the American Frontier_. St. Louis: Eden Publishing House, 1939.

Summarizes the development of Evangelical parochial schools in America from about 1840 to 1866, pp. 279-287. Includes scholarly footnotes.

587. Spotts, Charles D. "Our Educational Heritage Through the Reformed Tradition." _Church School Worker_ 17 (October 1966): 15-17.

Provides a brief summary of educational work, including parochial schools, throughout German Reformed history.

CHAPTER 11
FRIENDS, RELIGIOUS SOCIETY OF, SCHOOLS
Clayton L. Farraday

Part I: Historical

588. A Man and a School. Newtown, PA: George
      School, 1965.

      Contains six essays and a tribute to George
Walton. Of particular interest are the four
sections on "Expanding Horizons," "Concern for
all Students--the General Curriculum,"
"Religion and Education," and "The Educational
Philosophy."

589. Bickley, William Phillips. "Education as
      Reformation: An Examination of Orthodox
      Quakers' Formation of the Haverford School
      Association and Founding of Haverford
      School, 1815-1840." Ed.D. dissertation.
      Harvard University, 1983.

      Discusses the founding of the Haverford
School; Orthodox Quakers were responding to
what they viewed as the dissolution of their
religious community. It was their attempt to
use an educational institution to reform their
community. The School is examined as a
response to conflict, schism, and
disintegration of the American Quaker
community.

590.   Biddle, Owen. A Plan for a School on an
        Establishment Similar to that at Ackworth,
        in Yorkshire, Great Britain, varied to suite
        the Circumstances of the Youth within the
        Limits of the Yearly Meeting for
        Pennsylvania and New Jersey. Philadelphia:
        Joseph Crukshank, 1790.

591.   Brinton, Howard H. Quaker Education in Theory
        and Practice. Wallingford, PA: Pendle Hill
        Publications, Pamphlet #9, 1969.

        Discusses how the clear-cut philosophy of
        education planned by the Society of Friends was
        based solidly on its religious faith and
        practice. This book attempts to show that
        these principles grow out of a special type of
        community which has a pattern of living
        somewhat differently from that of the world
        around it. This pattern seeks to propagate in
        the world the divine-human and inter-human
        relationships developed within itself.

592.   Brown, Miriam Jones. Friends School Haverford
        1885-1985. Exton, PA: Schiffer Publishing,
        Ltd., 1985.

        Mirrors many of the changes which occurred
        in elementary education; this is the history of
        an elementary school in suburban Philadelphia
        through its first century. Changes are
        modified and adopted in this school under the
        influence of the principles governing the
        Society of Friends.

593.   Deweess, Watson W. and Sarah B. History of
        Westtown Boarding School 1799-1899.
        Westtown, PA: Westtown Alumni Association,
        1899.

Discusses the account of the trials and tribulations, the fires, the joys and successes of a rural, coeducational boarding school through the fourteen administrations of school principals and the Committee on Education for the school.

594. Dunlap, William Cook. Quaker education in Baltimore and Virginia Yearly Meeting. Lancaster, PA: Science Press Printing Co., 1936.

595. Farraday, Clayton L. Friends' Central School 1845-1984. Philadelphia: Friends Central School, 1984.

Contains references to the Eight Year Study of the Progressive Education Association, and to Exchange Programs with schools outside the U.S.A.

596. "First things first, the case for Friends Schools." Philadelphia: Philadelphia Yearly Meeting, 1942.

Presents an anonymous account written by a parent in appreciation of the little Friends School in his community. In this school there was security, serenity, scholarship, spirituality and sensitivity for the children in contrast to the hectic world.

597. Fox, George. Instructions for Spelling, Reading, Writing. Boston: Rogers and Fowle, 1743.

Instructions for correct spelling and plain directions for reading and writing true English. With several delightful things, very useful and necessary both for young and old, to read and learn.

598.   Griscom, John. Considerations relative to an
        establishment for perfecting the education
        of young men within the Society of Friends.
        New York: Samuel Wood & Sons, 1915.

599.   Harrison, Earl G., Jr. "Friends Work with
        Youth," in Seven Essays, Break the New
        Ground. Birmingham, England: Friends World
        Committee for Consultation, 1969.

        Discusses Quaker work with youth which must
        speak to needs not numbers. Our youth are an
        insignificant fraction of the teenage
        multitudes. We must demand the highest
        standards of preparation, caring, productivity;
        update our thinking; meet the youth where they
        are; lead toward experiences that will have
        meaning.

600.   Heath, Douglas H. Why a Friends School?
        Wallingford, PA: Pendle Hill Publications,
        Pamphlet #164, 1969.

        States that Friends should keep science and
        technology and their associated secularizing
        effects integrated within a larger
        humanistically patterned way of life. Keep the
        sciences strong, but keep the humanities,
        religious and ethical traditions stronger. The
        enduring strength of Quakerism lies in the
        reciprocal and integral combination of its
        individualistic and communal tradition.

601.   Hinshaw, Edwin E. Adventuring with Youth.
        Richmond, IN: Friends United Press, 1969.

        Contains the answers to a great number of
        requests for something new and different in the
        area of youth work. It is an idea-resource
        volume aimed at building a group--not just a
        gathering of people--but a closely knit group

in which each member is sensitive to the needs, concerns and feelings of others. It is intended to be used anywhere and anytime that young people and their adult coaches get together for a meeting, a good time or a happening.

602. Hole, Helen G. Things Civil and Useful, A Personal View of Quaker Education. Richmond, IN: Friends United Press, 1978.

Contains essays that demonstrate that Quaker schools and colleges can no longer even pretend to be principally of service to Quaker families. The schools and colleges have, therefore, an extraordinary challenge which they are meeting in diverse ways and degrees. Their staffs and students constitute the largest bodies of non-Friends gathered daily under Quaker influence anywhere in the world.

603. Jones, Richard M. Fantasy and Feeling in Education. New York: Harper and Row, 1968.

Contains in chapters 2 and 3, "The Challenge of the 'New Social Studies'" and "Meeting the Challenge," a discussion of the course of study entitled: "Man: A Course of Study." This social studies program was used in classrooms in several Quaker schools.

604. Lester, John Ashby. "The Ideals and Objectives of Quaker Education." Philadelphia: Friends Council on Education, 1939.

Identifies the central values and purposes of Quakerism and examines the relationship between Quaker religious ideals in the light of conditions markedly different from those which influenced Friends in the beginning and Quaker education.

605.   Lester, John Ashby.   "The Place of the Quaker
       School in Contemporary Education."
       Philadelphia: Friends Council on Education,
       1931.

       Discusses that only as they turn their
       advantage of position to the enlargement of the
       vision of their boys and girls, as this vision
       is given them, can the independent schools,
       relying upon their individual character,
       justify themselves in the educational fabric.
       Quaker schools will need the courage and will
       to consolidate their position through giving
       the potential leaders entrusted to them a full
       share of the Quaker view of this great and
       immediate service.

606.   Loukes, Harold.   Friends and their Children.   A
       Study in Quaker Education.   London: George
       G. Harrap & Co. , Ltd. , 1958.

       Discusses the responsibility of parents for
       their children's religious education.   The
       author carries the concern through the
       preschool time and into the years of elementary
       training, adolescence, secondary schooling.
       All is leading toward a mature religion.

607.   Poley, Irvin C.   Speaking of Teaching.
       Philadelphia: Germantown Friends Schools,
       1957.

       Contains a selection of writings in honor of
       Poley's contributions to education and his
       forty-five years as an exciting teacher of
       English in Germantown Friends School.
       Amusement, concrete suggestions, scholarships,
       and wisdom for all teachers, particularly those
       who teach English or drama.

608. Preston, Ralph C. , ed. <u>Teaching World</u>
      <u>Understanding</u>. New York: Prentice Hall,
      1955.

      Describes tested procedures for developing
      understanding of the people of the world among
      young Americans. The authors have been
      associated with Quaker schools and other Quaker
      educational agencies. All have experimented in
      educating for world understanding and were
      encouraged by their affiliation with Quaker
      education.

609. Richie, David S. <u>Memories</u> <u>and</u> <u>Meditations</u> <u>of</u> <u>a</u>
      <u>Workcamper</u>. Wallingford, PA: Pendle Hill
      Publications, Pamphlet #190, 1973.

      Discusses how weekend work camps became an
      important part of high school social studies
      classes. They were intended as an educational
      instrument. The camp enabled young men and
      women of privileged groups to buy, with hard
      physical labor, their ticket into troubled
      communities where they could learn at firsthand
      about the problems and peoples concerned.
      Campers have met hostility and acceptance and
      learned to understand these responses.

610. <u>Sketch</u> <u>of</u> <u>the</u> <u>History</u> <u>of</u> <u>Education</u> <u>in</u> <u>the</u>
      <u>Society</u> <u>of</u> <u>Friends</u>. York, England: William
      Sessions, Friends' Educational Society,
      1871.

      Contains lectures on experiences in
      education in England and Ireland. Concerned
      with the influence and Authority, Duties and
      Difficulties of Young Teachers.

611. Speight, Harold E. B. <u>Why</u> <u>Quaker</u> <u>Schools</u>?
      Philadelphia: Friends Council on Education,
      1935.

Discusses one kind of the many independent schools. Holds that Friends have a special opportunity for service, first because they have been pioneers in education since the 17th century, and more important, because the kind of education which aims at socializing the child while preserving and strengthening his individuality is in accord with the religious conviction of Friends.

612. Steere, Douglas V. A Quaker Meeting for Worship. Philadelphia: Philadelphia Yearly Meeting, 1962.

Explains the Meeting for Worship for the Quakers who attend an unprogrammed meeting: the value of the silence, the development of vocal ministry, the value of the occasion to those who attend.

613. Stewart, W. A. Campbell. Quakers and Education as seen in their Schools in England. London: The Epworth Press, 1953.

Presents a fully integrated account of the outlook of the Society of Friends since the 17th century upon the subject of education. Complete information on principles, details of cost, staffing, curriculum, school government, coeducation.

614. Taber, William P. Jr. Be Gentle, Be Plain. A history of Olney Friends School. Barnesville, OH: Olney School, Alumni Association, 1976.

This is the story of a small boarding school following the orthodox philosophy of the Friends in the Ohio Yearly Meeting--more conservative in the approach to education than the more liberal philosophy. A religious and

intentive emphasis within the school community
of caring in which people may grow in the
useful blend of moral intensity, physical work,
and intellectual development.

615. "Two-and-a-Half Centuries of Quaker Education."
      The Friend (Phila.), Vol. 113 (1939) No. 9,
      pp. 153-160; No. 10, pp. 171-175.

      Presents a series of five lectures on Quaker
      education. The first three by Henry Cadbury,
      Wilmot Jones, and William Comfort emphasize the
      historical background, the problems of today,
      and the future of Quaker education.

616. Woody, Thomas. "Early Quaker Education in
      Pennsylvania." Ph.D. dissertation.
      Columbia University, 1918.

      Contains a detailed account of the founding
      of the schools in Pennsylvania, in Philadelphia
      and the surrounding counties, Bucks,
      Montgomery, Chester, and Delaware. William
      Penn's Charter (1697) for establishing schools
      is quoted in full. Problems of financial
      support, providing teachers and preparing
      curriculum are clearly stated.

Part II: Contemporary

617. Ball, Earl John, III. "Structuring a
      Differentiated Supervisory Program in an
      Independent School." Ed.D. dissertation.
      University of Pennsylvania, 1981.

      Describes the planning, implementation and
      evaluation of a program of differentiated
      teacher supervision and development designed
      for the upper and middle school faculty at the
      William Penn Charter School in Philadelphia.
      The concepts and procedures of clinical

supervision of Goldhammer and collegial and
differentiated supervision of Glatthorn were
key to the study. The personal reflections of
the author who was the headmaster form part of
the analysis.

618.   Boulding, Elise.   The Family as a Way into the
       Future. Wallingford, PA: Pendle Hill
       Publications, Pamphlet #222, 1978.

       Discusses the future of the Family as a
       subject approached with great anxiety now.
       Family-type togetherness is the oldest and
       longest continuing human experience. The way
       of the family is not a barrier between us and a
       better society but a path to that better
       society.

619.   Brown, Thomas S., ed.   "Friends as Leaders: The
       Vision, Instrument, and Methods."
       Philadelphia: Friends Council on Education,
       1980.

       Presents the summary of a workshop to study
       leaderships, divided into three groups seeking
       the vision of Quakerism engendering leadership,
       the traditions of Quakers defining leaders, the
       ways and means of discovering, educating,
       nurturing and supporting those who respond to
       the call to lead.

620.   Caldwell, Samuel.   "New Eyes for Invisibles in
       Quaker Education." Philadelphia: Committee
       on Education, Philadelphia Yearly Meeting,
       1980.

       Presents the opening speech on Friends
       Schools Day, 1980, asking the questions, "What
       can properly be said to the 'Quaker' about
       Quaker Education? What sort of education is
       this? What can be said to be its distinctive
       attributes?"

621. "Celebration for Friends Schools' Heads."
     Philadelphia: Friends Council on Education,
     1983.

     Contains two speeches presented to the heads
     of Quaker schools.
     1.   "The Joys of our Vocation and the
     Opportunities Ahead" by Elise Boulding.
     2.   "Quaker Education: Irresistible Forces
     Meeting Immovable Objects" by Tom Mullen.
     In #1 imagining is learning, opening up the
     self where new relationships are seen.   In #2
     if a Friend's school will confront my child,
     value my child, and share laughter with my
     child, it will be worth its tuition and
     religious heritage.

622. Currie, Julia Patton.   "The Description of a
     Process for the Development and Initial
     Implementation of a Course in Human
     Development and Parenting Education for
     Juniors and Seniors in High School: A Case
     Study." Ed. D. dissertation.   University of
     Pennsylvania, 1980.

     Discusses an attempt to answer five
     questions: 1) What research is available for
     developing curriculum materials? 2) What
     processes were used and what obstacles were
     encountered in the use of the processes? 3)
     What curriculum materials were produced and
     what alternatives suggested? 4) How successful
     were the materials? and 5) What conclusions can
     be drawn from a course on parenting?

623. Dorrance, Christopher A. , ed.   "Reflections
     from a Friends Education." Philadelphia:
     Friends Council on Education, Philadelphia
     Yearly Meeting, 1982.

Contains a series of articles written by students, teachers, and administrators telling their thoughts about Quaker School education as they participated in it.

624.   Faith and Practice.   Philadelphia:
        Philadelphia Yearly Meeting, 1978.

Contains the basics for the Society of Friends: Historical statement, Quaker faith, meeting community, human brotherhood, selections from the writing of Friends, practices and procedures.   This book is called, "A Book of Christian Discipline."

625.   Heath, Douglas H.   The Peculiar Mission of a
        Quaker School.   Wallingford, PA: Pendle
        Hill Publications, Pamphlet #225, 1979.

Reflects Heath's continuing interest in the meaning of a Friends education first described in his Pendle Hill Pamphlet, Why a Friends' School?   (Pamphlet #164, 1969).

626.   Kenworthy, Leonard S.   Quakerism--A Study Guide
        on the Religious Society of Friends.
        Dublin, IN: Prinit Press, 1981.

Presents a textbook approach to studying about Quakers.   History, philosophy, practices and procedures are presented with test questions at the end of each chapter.

627.   Kratzer, Jerod John.   "An Ethnography of an
        Advisor-Advisee Program in a Quaker Middle
        School."   Ed. D. dissertation.   North
        Carolina State University, 1984.

Discusses how most middle school experts have identified an Advisor-Advisee program as essential for an effective middle school program. This study is intended to add to the base of middle school philosophy and identify practical ideas for teachers and administrators.

628. Letchworth, Rachel K. "Friends Schools Handbook for Beginning Teachers and Those New to a Friends School." Philadelphia: Friends Council on Education, 1978.

Presents a summary of Quakerism, Quaker organizations, Testimonies and Concerns, Educational Organizations, and Advice for classroom procedures for beginning teachers.

629. Letchworth, Rachel K. "Yesterday, Today and Tomorrow?" Philadelphia: Friends Council on Education, 1981.

Tells the story of this national organization (1931-1981) for Friends schools. The Council offers leadership and inspiration for school committees, administrators and teachers through its many services in education.

630. Making Sense out of Consensus. Philadelphia: Friends Council on Education, 1982.

Discusses how consensus is a practice within the Society of Friends to come to a decision, though not necessarily a unanimous one, in a spirit of unity. It is an expression of a fundamental attitude. Contains actual procedure in a school.

631. Mallery, David. The Strength of a Good School Faculty: Notes on Education, Growth and Professional Partnership of Teachers. Boston, MA: National Association of Independent Schools, 1975.

Presents a plea for building on the strength of teachers through evaluation carried on by those who feel themselves to be partners, "Not car parts on an inspection line." Following the plea (pages 1-28) are a number of varied instruments of teacher evaluations and a bibliography. David Mallery was a very successful and creative teacher in a Quaker school and program director for the Friends Council on Education.

632.   "Occasional Papers on the Meeting for Worship for Friends Schools." Philadelphia: Friends Council on Education, 1985.

Presents a collection of essays relating to Meeting for Worship as an integral part of the program in a Quaker school. Includes reactions, practices, procedures within elementary and secondary schools.

633.   Palmer, Parker J. Meeting for Learning. Wallingford, PA: Pendle Hill Publications, Pamphlet #284, 1976.

Discusses how in a meeting for learning the individual is always in relationship, and knowledge emerges in dialogue. It is not only what the student hears but what the student says back that counts. Here, learning happens between persons and not simply within the learner. In a dialogue there is also a third party: an idea, a text, data, or a concrete experience.

634.   Reader, John. "Of Schools and Schoolmasters." Swarthmore Lecture. London: Quaker Home Service, 1979.

Contains a forthright account about Quaker strengths and weaknesses in education through

the years since 1650.   Discusses the
differences between schoolmaster and teacher
and the need for a merger of the
characteristics of each in the school person
through two examples: Abelard the teacher and
Aelred the schoolmaster.   Contains suggestions
for the present for schools.

635.   "Religious Education in Friends Elementary
         Schools."   Philadelphia: Friends Council on
         Education, 1983.

         Discusses the elementary principals'
concerns for more specific directions to
strengthen the area of religious education in
the schools.   Approaches and preparation for
Meeting for Worship, religious education in the
classroom, assemblies, and use of the Bible are
carefully presented with bibliographies and
list of materials.

CHAPTER 12
INDEPENDENT CHRISTIAN DAY SCHOOLS
James C. Carper

Part I: Historical

636. Banta, Forrest D. "The Status and Quality of
      Education in the National Association of
      Christian Schools." Ed.D. dissertation.
      University of Buffalo, 1953.

      Surveys the facilities, community
      relationships, organization and administration,
      teacher characteristics, and curricula of
      seventy-two of the seventy-seven school
      affiliated with the National Association of
      Christian Schools.

637. Benson, Warren S. "A History of the National
      Association of Christian Schools During the
      Period of 1947-1972." Ph.D. dissertation.
      Loyola University of Chicago, 1975.

      Examines the development of the National
      Association of Christian Schools, and clarifies
      its educational philosophy as it emerged
      historically. Notes that the Association was
      formed because of the Calvinistic stance of the
      National Union of Christian Schools.

163

638. Buchanan, Henry A. , and Bob W. Brown. "Will
     Protestant Church Schools Become a Third
     Force?" Christianity Today, May 12, 1967,
     pp. 3-5.

     Describes the growth of Protestant day
     schools in the 1950s and 1960s. Argues that
     there will be a rapid and significant expansion
     of the Protestant school movement as society
     and the public schools become more secularized.

639. Encyclopedia of Educational Research, 5th ed.
     S. v. "Protestant Education," by D. Bruce
     Lockerbie.

     Surveys the history of Protestant education,
     including the Christian school movement.
     Includes a useful bibliography.

640. Erickson, Donald A. "Religious Consequences of
     Public and Sectarian Schooling." School
     Review 72 (Spring 1964): 22-33.

     Reports that public school students were as
     "religious" as students attending selected
     fundamentalist schools in urban and suburban
     areas in midwestern and southwestern states.

641. Fakkema, Mark. "The Christian Day School
     Movement." In An Introduction to
     Evangelical Christian Education, pp.
     370-378. Edited by J. Edward Hakes.
     Chicago: Moody Press, 1964.

     Asserts that Christian day schools exist
     because the aims of the public schools do not
     correspond with the educational goals of many
     evangelical Christians. Provides a statistical
     portrait of evangelical schools in 1963-64.

642. Fortosis, Anthony C. "A Study of Certain
     Characteristics of the Christian High
     Schools Holding Membership in the National
     Association of Christian Schools." Ed. D.
     dissertation. Duke University, 1964.

     Finds that the Christian high schools
     surveyed were small (median of seventy-four
     students and five teachers), accredited in
     about half the cases, expensive to operate,
     under-financed, academically adequate, and
     populated by dedicated teachers and
     administrators.

643. Hautt, William D. "The Efficacy of Christian
     Schools in Achieving Religious Objectives."
     Ed. D. dissertation. Columbia University,
     1971.

     Reports that Christian school attendance was
     an important predictor of doctrinal belief, but
     not of indices representing consequential,
     ideological, and ritualistic dimensions of
     religiousness.

644. Lowrie, Roy W., Jr. "The Administration of
     Schools Holding Membership in the National
     Association of Christian Schools." Ed. D.
     dissertation. Temple University, 1962.

     Describes the characteristics, philosophy,
     administration, and problems of 129 schools
     holding membership in the National Association
     of Christian Schools.

645. Nevin, David, and Robert E. Bills. The Schools
     That Fear Built: Segregationist Academies
     in the South. Washington, DC: Arcopolis
     Books, 1976.

Argues that race was a key ingredient in
formation of private academies in the South in
the 1960s and early 1970s. Claims that it is
difficult to distinguish between secular and
"Christian" academies.

646.   Palmer, James M. The Impact of Private
       Education on the Rural South. Arlington,
       VA: ERIC Document Reproduction Service, ED
       088 643, 1974.

       Describes six basic types of private
       (nonparochial) schools, including segregation
       academies and Christian day schools.

647.   Roth, David L. "A Historical Study of the
       Association of Teachers of Christian
       Schools, 1958-1979." Ed. D. dissertation.
       Northern Illinois University, 1981.

       Examines the origin, development, and
       contributions of the Association of Teachers of
       Christian Schools (ATCS). Concludes that ATCS
       played a significant role in the spiritual and
       professional maturation of Christian day
       schools in the Midwest.

648.   Scoggin, Pharis E. "A History of the
       Evangelical Christian School Movement in
       American from 1880 to Present." Ph. D.
       dissertation. Bob Jones University, 1974.

       Describes the origin and development of
       several groups of Protestant schools, including
       independent Christian schools. Discusses the
       significance of school associations and
       publishing houses that service these schools.

649.   Stone, Kenneth A. "A Status Study of
       Elementary Schools in the National
       Association of Christian Schools with

Emphasis on the Principalship." Ph. D. dissertation. Florida State University, 1972.

Reports that the schools surveyed tend to be small, unaccredited units headed by principals with little or no professional training in educational administration.

650.   Travis, Paul. "Where Christian Schools Mushroom." Christian Life, June 1957, pp. 17-19.

Describes the growth of Christian day schools in southern California in the 1950s.

651.   Wilson, Fred. "Why Are Fundamentalist Day Schools Growing?" Paper presented at History Department Seminar, Kansas State University, Manhattan, KS, April 20, 1982.

Argues that intensification of religious commitment and reaction to the secularization of public education, the development of Christian school associations, and improvement of the economic situation of fundamentalist parents spurred the growth of fundamentalist schools between 1945 and 1982.

652.   Wyckoff, D. Campbell. "The Protestant Day School." School and Society 82 (October 1, 1955): 98-101.

Asserts that Protestantism is committed to the support of public education. Maintains that the Protestant day school will flourish only within tightly-knit sectarian or cultural groups.

653.   Young, Donald R. "The Historical Development of Selected Independent Fundamentalist

168 Religious Schools in America

Christian Schools." Ph. D. dissertation.
Miami University, 1981.

Examines the influences and factors that
have contributed to the Christian school
movement.

Part II: Contemporary

654. Adams, Alice C. "A Comparative Study of Values
Among Christian School Parents, Christian
School Teachers, and Public School Teachers.
Ph. D. dissertation. Georgia State
University, 1983.

Finds that in this DeKalb County (GA) survey
Christian school parents and teachers were
significantly similar to one another and
different from public school teachers.

655. Alcorn, Bruce K. "Christian Schools and
Teacher Licensing." Phi Delta Kappan 66
(May 1985): 646-647.

Reports that Christian schools are
interested in hiring qualified teachers and
most of those surveyed (Association of
Christian Schools International members in the
midwestern region) favored certification of
some kind.

656. Allen, Douglas L. "A Study of Middle School
Parents Reasons for Choice and Satisfaction
in Christian, Catholic, and Public Schools
in Northcentral Pennsylvania. D. Ed.
dissertation. Pennsylvania State
University, 1984.

Reports that Christian school parents were
most satisfied with the schools their children
attended followed by Catholic and public school

parents. Suggests that Christian day school
parents desired a more particular kind of
school climate than other parents. Indicates
that parents chose Christian day schools for
religious and moral training, discipline,
reinforcement of parental values, and academic
standards.

657. Allison, Kenneth L. "An Investigation of the
      Influence of the Accelerated Christian
      Education Program of Instruction Upon
      Student Academic Achievement in a Christian
      College Environment." Ed.D. dissertation.
      Bob Jones University, 1982.

      Finds that on at least one measure, second
      semester grade point average, public high
      school students at Bob Jones University ranked
      significantly higher than either ACE or non-ACE
      Christian school graduates.

658. Ballweg, George E., Jr. "The Growth in the
      Number and Population of Christian Schools
      Since 1966: A Profile of Parental Views
      Concerning Factors Which Led Them to Enroll
      Their Children in a Christian School."
      Ed.D. dissertation. Boston University,
      1980.

      Maintains that the underlying reason why
      parents enroll their children in Christian day
      schools is to exercise their parental right to
      remove their children from an educational
      environment that is perceived to be in direct
      conflict with their values that they wish to
      have instilled in their children.

659. Bayly, Joseph. "How Wide Is the Spectrum in
      Christian Schools?" Eternity, September
      1980, pp. 24-31.

Describes the educational climate of a wide variety of Christian schools.

660. Beadle, R. Mark. "Fundamentalist Schools: What Do We Know?" Paper presented at the annual meeting of the American Educational Research Association, Chicago, April 4, 1985.

Reviews the literature on fundamentalist Christian schools. Describes characteristics of these schools, including philosophy, number and enrollment, and finances.

661. Bleggi, Douglas R. "A Study of Parent Choice and Satisfaction in Elementary Private and Public Schools in Rural Pennsylvania." D. Ed. dissertation. Pennsylvania State University, 1984.

Reports that religious/moral teaching and reinforcement of home values were more important to Christian school parents than to Catholic or public school parents. Finds that racial integration was not a factor in Christian school choice.

662. Brown, Dennis J. "An Investigation into the Philosophy of Education of Christian Elementary and Secondary Schools." Ph. D. dissertation. Indiana University, 1977.

Reports that in schools surveyed in southern California a Christian philosophy of education was only minimally developed.

663. Carper, James C. "Nuts and Bolts of the Excellence Movement--Christian Day Schools." American Spectator, September 1984, pp. 17-18.

Reviews the reasons for the growth of
Christian day schools. Argues that these
institutions may contribute to the quest for
excellence in education because, unlike public
schools, they are based on the values of
voluntarism, community, and decentralization.

664. Carper, James C. "The Christian Day School
      Movement." Educational Forum 47 (Winter
      1983): 135-149.

      Provides a general overview of the Christian
      day school movement. Surveys current
      criticisms of the movement and future concerns.

665. Carper, James C. "The Christian Day School."
      In Religious Schooling in America, pp.
      110-129. Edited by James C. Carper and
      Thomas C. Hunt. Birmingham, AL: Religious
      Education Press, 1984.

      Discusses the origins and characteristics of
      the Christian day school. Asserts that
      alienation from secular American culture and
      religious awakening are the primary forces
      behind the rapid growth of these institutions.
      Concludes that the Christian day school is a
      permanent fixture on the American educational
      landscape.

666. Catterall, James S. "Private School
      Participation and Public Policy." Paper
      presented at the Comparing Public and
      Private Schools conference, Stanford
      University, October 25-26, 1984.

      Analyzes patterns and trends in enrollment
      in American private schools. Argues that there
      has been a decline in the growth of Christian
      school enrollments in recent years, from nearly
      25 percent per year in 1976 to approximately 9
      percent in 1983.

667. Clerico, Donald R. "Searching for Peace of Mind: Parents Rationales for Enrolling Their Children in a Christian School." Ph.D. dissertation. Syracuse University, 1982.

   Argues that gross dissatisfaction with the organization, administration, and instruction in public schools led parents to enroll their children in the Central New York Christian School. Reports that parents desired a school that complemented their social, moral, political, and religious perspectives.

668. Cole, John D. "Religion in the Nonpublic Schools: A Selective Study Comparing Pillar of Fire Schools with Those of Six Major Denominations." Ph.D. dissertation. University of Colorado at Boulder, 1978.

   Describes the place of religion in recently founded Christian schools.

669. Cooper, Bruce S. "The Changing Demography of Private Schools: Trends and Implications. Education and Urban Society 16 (August 1984): 429-442.

   Analyzes the role of the Christian day school in the expanding and increasingly diverse private school sector.

670. Decker, Margaret S. "A Prospectus for the Establishment of a Twelve Grade Christian School." Ph.D. dissertation. University of Michigan, 1982.

   Describes a model Christian day school based on interview data and school visitation.

671. Dorsey, Jeffrey D.   "The Christian Day School,
      in the Black Community." D. Min.
      dissertation.   School of Theology at
      Claremont, 1977.

      Examines the Christian day school movement
      and its relevance to the Black community.
      Argues that a theology of liberation and
      reconciliation is the best theological approach
      for Christian day schools that educate Blacks.

672. Doyle, Denis P.   "A Din of Inequity: Private
      Schools Reconsidered." Teachers College
      Record 82 (Summer 1981): 661-673.

      Reviews factors that affect current public
      policy debates about private education,
      including Christian day schools.

673. Erickson, Donald A.   "Choice and Private
      Schools: Dynamics of Supply and Demand."
      In Private Education and Public Policy.
      Edited by Daniel C. Levy.   New York: Oxford
      University Press, forthcoming.

      Discusses the ebb and flow of private school
      options and public policy implications.
      Includes a section on fundamentalist schools.
      Concludes with a summary of recent research on
      the effects of government aid on Catholic and
      other private schools in Canada.

674. Evearitt, Timothy C.   "An Analysis of Why
      Parents Enroll Their Children in Private
      Christian Schools." Ed. D. dissertation.
      Illinois State University, 1979.

      Reports that parents in two Illinois
      counties noted the following reasons for
      enrolling their children in Christian schools
      as "very important": desire for moral training,

lack of discipline in the public school, and
the need for Christian teachers.

675.   Foreman, Chris A.   "Why Parents in Oregon
       Enroll Their Children in Protestant
       Christian Schools."   Ph.D. Dissertation.
       University of Oregon, 1982.

       Examines religious, social, and academic
reasons for Christian school enrollment.

676.   Gleason, Daniel M.   "A Study of the Christian
       School Movement."   Ed.D. dissertation.
       University of North Dakota, 1980.

       Discusses the history and philosophy of the
Christian day school movement, as well as
recent legal clashes with state governments.
Argues that though the movement is basically
sound, advocates must avoid the tendency to
overreact to real and perceived problems in
public schools.

677.   Glesne, Corrine, and Alan Peshkin.   "The
       Christian Day School: A Literature Review."
       Private School Monitor, forthcoming.

       Reviews significant literature on the
Christian day school movement.   Includes non-
Christian journal articles, papers presented at
professional meetings, and dissertations which
focus on national Christian school
associations, demographics, reasons for growth,
curriculum, teachers, student finances, state
regulation, and impact on public education and
society.   Argues that assessments of the
Christian school movement are closely tied to
the issue of cultural pluralism.

678.   Ham, Dalton E.   "Reasons Why Parents Enroll
       Their Children in Fundamentalist Christian

Schools and Why Churches Sponsor Them."
Ed. D. dissertation. University of Missouri-
Columbia, 1982.

Describes the characteristics of Christian
day schools in Missouri. Reports that while
parents indicated concern over discipline in
the public schools and teaching of evolution,
churches sponsoring schools expressed a need
for moral and religious instruction, Christian
teachers, and stronger discipline.

679. Hattan, Walter E. "Protestant Christian Day
Schools in Connecticut, 1900-1980." Ph. D.
dissertation. University of Connecticut,
1983.

Reports that evangelical and fundamentalist
churches established their schools primarily
for religious reasons, chiefly to counter the
perceived secularism of the public schools.
Concludes that the schools included in the
study, all of which were founded after 1970,
are nondenominational in theological outlook
and open to all religious and racial groups.

680. Holmes, John C. "A Comparison Among Black,
Hispanic, and White Parental Expectations of
the Evangelical Christian School." Ed. D.
dissertation. Pepperdine University, 1982.

Reports that over two-thirds of each group
of parents (Black, Hispanic, and White)
surveyed in South Los Angeles County indicated
"Christ-centered academics" as the primary
reason for enrolling their children in
elementary, evangelical Christian schools.
Claims that the development of alternative
public schools would not draw these parents
back to public education.

681.   Johnson, David A. "The Current Status of
       Christian School Industrial Arts Education
       Programs." Ph.D. dissertation. University
       of Minnesota, 1983.

       Reports that the industrial arts education
       programs were offered in approximately 20
       percent of the 130 Association of Christian
       Schools International member schools surveyed
       in the Mid-American region.

682.   Johnston, A.P., and David K. Wiles. Christian
       Schools and Public Schools in Small Rural
       Communities in the Northeast. Arlington,
       VA: ERIC Document Reproduction Service, ED
       235 948, 1982.

       Reports that fundamentalist schools surveyed
       were localistic, autonomous, and virtually
       unregulated educational communities.

683.   Joss, Charles A. "A Survey of the Science
       Teaching Practices in Selected Elementary
       Christian Schools in the United States."
       Ph.D. dissertation. Michigan State
       University, 1982.

       Reports similarities between public school
       and Christian school science instruction,
       including low priority, dependence upon
       teacher-centered methods, and reliance upon a
       single textbook.

684.   Kienel, Paul A., ed. The Philosophy of
       Christian School Education. Whittier, CA:
       Western Association of Christian Schools,
       1978.

       Contains essays on the principles and
       practices of Christian school education.
       Includes a useful bibliography.

685. Letcher, Stanley E. "An Appraisal of the
       Private School As Established by the
       Christian Church (Churches of Christ) in the
       United States." D. Ed. dissertation.
       University of South Africa, 1981.

       Finds that lack of discipline in the public
       school was the major reason why parents
       enrolled children in Christian schools.

686. Lyons, Ralph O. "Compulsory School Attendance
       Laws and Their Application to Students in
       Christian Schools." Ed. D. dissertation,
       Northern Arizona University, 1983.

       Reviews the application of compulsory school
       attendance laws to nonpublic schools,
       particularly Christian day schools.

687. MacCullough, Martha E. "Factors Which Led
       Parents to Leave Public School." Ed. D.
       dissertation. Temple University, 1984.

       Reports that Philadelphia-area parents
       transferred their children from public to
       Christian schools primarily for religious
       reasons.

688. Maffett, Gregory J. "The Educational Thought
       of Cornelius Van Til: An Analysis of the
       Ideological Foundations of His Christian
       Philosophy of Education." Ed. D.
       dissertation. University of Akron, 1984.

       Analyzes Van Til's educational theory.
       Compares his beliefs with humanistic and other
       Christian belief systems as they relate to
       education.

689. Massey, Dorothy M. B. "A Comparison of the
       Stated Values of Selected Principals of

Evangelical Christian and Public Elementary
Schools in Texas." Ed. D. dissertation.
Baylor University, 1982.

Reports that Christian school principals
ranked the following values higher than public
school principals: salvation, forgiveness,
helpful, obedient, and wisdom; while public
school principals ranked the following higher
than Christian school principals: broadminded
and independent.

690. Maynor, William W. "Factors Related to
     Children's Attending Selected Christian Day
     Schools As Reported by Administrators and
     Parents." Ph. D. dissertation. University
     of Alabama, 1982.

     Reports that respondents in six southern and
     border states gave religious reasons for
     sending their children to Christian schools.
     Notes that two of the schools surveyed had
     significant minority enrollment (21 and 14
     percent), while the remaining schools indicated
     minority enrollment of less than 1 percent.

691. McDearmid, Andrew M. "Student Achievement in
     Accelerated Christian Education Schools in
     Pennsylvania." Ed. D. dissertation. Temple
     University, 1980.

     Reports that Accelerated Christian Education
     schools prepared students for college entrance
     when SAT scores and college attendance were
     compared with those of all high school
     graduates in the state.

692. McKenzie, Lois J. "The Relationship of Self-
     Concept and Academic Achievement of Students
     After Leaving Private/Christian Schools and
     Entering Public Schools." Ed. D.

dissertation.   Northern Arizona University,
1984.

Reports that Christian school students and
those who had left Christian schools and
entered public schools demonstrated equal
ability in academic achievement and self-
concept.

693.   Murphy, William M.   "Why Parents Send Their
       Children to Luckett Christian Academy:
       Comparative Attitudes and Objectives of
       Luckett Christian Academy Patrons: A Case
       Study."   Ph.D. dissertation.   Southern
       Illinois University at Carbondale, 1981.

       Finds that black respondents gave academics
       as the primary reason for sending their
       children to the academy, while whites cited
       moral/religious instruction as the primary
       reason for enrolling their children.

694.   Nordin, Virginia D., and Turner, William L.
       "More Than Segregation Academies: The
       Growing Protestant Fundamentalist Schools."
       Phi Delta Kappan 61 (February 1980):
       391-394.

       Claims that the motivation for establishing
       Christian day schools involves much more than
       racism.   Suggests that a growing number of
       evangelicals believe that public schools
       espouse a philosophy that is secular, perhaps
       even anti-Christian.

695.   Ostling, Richard N.   "Why Protestant Schools
       Are Booming."   Christian Herald, July-August
       1977, pp. 44-47.

       Asserts that the changing value orientation
       of American society, declining academic

standards, disenchantment with certain aspects of the public school curriculum, and a revival of religious fundamentalism have led an increasing number of parents to choose the Christian day school over the public school.

696.   Peshkin, Alan. God's Choice: The Total World of a Fundamentalist Christian School. Chicago: University of Chicago Press, 1986.

Analyzes the "climate" of Bethany Baptist Academy, a fundamentalist Christian high school. Concludes that the school well serves the educational ends of a fundamentalist Christian community. Raises questions concerning the relationships of this "total institution," with its emphasis on "absolutes," to "American pluralism."

697.   Reese, William J. "Soldiers of Christ in the Army of God: The Christian School Movement in America." Educational Theory 35 (Spring 1985): 175-194.

Argues that racism is an inadequate explanatory device in analyzing the origins of Christian day schools. Claims that other socio-cultural factors, e.g., secularism, are far more significant. Provides a general overview of the characteristics of these institutions and problems facing them.

698.   Rose, Susan D. "Christian Schools in Secular Society." Ph.D. dissertation. Cornell University, 1984.

Analyzes the goals, content, and socialization processes in a Baptist school that uses Accelerated Christian Education (ACE) and in an independent, charismatic fellowship that uses secular texts. Finds that the former stresses conformity, constraint, and consolation, while the latter emphasizes internalization of values, exploration, and confrontation.

699. Schaller, Lyle E. "Public Versus Private Schools: A Divisive Issue for the 1980s." Christian Century, November 7, 1979, pp. 1086-1090.

Explores policy issues related to the growth in the number of Christian day schools that will confront Protestants and Catholics in the 1980s, including tuition tax credits, public school loyalty among many Protestant denominations, and social integration.

700. Skerry, Peter. "Christian School Versus the I.R.S." Public Interest 61 (Fall 1980): 18-41.

Describes Christian schools visited in North Carolina and asserts that the effort to attribute their emergence to racism is an oversimplification. Suggests that religious factors are primary.

701. Smith, Harvey A. "A Study of Teachers in Independent Christian Schools." Ed. D. dissertation. Syracuse University, 1979.

Describes the background, training, professional roles, and needs of teachers in independent Christian schools in New York. Notes that these teachers viewed teaching as a ministry.

702. Stiles, Gerald J. "Evangelicals and Public Education." Ed. D. dissertation. Virginia Polytechnic Institute and State University, 1980.

Explores evangelicals' current dissatisfaction with public education and its impact, including the formation of private schools.

703.   Stoker, W. M. , and Robert Splawn. A Study of Accelerated Christian Education Schools in Northwest Texas. Arlington, VA: ERIC Document Reproduction Service, ED 206 095, 1980.

Relates the growth of Accelerated Christian Education (ACE) to the expansion of Christian day schools and dissatisfaction with public education.   Includes observations concerning which aspects of ACE schools may or may not be useful to public schools.

704.   Stoms, William K. , Jr.   "The Growth of Evangelical Schools: A Study of Parental Concerns and Other Contributing Factors." Ed. D. dissertation.   Rutgers University, 1982.

Describes the forces behind the growth of Christian day schools in New Jersey.   Asserts that the lack of religious practices in the public schools is a significant contributing factor.   Reports that abandonment of public education can also be attributed to racial, discipline, and drug problems, as well as declining academic standards.

705.   Turner, William L.   "Reasons for Enrollment in Religious Schools: A Case Study of Three Recently Established Fundamentalist Schools in Kentucky and Wisconsin."   Ph. D. dissertation.   University of Wisconsin-Madison, 1979.

Asserts that fundamentalist schools are not havens for those seeking to avoid desegregation. Claims that researchers have often confused fundamentalist religious schools with segregation academies.

706. Turner, William L. Understanding the Growth of Christian Schools. Arlington, VA: ERIC Document Reproduction Service, ED 212 043, 1981.

Attributes that establishment and growth of Christian day schools to religious reasons, though academic and discipline concerns are also important. Asserts that the disintegration of consensus on common American values contributes to their growth as well.

707. Vankleek, Paul H. "A Descriptive Study of Christian School Distinctives and How They Are Put into Action by Teachers and Administrators." Ph.D. dissertation. Michigan State University, 1983.

Finds that human dimension (teacher) was the most outstanding distinctive of the Christian schools studied.

708. Willimon, William H. "Should Churches Buy Into the Education Business?" Christianity Today, May 5, 1978, pp. 20-23.

Expresses misgivings about the Christian day school movement. Claims that racism, elitism, and low academic standards characterize many of these schools. Asserts that the public school is a mission field that should not be abandoned.

CHAPTER 13
JEWISH SCHOOLS
Bruce S. Cooper

Part I: Historical

709. Ackerman, Walter I. "From Past to Present:
Notes from the History of Jewish Education
in Boston." Jewish Education 51 (Summer
1983): 32-37.

Describes the role of the Boston Bureau of
Jewish Education in building religious
schooling for its children. Analyzes the role
of leadership, organization, and programs, in
pressing the development of Talmud-Torahs and
afternoon schools, and the importance of strong
school principals.

710. Adar, Zvi. Jewish Education in Israel and the
United States. Jerusalem. Hebrew
University, Samuel Mendel Melton Center,
1977.

An Israeli educator's interesting view of
Jewish schooling overall in both countries.
Defines the nature of Jewish schooling, its
background, characteristics, from an Orthodox,
Conservative, and Reform in U. S. , as well as
examples from Israel.

711.   Alper, Michael. <u>Reconstructing Jewish
       Education</u>. New York: Reconstructionist
       Press, 1957.

       Provides a philosophical basis and rationale
       for the "Reconstructionist" (pun in title is
       intentional) approach to Jewish education and
       Judaism--one that is "naturalistic" (not
       mystical), based on "self-realization," growth,
       and one which is scientific and worldly (not
       directed toward the afterlife). Schools should
       reflect, in other words, Rabbi Mordecai
       Kaplan's viewpoint, which is organismic,
       democratic, and pragmatic. Favors "community"
       rather than congregational schools that present
       the Reconstructionist philosophy.

712.   Baradon, Eunice. "Ethical Values of Jewish
       Adolescents and Implications for the Jewish
       Religious School Curriculum." Ed. D.
       dissertation. University of Pittsburgh,
       1964.

       Examines the attitudes of a number of
       graduates of Jewish schools concerning Jewish
       ethics and values, based on a set of situations
       requiring ethical decision-making. Finds that
       60% of these students profess ethical positions
       consistent with Jewish teachings. Finds that
       girls are more positive in their attitudes, and
       that a Hebrew background was significant in
       predicting the level of development of ethical
       standards. Feels that these findings are
       important for the teaching of God, rituals,
       Torah, and prayers in the school curriculum.

713.   Berdugo, Yehuda. "The Design, Implementation,
       and Evaluation of a Theme-Centered
       Interaction Program for Adolescents in a
       Jewish Day School." Ph. D. dissertation.
       University of Pittsburgh, 1978.

Analyzes a program to improve Jewish identification and school acceptance for disenchanted teenagers in the Hebrew Academy of Pittsburgh. Finds that group sessions enhanced self-awareness, openness, and Jewish awareness.

714. Birnbaum, Herbert. "A Study of the Religious Attitudes, Beliefs, and Observances of Jewish Pupils with Varying Religious Educational Experience." Ed. D. dissertation. University of Maryland, 1963.

Investigates the patterns of beliefs of 6th grade (12 year olds) elementary school children. Looks at the impact of varying amounts of Jewish education by various religious agencies. Concludes that the Jewish day school seems to lead to greater self-acceptance as Jews than the afternoon, supplemental schools. Conservative Jews attitude toward Israel is significantly more favorable than Reform students. Greater tradition leads to more positive attitudes.

715. Brickman, Benjamin. "Two Day Schools." Jewish Education 50 (Fall 1982): 6-8.

Personal reminiscences of two Orthodox day schools, Ramaz Schoo (found in Manhattan, NYC) started by Rabbi Joseph A. Lookstein (z"1) and the Yeshivah of Flatbush (in Brooklyn), founded by Mr. Joel Braverman (z"1).

716. Chanover, Hyman. "A History of the National Board of License for Teachers and Supervisory Personnel in American Jewish Schools: The Struggle to Improve the Quality of Instruction in Jewish Schools in the United States." Ed. D. dissertation. New York University, 1971.

Studies the licensing processes in key
cities (Chicago, Cleveland, Philadelphia, and
New York) and the importance of the National
Board of License. Examines its influence in
professionalizing the preparation of teachers
for Jewish schools. Finds the overall need to
strengthen the profession, for greater
supervision of teacher preparation, expansion
of the accrediting bodies, improving teacher
education, greater liaison between the National
Board of License and local schools on key
issues and requirements, recruitment and
stringent requirements, better training and
licensing procedures, and certification to meet
the needs of children and day school
instruction.

717. Cohen, Jack J. "New Trends in Jewish
      Education. " In A History of Jewish
      Education in America, pp. 201-223. Edited
      by Judah Pilch. New York: The National
      Curriculum Research Institute of the
      American Association for Jewish Education,
      1969.

      Provides extensive history of recent
      developments in Jewish education in the U.S. ,
      starting with the 1959 national study of
      Dushkin and Engelman. Notes the impact of
      "surrounding culture" on the curriculum of
      Jewish schools, away from the Talmudic-Gemara
      tradition, and toward a modern, "secular"
      curriculum (history, arts, music, dance,
      literature), based on renewed interest in
      classical Judaism as a basis of Western thought
      and development. Offers the need to improve
      secondary Jewish education, which must compete
      with the attractions of the core culture.
      Discusses the important rise in the Jewish day
      school. Notes that Jews now are supporting
      separate all-Jewish schools, and even

state/government support for nonpublic schools.
Raises important questions of the separation of
Jews from other non-Jewish children and youth.

718.   Colodner, Solomon. School Management: A
        Practical Manual and Guide for Principals of
        Jewish Schools. New York: Cole
        Publications, 1967.

        Provides a ready reference and guide to the
        administration and supervision of Jewish
        Schools. Includes steps for preparation,
        evaluation, curriculum, report cards,
        observation and evaluation of teachers.

719.   Donin, Hayim. "An Inquiry into the Value
        Propositions Underlying Jewish Education in
        Metropolitan Detroit." Ph.D. dissertation.
        Wayne State University, 1966.

        Explores the stress of Jewish faith and its
        values in religious schools in greater Detroit.
        Schools included Right-Orthodox, Orthodox,
        Conservative, Reform, Labor Zionist, Secular,
        and Community schools. Finds that Halakha
        (Torah based education, as the means for
        understanding the Law) to be best way to
        improve the Jewish "way of life" and for
        securing the spiritual survival of the Jewish
        people.

720.   Dushkin, Alexander M. , ed. Dr. Samson
        Benderly: Leader in American Jewish
        Education. New York: National Council for
        Jewish Education, 1949.

        A memorial volume dedicated to Dr. Benderly,
        provides background, writings, contributions,
        and community leadership on this great Jewish
        educator.

721.   Dushkin, Alexander M. Living Bridges: Memoirs
        of an Educator. Jerusalem: Keter, 1975.

        Fascinating memoir of a key Jewish leader
        who worked in both Chicago and New York,
        establishing the Jewish Education Committee in
        1938. Describes the development of resources
        for Jewish education from a personal
        perspective.

722.   Dushkin, Alexander M. and Uriah Engelman.
        Jewish Education in the United States. New
        York: American Association for Jewish
        Education, 1959.

        Provides background on the origin,
        definitions, surveys, demographics, attitudes
        of families and Jewish leaders. Explains the
        organization, staffing, administration,
        funding, interorganizational relations, and
        curriculum of these schools, with a discussion
        of ways to improve these schools.

723.   Fatto, Zahawa. "Role Congruency and Job
        Satisfaction of Principals in Jewish Day
        Schools." Ph. D. dissertation. Yeshiva
        University, 1978.

        Studies role congruency and satisfaction of
        24 principals in 12 Jewish schools (one for
        Religious Studies and one for General Studies
        in each school). Inconclusive findings, though
        role expectations were different from school
        boards and teachers. Satisfaction was not
        significantly affected by role congruency.

724.   Finkelstein, Eleanor. "A Study of Female Role
        Identification in a Yeshiva High School."
        Ph. D. dissertation. New York University,
        1980.

Examines the impact of the women's movement
on girls in an Orthodox yeshiva. Finds that
girls and boys belong to different cultures
because of differential treatment of the sexes
by teachers. Learns of significant differences
in role and status of girls and boys. Judaic
program reinforces differences and was deemed
inadequate in providing useful role models.
Female students were concerned for success in
careers and for traditional roles as wives and
mothers.

725. Fuchs, Jay Levi. "Relationship of Day School
     Education to Student Self-Concepts and
     Jewish Identity." Ed.D. dissertation.
     University of California at Los Angeles,
     1978.

     Explores the relationship between Jewish
schooling types and self-concepts, Jewish
identity, practice and beliefs, among 384
Kansas City Jewish children. Finds that the
more the students' education, the greater their
identity, ritual, and beliefs. Reports that
parent activities positively influence pupil
identity, and that Jewish education affects
attitudes toward intermarriage, ritual, Israel,
commitment, and pride and values.

726. Geller, Joshua S. "A Study of Early Adolescent
     Attitudes Towards Ethnic and Democratic
     Beliefs as Related to Attendance in Public
     and Jewish Schools." Ph.D. dissertation.
     University of Michigan, 1968.

     Examines differences in ethnic and
democratic values between groups attending
different schools. Seeks also to determine the
relationship between Judaic concepts of freedom
and the ideals of American democracy. Finds
that Jewish children attending public schools

and afternoon Jewish programs have a greater
commitment to liberal American values than
those who receive only a public education (and
have no contact with synagogue schools) or
those attending Jewish day schools. Finds
Jewish day school pupils accept ethnic beliefs
and religious practices more than other two
groups.

727.   Goodman, Isaac M. "Jewish Education and
        Religious Attitudes." Ed. D. dissertation.
        Yeshiva University, 1978.

Measures the relationship between Jewish
education and religious attitudes among
Orthodox Jewish graduates of day schools, with
515 participating in the study. Finds that
greater Jewish education increases Orthodox
religious attitudes. No difference between
elementary only versus high school graduation.
Late starters in Jewish education also attained
the same level of religious beliefs as rabbinic
trainees. Advocates day schools for older and
younger people.

728.   Heimowitz, Joseph. "A Study of the Graduates
        of the Yeshiva of Flatbush High School."
        Ed. D. dissertation. Yeshiva University,
        1979.

Study of 404 graduates of the school. Finds
that 94% graduated college; 60% continued their
Jewish schooling; half are professionals; the
majority keep kosher, the sabbath, and pray
daily. Ninety percent found the school to be a
positive experience and send their own children
there, and indicated a positive attitude toward
the State of Israel.

729.   Hertz, Richard C. The Education of the Jewish
        Child. New York: Union of American Hebrew
        Congregations, 1953.

Gives background on Jewish education from
the Reform perspective, comparing a survey done
in 1924 and this one conducted in 1948.
Provides useful background on the philosophy,
expectations, programs, and facilities of
afternoon schools, as a step toward
understanding the rise of the Reform day
schools.

730. Himmelfarb, Harold S.   "Agents of Religious
      Socialization Among American Jews." The
      Sociological Quarterly 20 (Autumn 1979):
      477-494.

Analyzes the process of religious
socialization among American Jews in the
Chicago area, using framework by Andrew Greeley
and colleagues. Considers the effects of
parents, spouse, peer influence, participating
in Jewish youth groups and summer camping on
religiosity of adult Jews, using path analysis.
Finds four agents of socialization to be most
important: parents' ritual observance,
spouse's observance, total hours of religious
training, and peer influence in high school and
college. Parents seem to "channel" children
into religious school, marriage within the
faith, camping, schooling, and life with peers.
The religiousness of the spouse is the
strongest determinant of religiosity, not
parents as previously believed. Overall,
Jewish education appears to be a more powerful
socializing force than Catholic schools,
perhaps because of greater time spent on
religious subjects in the Jewish programs.

731. Himmelfarb, Harold S.   "The Non-Linear Impact
      of Schooling: Comparing Different Types and
      Amounts of Jewish Education." Sociology of
      Education 42 (April 1977): 114-129.

Assesses the impact of Jewish schooling
(types and amounts) in producing adult
religiousness, using a covariance design.
Finds afternoon Jewish schools to have little
lasting impact on adult religiosity. Jewish
all-day schools have a significant impact,
particularly after six uninterrupted years,
though no real difference in religiousness
between 7 and 12 years of day schooling.
Asserts that the quantity of education is not
linear in producing a religious adult: certain
thresholds and plateaus exist in producing the
eight orthogonal factors of religious
involvement: Devotional, Doctrinal-
Experiential, Associational, Fraternal,
Parental, Ideological, Intellectual-Esthetic,
and Ethical-Moral. Relates to other religious
schools and public ones.

732.   Himmelfarb, Milton. The Jews of Modernity.
        New York: Basic Books, 1973.

        In Chapter 22, author places federal aid to
Jewish day schools in an interesting context.
Discusses the origins of church-state
separation, support by Jews for several
reasons. First, Jews were persecuted by
"Christian" governments; Jews see the public
schools as life-lines to a better life and fear
anything which might erode the public approach.
Classic view of Jews on federal aid to private
schools.

733.   Kaminetsky, Joseph, ed. Hebrew Day School
        Education: An Overview. New York: The
        National Society for Hebrew Day Schools,
        1970.

        Provides a valuable set of readings by
various authors on a wide range of issues
relating to Jewish all-day schools. Includes

topics such as development, dimensions,
educational program, federal relations,
relations to the home, curricula, and special
concerns. Focus on the special child -
exceptional, the slow learner, and preparation
of children for future learning and life.

734. Karan, Val Elliot. "An Empirical Investigation
      of the Relationship between Exposure to
      Formal Jewish Education, Personal-Social
      Factors, and Moral Judgment." Ph. D.
      dissertation. New York University, 1973.

      Seeks to learn the relationship between
      Jewish schooling and key factors: moral
      development and personal development. Moral
      judgment was more related to intelligence and
      high self-concept than to age, sex, SES.
      Religious instruction was significantly related
      to moral judgment, though personal/intelligence
      variables were more important. Draws
      implications for the teaching of moral values
      in all Jewish schools.

735. Katzoff, Louis. Issues in Jewish Education.
      New York: Block, 1949.

      Reviews the development of Conservative
      Jewish education. Gives history, structure,
      objectives, and climate in schools mainly in
      congregations but useful as background to the
      rise of the Solomon Schechter day schools.

736. Kelman, Stuart Lawrence. "Motivation and
      Goals: Why Parents Send Their Children to
      Non-Orthodox Jewish Day Schools." Ph. D.
      dissertation. University of California,
      1978.

      Analyzes descriptive information concerning
      why parents selected one of seven non-Orthodox

Jewish day schools in Los Angeles in 1977. Finds that these parents were seeking primarily an excellent, quality secular education, though these respondents were also interested in "Jewish" subjects and the "integration of Judaic and secular" subjects. This integrated curriculum seemed less important than "predominantly secular" ones, even though the desire for a Jewish education was important in tipping the scale in favor of this school.

737. Kurzweil, Zvi E. <u>Modern Trends in Jewish Education</u>. New York: Thomas Yoseloff, 1964.

Presents 12 essays on Jewish education, scholarship, and philosophy, including the ideas of N. H. Weisel, Rabbi Samson Raphael Hirsh, Rabbi Israel Salauter, and the <u>Mussar</u> movement, and A. D. Gordon, Januesz Korcsah, Franz Rosenzweig, Martin Buber, and Sara Schenirer. Shows the influence of these educators on Jewish schools. Relates Zionism, the revival of modern Hebrew as the language of instruction in day and afternoon schools. Gives background on Jewish thought and education.

738. Lazar, Meyer. "Religious Academic Achievement of Boys and Girls of Hebraic Jewish Orthodox Day Schools as Related to Selected Variables." Ph.D. dissertation. St. John's University, 1969.

Studies relationship of (1) student intelligence, (2) student adjustment, (3) parents' religious practices, (4) religious education of the father and mother, and (5) socio-economic status, as independent variables, and <u>achievement</u> in religious subjects as the dependent variable. Performed

study with 6th to 8th grade boys and girls in
Orthodox schools. Finds a significant
statistical relationship between the five
variables and religious academic achievement.

739. Leary, Carolyn F. "Perceived Goals and
      Characteristics of Jewish Day Schools and
      Catholic Parochial Schools." Ed.D.
      dissertation. Fordham University, 1978.

      Compares seven Jewish and twelve Catholic
      all-day schools. Both types stress values and
      morals; both wanted the religious emphasis to
      be an integral part of their schools. Jews had
      greater stress on openness and independence
      than their Catholic counterparts; both were
      concerned about special needs pupils,
      counseling, and better pay for staff.

740. Margolis, Isidor. Jewish Teacher Training
      Schools in the United States. New York:
      National Council for Torah Education of
      Mitzrachi-Hapoel Hamizrachi, 1964.

      Traces the origin and development of
      training colleges for Jewish teachers from 1897
      to 1960, with background on the conditions in
      the American Jewish community which influence
      this evolution. Highlights the "appalling"
      shortage of Jewish teachers and what 6
      institutions have done to meet the needs.
      Include analysis of such colleges as (1) Gratz
      college, Philadelphia, founded 1897, which now
      provides a full program for teachers and
      administrators in Jewish schools; (2) Teachers
      Institute of Jewish Theological Seminary of
      America, founded 1904 in New York City; (3)
      Teachers Institute of Yeshiva University,
      started 1917, in New York City; (4) Hebrew
      Teachers College of Boston, founded, 1921, and
      is the only one in that city; (5) Herzliah

Hebrew Teachers Institute, 1921, New York City, is an early Zionist teachers program, named after founder of modern Zionism, Theodore Herzl; and (6) College of Jewish Studies, Chicago, 1924. Details the program, staff, development, and schedules of these teachers colleges, up to about 1960.

741. Morris, Nathan. The Jewish School: An Introduction to the History of Jewish Education. New York: Jewish Education Comm. Press, 1964.

Gives full background on the philosophical, religious, and social roots and development of Jewish schooling. Covers curriculum, theories, pedagogy and learning, manual work and the child at home and at school.

742. Pilch, Judah. "From the Early Forties to the Mid-Sixties." In A History of Jewish Education in America, pp. 119-176. Edited by Judah Pilch. New York: American Association for Jewish Education, 1969.

Details the complex influences on American Jewish education post-World War II. Shows rise of day schools, origins of the Hasidic schools, particularly those started by the Lubavitcher Rebbe starting in 1940. Ties in with renewed interest in religion, growth of the American Jewish community, birth of Israel, and growing centralization of Jewish "federations," bureau of Jewish education, and the willingness of the Jewish community to support all-day schools. Leads to the "professionalization" of schooling, including boards of licensure, placement bureaus, fringe benefits, Israeli-U.S.A. exchanges, in-service education, codes of practice, and the rise of Jewish teachers colleges, cultural centers, and Hebrew studies programs.

743. Pollak, George. Doctoral Dissertations in
          Jewish Education. New York: Jewish
          Education Services of North America, 1982.

          Reviews important doctoral theses on the
      topic of Jewish education. Good source and
      reviews.

744. Pollak, George. "The Graduates of the Jewish
          Day Schools -- A Follow-Up Study." Ph.D.
          dissertation. Western Reserve University,
          1961.

          Studying the graduates of 25 day schools of
      all types (166 respondents), to learn
      education, prayer and observances, dietary
      laws, congregational-communal activities, and
      cultural involvement.

          Finds 66% attend synagogue, 25% recite
      prayers at home, and are active in Jewish life
      and culture. Spouse's religious affiliation
      and higher Jewish education were significantly
      related to religious practices.

745. Pollak, George. "A Review of Doctoral
          Dissertations in Jewish Education." Jewish
          Education 47 (Spring 1979): 35-43.

          Reviews and summarizes the hard-to-find
      studies done as doctoral theses on the topic of
      Jewish education. Invaluable source. Includes
      topics such as "adult education," "attitudes,"
      "audio-visual," "camping," "youth,"
      "curriculum," "day schools," "ethical values,"
      "ideological schools," "innovation," "Jewish
      education history," "licensing,"
      "personalities," "philosophies," and
      "withdrawal from Jewish schools." Gives brief
      summary of dissertations.

746.   Rauch, Eduardo.   "The Jewish Day School in
            America: A Critical History and
            Contemporary Dilemmas."   In Religious
            Schooling in America, pp. 130-168.   Edited
            by James C. Carper and Thomas C. Hunt.
            Birmingham, AL: Religious Education Press,
            1984.

        Reviews the definitions of Jewish day
        schools: their history, curriculum, finances,
        growth, criticism, and future of Orthodox,
        Conservative, and Reform all-day Jewish
        schools.   Focuses on the paradox represented by
        separate (and separated) Jewish schools and the
        need for integration, tradition and modernity,
        Judaism and Americanism, stubborn identity
        versus total assimilation.

747.   Schiff, Alvin I.   The Jewish Day School in
            America.   New York: Jewish Education
            Committee Press, 1966.

        Only book devoted totally to the topic of
        Jewish day schools to this date.   Presents
        exhaustive descriptions of the development,
        history, types, impact, and challenge of these
        schools.   Provides comprehensive view of the
        schools' workings of these schools from the
        various Orthodox, Conservative, and Reform
        traditions.   Ties schools into wider Jewish
        communal life, and trends in the integration
        (Jewish and secular subjects), expansion, and
        intensification of religious schooling through
        all-day Jewish education.

748.   Schiff, Alvin I.   "From Sunday School to Day
            School."   Jewish Education 50 (Summer 1982):
            6-13.

        Addresses a conference on 100 years of
        Jewish education in North America.   Traces

development of full-day Jewish schools from
their inception. Finds that Jewish schooling
reflects the dreams and paradoxes of each and
every generation and community. Today, 40% of
Jewish youth have no formal Jewish education at
all; 120,000 do receive day school
experiences--of which 85% are Orthodox;
remaining Jewish children attend afternoon
supplemental schools, though this late-day
alternative appears to produce many Jewish
"illiterates."

749. Willner, Eric. "The Adjustment of Jewish All-
       Day School Students Compared to that of
       Public School Students Attending Afternoon
       Hebrew Schools: as Determined by the Mooney
       Problem Check List of Problems Related to
       Religion and an Adoption of the Maslow S-L
       Inventory." Ph.D. dissertation. New York
       University, 1963.

       Compares students in Jewish day schools with
       those attending public schools to examine their
       adjustment and security. Finds that all-day
       students manifest significantly greater
       insecurity than the afternoon Hebrew school
       students; the all-day group gives higher
       priority to areas of "health and physical
       development," and less priority than that group
       in "Problems Related to Religion" and "boy-girl
       relations," and "relations to people in
       general." Recommends guidance programs for
       Hebrew day schools, and further research.

750. Zissenwine, David William. "A
       Conceptualization of Foundations for
       Curriculum Development in Jewish Education."
       Ph.D. dissertation. Ohio State University,
       1974.

Finds that most Jewish school curricula are "text-centered." Thinks that curricula fail to meet the needs of the times; proposes new educational approaches and new models for developing and using curricula. Even suggests the creation of "model" Jewish schools, providing some empirical bases for new approaches, methods and materials.

Part II: Contemporary

751. Adiv, Ellen. "Jewish Day Schools as Multilingual Models of Education." Jewish Education 53 (Fall 1984): 10-14.

Examines the adaptability and effectiveness of tri-lingual Jewish Schools (Hebrew, French and English) in Montreal. Finds schools able to provide a diverse language experience without compromising quality. Finds ability of Jews to handle all 3 languages advantageous in Quebec life.

752. Bank, Adrianne. "Evaluation: Is It Good for Jewish Education?" The Pedagogic Reporter 3 (September 1985): 1-6.

Discusses the background and need for good evaluation to improve Jewish education, by setting an agenda. Reviews the purposes, subject matter, and instruction by understanding the context and governance of Jewish schools.

753. "Challenges Facing the Jewish Day School." Jewish Education, Fiftieth Anniversary Issue 51 (Spring 1983): 2-48.

Entire issue devoted to background, examples, needs and growth of Hebrew day schools. Includes articles on related topics

by 14 authors on a range of topics, including
past and current.

754. Feder, Avraham. "Kohlberg's Theory and the
Religious Jew." Religious Education 79
(Spring 1984): 163-182.

Discusses whether a religious Jew can
support Kohlberg's theory of moral development,
reasoning, and education. Finds Kohlberg's
Kantian view basically unacceptable since it
stresses formal rather than contextual
criteria; unacceptable since Kohlberg is
categorial whereas Jewish morality is
tentative; unacceptable because Kohlberg
stresses autonomy and free will while Judaism
rests on the revealed order of the commandments
of God. Kohlberg presses moral reasoning,
Jewish morality rests on behavior or "mitzvot
Massiyot" (normative behavior). Jews perform
good deeds ("Mitzvot") "not because it is moral
but because God commands it."

755. Feuerman, Chaim. "Critical Challenges Facing
the Jewish Day School in the Coming Decade."
Jewish Education 51 (Summer 1983): 20-22.

Relates six challenges to continued day
school growth: (1) finding a Torah approach to
teaching; (2) teacher recruitment and training;
(3) financing schools adequately; (4) expanding
the numbers of children who benefit from
intensive Jewish schooling, regardless of
handicaps and needs; (5) integrating new Jewish
immigrants such as Russian and Iranian Jews;
and (6) computer literacy.

756. Freidenreich, Fradle Pomerantz. "The Unwritten
School Curriculum in the Jewish School."
Jewish Education 52 (Spring 1984): 3-9.

Analyzes the "unstudied" curriculum of
Jewish Schools. Finds schools are rich human
and religious environments, based on
mentchlekheit, humaneness and concern for
people, practices, the Covenant, Messianic
ideals, and belief in God.

757.   Friedman, Norman L. "On the Non-Effects' of
       Jewish Education on Most Students - A
       Critique." Jewish Education 52 (Summer
       1984): 30-33.

Critiques research on effects of Jewish
schooling. Finds much is lost by quantitative
approaches - need to know more about the impact
of education on each child. Even some
religious education may be better than none!

758.   Israel, Sherry. "Structural Experiences in
       Jewish Education." Religious Education 76
       (July-August 1981): 403-415.

Advocates the use of structured experiences
in groups as a means of bringing out feelings
and values in Jewish schools. Stresses these
experiences in addition to texts, languages,
laws, and facts, the "intellectual substance"
of Jewish tradition.

759.   Kobrin, Lawrence A. "A Layman Views the
       Organization and Structure of a Day School."
       Jewish Education 51 (Winter 1983): 31-35.

Examines the formal structure of a day
school -- its legal organization, tax
compliance, sponsorship, boards, committees,
parent involvement, as well as relations to
natural and regional associations. Urges
greater community participation and support.

760. Kraemer, David C. "Critical Aids to Teaching
      Talmud." Jewish Education 49 (Spring 1981):
      37-40.

          Asserts interest in Talmud instruction among
      Conservative Jewish Solomon Schechter day
      schools, though qualified staff are lacking.
      Method of teaching Talmud is presented.

761. Kramer, Doniel Zvi. The Day Schools and Torah
      Umesorah: The Seeding of Traditional
      Judaism in America. New York: Yeshiva
      University Press, 1985.

          Traces the development of Jewish day schools
      and their impact on Jewish American life.
      Focuses on the Torah Umesorah schools, those
      run by the National Society for Hebrew Day
      schools. Includes the history, philosophy,
      establishment, licensing, publications,
      parental and student involvement, curriculum
      development, Church-state relations, and
      relations between local day schools and
      state/national associations. Looks too at the
      effects of day schools and their graduates upon
      the general Jewish community.

762. Mars, Alvin. "A Staff Development Model for
      the Jewish Day School." Jewish Education 52
      (Winter 1984-85): 18-21, 28.

          Seeks methods of teaching staff of Jewish
      day schools the "concept of curriculum
      integration," particularly thinking skills
      across both the Hebraic and general studies
      areas. Difficulty exists because many day
      schools have half-day Jewish studies and half-
      day general academics. Encourages "critical
      thinking," "peer coaching," and "peer
      observations" as means of effective staff
      development. Then presses direct

implementation of integrated critical skill-
building in all subjects, using observation,
coaching, and evaluation.

763.   Rand, Baruch.   "Jewish Education Under Communal
       Auspices."   Jewish Education 50 (Summer
       1982):   18-23.

Describes and analyzes the "communal" or
"inter-congregational" schools--those run by
independent trustees rather than a particular
synagogue--and its role and importance in
Jewish life.   In 1978, 327 Jewish day schools
had community-wide sponsors, philosophies, and
outlooks.   Analyzes the pros and cons of these
communal approaches, using a joint Orthodox-
Conservative-Reform Jewish school in Toledo,
Ohio, and the consolidation of five day schools
into one "system" in Winnipeg, Canada, under a
superintendent.   Argues for the advantages of
community, central auspices, though many
"political" problems occur when trying to have
congregations to "give over" their schools.

764.   Ravin, Noach.   "The Effects of Individual and
       Job Characteristics on Job Satisfaction of
       Supplemental and Hebrew Day Schools' Hebrew
       Teachers."   Jewish Education 50 (Spring
       1982): 28-36.

Applies Herzberg's "Motivation-Hygiene
theory" and job satisfaction of Hebrew teachers
to the problem of locating and retaining these
teachers.   Herzberg believes that people have
basic needs such as salaries and decent working
conditions (the hygiene factors) and higher
order human longings for fulfillment,
accomplishments, and recognition (the
motivation factors).   Thus, more money removes
the "dissatisfiers" (hygiene needs) but does
not provide recognition and other higher needs
or "satisfiers."

Uses three scales in 12 Jewish schools in the Washington, D.C. area (4 day schools; 8 afternoon schools). Findings include no significant difference between day and supplemental school teachers in terms of satisfaction and hygiene/motivational factors; found some significant difference according to background and experience across types of schools; and (astoundingly) money affected levels of satisfaction ("motivation factors"), despite Herzberg's theory. Important to teachers were money, fringe benefits, interpersonal relations with students, and supervisor-teacher relations. Strong research approach.

765.   Resnick, David A. "Toward an Agenda for Research on Jewish Education." Jewish Education 50 (Summer 1982): 24-28.

Discusses problems in building a sound research foundation on Jewish education: hence, a vital study to future research in the field. Found that five reasons exist for the poor state of research on Jewish education: (1) unclear and confusing philosophy of Jewish education; (2) no on-going research enterprise in the field; (3) separation of Jewish research and publications from the social science mainstream; (4) the complex, unstudied politics surrounding Jewish schooling; and (5) the estranged relationship between general, secular education research and Jewish educational studies. Urges a cautious comparative approach.

766.   Rosman, Steven. "Process Thought and Jewish Education." Religious Education 79 (Fall 1984): 601-612.

Applies the concept of "Process Theology" of
Alfred North Whitehead to Jewish education, who
believes that the "essence of education is that
it be religious." Education, then, is a
process of nurturing and loving through God's
presence in the lives of pupils and teachers.

767. Schiff, Alvin I. "Public Education and the
     Jewish School." Journal of Jewish Communal
     Services 6 (Summer 1985): 305-311.

     Discusses four "imperatives" for Jewish
     education, given current developments in the
     field of education: (1) to put Jewish
     education on the community's agenda; (2)
     increase the number of Jewish educational
     professionals through more rigorous, active
     recruitment, higher standards, better training,
     more autonomy, better supervision, and more
     teacher responsibility; (3) clearer goals in
     building Jewish identity, sharper objectives,
     and stronger curricula; and (4) broader
     financial support from the national Jewish
     community--as well as grater government help
     for schools (see the Province of Quebec's
     support for Jewish schools in Montreal).

768. Schiff, Alvin I. and Botwinick, Chiam Y. "The
     Relevance of the Recommendations of Major
     National Studies on Education to Jewish
     Schooling." Jewish Education 52 (Summer
     1984): 7-18.

     Tests the relevance of recommendations of
     five national education reports to Jewish
     schools in Greater New York and other selected
     metropolitan areas, using a 32-item
     questionnaire to 1,076 Jewish educators,
     families, and lay leaders. Findings:
     "Extremely Relevant"--increased funding and
     better salaries in Jewish schools; "Very

Relevant"--improved leadership, freeing
teachers from administrative duties; "Somewhat
Relevant"--better texts, study skills, pre-
service education, recruiting of Hebrew school
principals, in-service training, and moral
development. Presents challenges for the
improvement of Jewish education, using new
awareness of education "engendered by national
studies. "

769.   Schwartzben, Sandon Howard. "Help Seeking
        Patterns Among Jewish Day Schools in
        Montreal." Jewish Education 50 (Summer
        1982): 32-38.

        Analyzes the use in 16 Jewish day schools of
        "helping personnel" such as community-based
        social workers, guidance counselors,
        psychologists and nurses in Montreal. Survey
        seeks information from day school educators on
        extent of problems among Jewish children in day
        schools and the use of helping personnel to
        assist them. Finds problems to be extensive
        throughout Jewish schools; finds that
        principals and teachers were aware of resources
        and needs; and that these school people are
        generally pleased with the services offered by
        Jewish community outside the immediate schools.

770.   Shevitz, Susan L. "Evaluation: A Tool for
        Program Evaluation (A Case Study)." The
        Pedagogic Reporter 36 (September 1985):
        10-13.

        Analyzes a case study of the Boston Bureau
        of Jewish Education and its efforts to improve
        Jewish schooling for adolescents. Abandoned
        the idea of a Judaic high school as too costly
        in favor of programming and built-in programs
        for this group. Stresses the importance of
        evaluation for program development and

improvement. Goals are to reach more teenagers
with better programs. Finds that this program,
the Program of Jewish Studies for High Schools,
was successful and becomes a permanent part of
the Burea, based on these evaluation
techniques.

771.   Soffer, Abraham. "Daily Prayer in a Day School
       Can Succeed!" The Pedagogic Reporter 33
       (December 1981): 22-23.

       Argues for daily prayers in Jewish schools -
       based on positive attitudes of leaders and
       staff and proper implementation in a proper
       setting for services, and should be related to
       the school's curriculum.

772.   Solovy, Dolores Kohl. "Potential and Reality:
       Can Computers Help Meet the Goals of the Day
       School?" Pedagogical Reporter 35 (January
       1984): 10-12.

       Discusses current and future uses of
       computers in Jewish schools. Finds schools now
       using computers for instruction, programming,
       word processing, and record keeping. Suggests
       new ways to integrate computer into the schools
       as useful tools as training and technology
       continue.

CHAPTER 14
LUTHERAN SCHOOLS
Jon Diefenthaler

Part I: Historical

773. Arden, G. Everett. Augustana Heritage. Rock
      Island, IL: Augustana Press, 1963.

      Furnishes a definitive denominational
      history of Swedish Lutheranism in America and
      focuses on the European background,
      organizational development, Americanization and
      ecumenical efforts of the Augustana Synod.
      Calls attention to 56 parochial schools
      maintained by 142 congregations in 1870, but
      emphasizes the more general tendency of these
      Lutherans to favor the public schools. Argues
      that parochial education during the early years
      of the Augustana Synod was for the
      "preservation of the Swedish language among the
      youth," and thus evolved into a more limited
      summer program known as "Swede school."

774. Beck, Walter A. Lutheran Elementary Schools in
      the United States. St. Louis: Concordia
      Publishing House, 1939.

Provides a comprehensive overview of
parochial education efforts on the part of all
Lutheran synods in America from colonial times
to the eve of World War II. Assesses attitudes
shaped by historical developments within the
contexts of the many German and Scandinavian
groups of Lutherans. Devotes a chapter to
mission schools established for Blacks,
Indians, orphans and handicapped.

775. Blegen, Theodore C. Norwegian Migration to
America: The American Transition.
Northfield, MN: The Norwegian-American
Historical Association, 1940.

Contains an important chapter on the
controversy over the "common school" in
Lutheran synods of Norwegian immigrants during
the second half of the 19th century.
Emphasizes the clash of values that pitted lay
persons seeking to fulfill their immigrant
aspirations in the New World against clergy of
the Norwegian Synod who denounced public
education as "religionless" and tended to favor
the establishment of separate parochial
schools.

776. Diefenthaler, Jon. "Lutheran Schools in
America."In Religious Schooling in America,
pp. 35-57. Edited by James C. Carper and
Thomas C. Hunt. Birmingham, AL: Religious
Education Press, 1984.

Focuses on the elementary school system of
the Missouri Synod and stresses that
"orthodoxy" was the reason schools were
established by congregations of this group's
immigrant forebears. Argues that America's
pluralistic environment has proven as
threatening as friendly to these Lutherans and
that their schools were often in the vanguard

of resistance to assimilation. Suggests that
the steady increase in the numbers of
nonLutherans enrolling in these same schools
since the early 1970s may precipitate some
modification of these historical attitudes.

777.   Dierker, Leonard J.   "Minutes of the First
       Lutheran Teachers Conference in St. Louis."
       Concordia Historical Institute Quarterly 57
       (Fall 1984): 118-126.

       Translates and summarizes minutes of
       conference of parochial school teachers from
       the Missouri Synod congregations in St. Louis
       between 1851 and 1869. Highlights publication
       of texts, exchanges of catechizations,
       discussions of professional standards and
       assigned readings on topics of common concern.

778.   Forster, Walter O.   Zion on the Mississippi.
       St. Louis: Concordia Publishing House,
       1953.

       Gives an indepth analysis of the settlement
       of Missouri, 1839 to 1841, of the Saxon
       Lutheran strain of immigrants who contributed
       to the formation of the Missouri Synod.
       Alludes only in passing to some of first forms
       that religious instruction took, but highlights
       the reaction to rationalism's influence and
       aversion to state church policies in Europe so
       crucial for understanding the synod's
       unwavering commitment to Lutheran orthodoxy and
       its preservation through the establishment of a
       parochial school in each congregation.

779.   "Growing in the Lord: 75 Years of Lutheran
       Secondary Education in Milwaukee."
       Concordia Historical Institute Quarterly 51
       (Spring 1978): 3-8.

Recounts history of Lutheran secondary education from its beginnings at Immanuel Lutheran School. Discusses the joint high school supported by congregations of Wisconsin and Missouri synods in Milwaukee and the eventual establishment of three separate schools in 1955, 1959, and 1968.

780.   Gude, George J. "Women Teachers in the Missouri Synod." Concordia Historical Institute Quarterly 44 (November 1971): 163-170.

Recounts the history of the long-standing debate over the propriety of women teachers in the parochial schools of the Missouri Synod. Focuses on inconsistencies between policy and practice. Shows that not only were women assuming classroom responsibilities prior to 1929, when the synod decreed that in "emergency situations" women could be employed in place of men, but asserts that while current synodical policy states that "the woman teacher is to be regarded as called in the same sense as the man," this position "is not practiced very widely."

781.   Hamre, James S. "Georg Sverdrug's Defense of Secular Education." The Lutheran Quarterly 17 (May 1965): 143-150.

Sets forth the school controversy among Norwegian Lutherans of the 19th century from the standpoint of Sverdrug's effort to establish a theological rationale (Martin Luther's doctrine of the two spheres) for public education.

782.   Hamre, James S. "Norwegian Immigrants Respond to the Common School: A Case Study of American Values and the Lutheran Tradition." Church History 50 (September 1981): 302-311.

Assesses the common school debate among
Norwegian immigrants of the 19th century as to
whether their children should attend America's
public schools or Lutheran parochial schools.
Focuses on Georg Sverdrug's effort to value
public education without surrendering
traditional Lutheran emphasis on thorough
instruction in the faith by interpreting Martin
Luther's writings to mean that church and state
had different mandates and could function
separately from each other.

783. Hunt, Thomas C. "The Bennett Law of 1890:
      Focus of Conflict Between Church and State
      in Education." Journal of Church and State
      23 (Winter 1981): 69-93.

Analyzes the controversy provoked by
Wisconsin's Bennett Law of 1890 from its
enactment to its repeal in 1891. Examines the
position and motives of Governor Hoard and
other supporters of such legislation, the
reactions of Roman Catholic and Lutheran
authorities who viewed the law a threat to
their systems of parochial schools, the
political campaigns of 1890 in which Catholics
and Lutherans joined forces to defeat
incumbents associated with the law.

784. Jahsmann, Allan Hart. What's Lutheran in
      Education? St. Louis: Concordia Publishing
      House, 1960.

Sets forth "Lutheran" theory of education
from theological, philosophical, and
educational standpoints. Provides summary of
Missouri Synod's understanding of its own
educational institutions, including parochial
schools. Reveals attitudes of synod concerning
"religion" in public school setting and
government aid to religious schools.

785.   Johnson, Neil A.   "The Patriotism and Anti-
            Prussianism of the Lutheran Church--Missouri
            Synod, 1914, 1918." Concordia Historical
            Institute Quarterly 39 (October 1966):
            99-118.

        Emphasizes the anti-German sentiment and
        mass hysteria that placed Lutherans of the
        Missouri Synod on the defensive during World
        War I and forced the closing of a number of
        their parochial schools. Asserts that such
        pressures prompted these Lutherans to adopt
        "loyalty resolutions" affirming their
        dedication to "the democratic principles of the
        Protestant Reformation" and accelerated their
        Americanization.

786.   Johnston, Paul I.   "Freedom of Speech Means
            Freedom to Teach: The Constitutional Battle
            of Nebraska, 1919-1923." Concordia
            Historical Institute Quarterly 52 (Fall
            1979): 118-124.

        Discusses the bellwether Meyer v. State of
        Nebraska case involving a Lutheran teacher
        indicted, convicted, and fined under state law
        enacted during World War I for conducting
        school lesson in "German." Shows how the due
        process clause of the 14th Amendment to the
        United State Constitution came to be used as a
        defense in freedom of speech cases pertaining
        to religious instruction.

787.   Johnstone, Ronald A.   The Effectiveness of
            Lutheran Elementary and Secondary Schools as
            Agencies of Christian Education.   St. Louis:
            Concordia Publishing House, 1966.

        Discounts the difference between parochial
        and public-school educated youth of the

Missouri Synod. Highlights the strength of the
Lutheran family, where both groups showed
remarkable similarities in their attitudes
toward worship attendance, stewardship,
beliefs, willingness to share their faith, and
social attitudes. Points out that while the
direct influence of parochial education was
more apparent in the "marginal" families
considered by this study, the children of such
families were the group least likely to receive
it.

788.   Johnstone, Ronald L.   "A Response to the Kramer
          Review." Concordia Theological Monthly 38
          (January 1967): 37-38.

        Expresses rebuttal of author of the
controversial "Johnstone Report" to his critics
within the Missouri Synod.

789.   Klein, Leonard. "A Parish School." Dialog 18
          (Summer 1979): 197-201.

        Describes the author's experience as pastor
of a Lutheran church with a parochial school in
New York City's Borough of Queens. Contains
reflections on the multi-ethnic character of
the surrounding community and discusses
challenges and mission opportunities it
presents to the church as well as school.

790.   Koehler, John Philipp.   The History of the
          Wisconsin Synod.   St. Cloud, MN: Sentinel
          Publishing Company, 1970.

        Gives an "insider's" (Koehler stood at the
center of a major controversy in the Wisconsin
Synod) view of the development of one of
Lutheranism's most conservative synods,
1850-1930, that sheds light on the purpose and
outlook of its educational institutions.

Reveals not only the strong commitment to orthodox Lutheran teaching, but the anti-cultural bias (Koehler suggests that education is not the business of government in the first place) at work in Wisconsin's system of parochial schools.

791.   Kramer, William A.   General Course of Study for Lutheran Elementary Schools.   St. Louis: Concordia Publishing House, 1943.

Sets forth philosophy and objectives of the educational process in elementary schools of the Missouri Synod.   Implies that goal of this process is not only thorough instruction in Lutheran doctrine, but presentation of all subjects from a Christian point of view.

792.   Kramer, William A.   "The Johnstone Study of Lutheran Schools."   Concordia Theological Monthly 38 (January 1967): 23-36.

Reveals the controversy by The Effectiveness of Lutheran Elementary and Secondary Schools as Agencies of Christian Education.   Asserts the criticisms of the educational establishment of the Missouri Synod.

793.   Kramer, William A.   "Life in Perry County, Missouri at the Turn of the Century."   Concordia Historical Institute Quarterly 48 (Spring 1955): 10-25.

Provides a firsthand set of recollections of the Lutheran subculture of which parochial schools were an important component at the beginning of the 20th century.   Describes Perry County, Missouri, the area in which the Missouri Synod's Saxon forebears settled in 1839, and in discussing the various facets of life in its agricultural communities of

Lutherans, examines the curriculum and teachers associated with the schools.

794. Kramer, William A. Lutheran Schools--15
      Crucial Years: History of the Schools of
      the Lutheran Church--Missouri Synod from
      1959 to 1973. St. Louis: Concordia
      Publishing House, 1975.

      Discusses challenges to all facets of
      Missouri Synod's parochial school system
      brought on by the changes of the 1960s in such
      areas as educational environment, teacher
      education, theological emphasis, and teaching
      methods. Focuses on enrollment trends,
      relationships between congregations and
      synodical agencies, local organization and
      administration, issue of "quality" education,
      teacher training, relationships to other
      private schools and public education.

795. Krause, Victor C. , ed. Lutheran Elementary
      Schools in Action. St. Louis: Concordia
      Publishing House, 1963.

      Provides insight into the philosophy and
      operating procedures of elementary schools of
      the Missouri Synod during years of growth and
      expansion following World War II. Expresses an
      "inside" point of view in separate chapters
      written by various authors that treat school
      purposes, personnel, and pupils; explores the
      school's relationships to the home,
      congregation, synod, and community; considers
      issues of instruction, guidance, worship, pupil
      activities, health services, facilities, and
      funding.

796. Manley, Robert N. "Language, Loyalty and
      Liberty: The Nebraska State Council of
      Defense and the Lutheran Churches,

1917-1918." Concordia Historical Institute
Quarterly 37 (April 1964): 1-16.

Discusses World War I efforts of Nebraska
State Council of Defense to "focus public
indignation" against Lutherans that led to the
banning of teaching or use of foreign languages
in parochial schools, restrictions on foreign-
language worship services, and mandatory
licensing of "alien teachers and preachers."
Describes reactions of Lutherans to these
measures and relates their trauma to nativism
in Nebraska during the early decades of the
20th century.

797.   Maurer, Charles L. Early Lutheran Education in
Pennsylvania. Philadelphia: Dorrance &
Company, 1932.

Collects data on parochial schools of
Lutheran congregations in colonial Pennsylvania
and organizes it both geographically and
chronologically. Also contains assessment of
18th century Lutheran attitudes toward such
education, their teachers and schoolmasters,
and the administrative methods they employed.

798.   Meier, Everette, and Herbert T. Mayer. "The
Process of Americanization." In Moving
Frontiers, pp. 334-385. Edited by Carl S.
Meyer. St. Louis: Concordia Publishing,
1964.

Consists of a collection of readings with
introduction and commentary on many aspects of
the Missouri Synod's "Americanization" from the
Civil War to World War I. Argues that the
parochial schools of the synod's congregations
tended to impede the process because they were
so heavily identified with "German" culture and
language. Furnishes primary source materials

from magazines and proceedings of synodical
conventions that illustrate Missouri's fear of
assimilation and the dynamics of its language
controversies.

799. Meyer, Carl S. "Early Growth of the Missouri
      Synod." In Moving Frontiers, pp. 194-246.
      Edited by Carl S. Meyer. St. Louis:
      Concordia Publishing House, 1964.

      Collects primary sources from 1839 to the
      Civil War that illustrate the outlook and
      concerns of the forebears of the Missouri Synod
      and reinforces the notion that indoctrination
      of the laity motivated them to encourage the
      establishment of Lutheran elementary schools.
      Also explores Missouri's view of the
      relationship between its own schools and the
      public school system and argues that while
      these Lutherans supported the latter as
      citizens of the state, they found such public
      institutions incapable of providing
      sufficiently orthodox religious training.
      Gives helpful examples of daily routine and
      administration of Lutheran elementary schools
      and discusses early (few and not always
      successful) efforts to establish secondary
      schools.

800. Meyer, Carl S., ed. Moving Frontiers. St.
      Louis: Concordia Publishing House, 1964.

      Contains items 798 and 799.

801. Miller, Arthur L. Educational Administration
      and Supervision of Lutheran Schools of the
      Missouri Synod. Chicago: University of
      Chicago Press, 1951.

      Contains an assessment of function and
      structure of Missouri Synod's elementary school

system written from the standpoint of an
"insider."

802.   Nelson, E. Clifford, ed.   The Lutherans in
          North America.   Philadelphia: Fortress
          Press, 1975.

          Contains the most comprehensive overview of
          the history of Lutheranism in America to date.
          Attends to parochial elementary schools among
          German and Scandinavian immigrant families of
          the late nineteenth century, describes the
          anti-foreign reaction the Lutheran schools
          among the Germans endured during World War I,
          and discusses threats (e. g. , Wayne County Civic
          Association) and adjustments made during the
          1920s.

803.   Nelson, E. Clifford, and Eugene L. Fevold.   The
          Lutheran Church Among Norwegian-Americans.
          Minneapolis: Augsburg Publishing House,
          1960.

          Surveys the organizational history of
          Norwegian Lutheran churches in America from
          1825 to 1890.   Asserts that parochial elemental
          schools chiefly in the Norwegian Synod where
          they were promoted by clergy concerned about
          the pure transmission of orthodox Lutheran
          doctrine.   Includes brief discussion of the
          rise of academies (secondary schools) and
          emphasizes the ethnic as well as religious
          rationale for their establishment.

804.   Repp, Arthur C. , ed.   One Hundred Years of
          Christian Education.   River Forest, IL:
          Lutheran Education Association, 1947.

          Contains essays recounting the development
          of all educational institutions of the Missouri
          Synod.   Breaks this history into distinct

periods and highlights the outstanding
characteristics of each.   Provides the "inside"
point of view of various authors.

805.   Rietschel, William C.   "A. C. Stellhorn and the
        Lutheran Teacher in Ministry." Lutheran
        Education 115 (January-February 1980):
        147-160.

        Delineates the high view of the Lutheran
        teacher advocated by A. C. Stellhorn during his
        56 years as superintendent of Missouri Synod
        parochial schools.   Argues that Stellhorn saw
        teachers as full participants in the public
        ministry of preaching and teaching the Word of
        God (even intimating that teachers might be
        ordained) in the face of many others in the
        synod who tended to diminish the scope and
        function of the office.

806.   Rietschel, William C.   "August C. Stellhorn--A
        Biographical Sketch." Concordia Historical
        Institute Quarterly 55 (Summer 1982): 52-65.

        Chronicles the life and career of the
        Missouri Synod's first secretary of schools and
        highlights his pivotal role in shaping the
        development of its system of elementary and
        secondary schools between 1920 and 1960.

807.   Schmidt, Stephen A.   "American Education: A
        Lutheran Footnote."   In The Lutheran Church
        in North American Life, pp. 168-193.   Edited
        by John E. Groh and Robert H. Smith.   St.
        Louis: Clayton Publishing House, 1979.

        Surveys Lutheran education in North America
        from colonial days to the present and argues
        that it has embodied a distinct subcultural set
        of values in viable communities of faith.
        Assesses musical achievements, liberal arts

colleges, day school system, definitive
theological systems, and vital parish life as
strengths of Lutheran education and points to
dogmatism, parochialism, and clericism as some
of its chief weaknesses.

808. Schmidt, Stephen A. Powerless Pedagogues.
      River Forest, IL: Lutheran Education
      Association, 1972.

      Interprets the history of the Lutheran
      teacher in the Missouri Synod as an agonizing
      search for professional identity. Asserts that
      while "almost a minister" was the status to
      which Lutheran teachers aspired, "almost a
      hireling" was the reality of their job.
      Concludes that such confusion led to a
      "weakened professional self-image" for which
      teachers were forced to compensate with "over-
      dedication."

809. Stellhorn, August C. History of the
      Superintendents Conference. St. Louis:
      Concordia Publishing House, 1956.

      Recounts the development of the bureaucracy
      governing the parochial school system of the
      Missouri Synod following World War I at the
      district and synodical levels of
      administration.

810. Stellhorn, August C. Schools of the Lutheran
      Church--Missouri Synod. St. Louis:
      Concordia Publishing House, 1963.

      Surveys the history of elementary and
      secondary schools of the Missouri Synod from
      1847 to 1961. Divides the period into quarter
      centuries and discusses schools in light of
      general developments in the synod. Gives
      attention to the relationship of Lutheran

schools to public schools, transitions from
German to the English language, development of
Lutheran high schools, and the educational
bureaucracy that began to evolve at the
synodical level following World War I.
Consistently treats the role of the Lutheran
teacher and the development of Missouri's
system of teacher-training institutions, as
well as principles of education, courses of
study, and textbooks. Provides a wealth of
information but fails to give us a critical
assessment of it because the author is an
"insider" who in fact served as Missouri's
Secretary for Schools for nearly forty years.

811.   Sylwester, Harold J. "Swedish Lutheran Schools
         on the Delaware, 1638-1755." Concordia
         Historical Institute Quarterly 40 (July
         1967): 51-66.

         Traces the history of educational efforts
from the founding of New Sweden in 1638 and
argues that prior to 1700, lack of leadership
(Swedish ministers were few in number and
tended to remain in America for relatively
short periods of time), frontier conditions,
and linguistic factors combined to hinder
instruction. Asserts that the intervention of
the Lutheran Church of Sweden in 1697 aided the
development of schools up until 1722, but that
America's Swedes were unable to sustain this
momentum due to financial problems, shortage of
schoolmasters, and decline of population.

812.   Wessler, Martin, ed. Planning for Lutheran
         Elementary Schools. St. Louis: Board of
         Parish Education, the Lutheran
         Church--Missouri Synod, 1978.

         Consists of collection of 13 booklets that
provide guidelines for all phases of operating

a Lutheran parochial school (e.g., starting a
new school, personnel, handbook, financial
planning, legal requirements, curriculum,
parents as partners). Reveals the "Lutheran"
points of view and their applications to
specific areas of elementary education.

Part II: Contemporary

813.   Bayer, Les. "More Needed--Less Available."
       Lutheran Education 118 (November-December
       1982): 61-68.

       Demonstrates Lutheran commitment of
       operating parochial schools in urban settings
       in second of five articles. Discusses promise
       and strains in beginning a teaching career in
       an urban Lutheran school.

814.   Einspahr, Glenn C. "State Certification
       Trends." Lutheran Education 119 (November-
       December 1983): 104-113.

       Examines such trends in state certification
       of teachers as testing, involvement of various
       political groups, requirement of specific
       courses, local control. Calls upon Lutheran
       teachers to obtain valid state certificates,
       whether their employers require them or not,
       for their own professional welfare and the good
       of the schools in which they teach.

815.   Engebrecht, Richard H. "Conceptualizing Your
       Urban Lutheran School." Lutheran Education
       118 (September-October 1982): 5-17.

       Demonstrates Lutheran commitment to
       operating parochial schools in urban settings
       in first of five articles. Presents a
       conceptual analysis model through which those
       involved in such schools can chart various

change realities (i.e., member/nonmember
enrollment, racial/ethnic diversity,
neighborhood demographics, economic support
relationships, makeup of faculty and staff)
converging upon them.

816. Engebrecht, Richard H. "'Role and Purpose'
      Models and Your Urban Lutheran School."
      Lutheran Education 118 (May-June 1983):
      262-271.

      Demonstrates Lutheran commitment to
      operating parochial schools in urban settings
      in last of five articles. Describes five
      different conceptual models for urban Lutheran
      schools (i.e., traditional outreach and service
      to community, new faith community, cathedral
      school, missionary school) and encourages
      greater efforts by those involved to discover
      and understand the role and purpose of a given
      urban school. Offers practical suggestions for
      reaching a desired model through goal setting
      and planning.

817. Hazard, William R. "Educational Malpractice:
      An Injury in Search of a Remedy." Lutheran
      Education 117 (March-April 1982): 181-186.

      Explores the boundaries of current questions
      concerning the extent to which schools are
      legally required to teach all children the
      skills and knowledge necessary to operate
      effectively in society. Warns that Peter W.
      v. San Francisco Unified School District
      (alleged failure of school to teach student to
      read) is not the last word and suggests that
      legal remedies (malpractice suits, etc.) for
      educational injuries may ultimately prevail.

818. Heinemeier, John. "Spirituality in the Urban
      Lutheran School." Lutheran Education 118
      (January-February 1983): 121-129.

Demonstrates Lutheran commitment to
operating parochial schools in urban settings
in third of five articles. Examines eleven
assumptions about urban Lutheran schools and
presents a checklist of suggestions for
developing spiritual life in them.

819.   Heinitz, Kenneth. "The Lutheran Teacher and
        Ministry." Lutheran Education 119
        (September-October 1983): 18-26.

Attempts to put problem of ecclesiastical
identity of parochial school teachers in the
Missouri Synod into biblical and historical
perspective and calls for a more formal
recognition of their "ministry" within the
church.

820.   Herzog, John A. "Tuition Tax Credits--An Issue
        of Education: Part One, The Case Against
        Tax Credits." Lutheran Education 119
        (September-October 1983): 38-47.

Provides background information and
discusses such issues raised by opponents of a
federal tax tuition credit for families with
children in parochial schools as cost to the
taxpayer, racial and ethnic segregation, loss
of enrollment in public schools, danger of
government interference, and the
constitutionality of the idea itself.

821.   Herzog, John A. "Tuition Tax Credits--An Issue
        of Education: Part Two, The Case for Tax
        Credits." Lutheran Education 119 (November-
        December 1983): 78-89.

Asserts that the purpose of the parochial
school is not to replace public education, but
to provide an "alternative" form of schooling,

one with a "distinctly religious bias." Cites
evidence that repudiates the arguments against
tuition tax credits (e.g., the reality of
integration in many nonpublic schools).

822. Linse, Eugene. "Church and State: Some
      Problems of Philosophy and Practice."
      Concordia Journal 6 (November 1980):
      242-256.

Sees secular humanism as an antibiblical
philosophy infecting American public education
and altering contemporary interpretations of
the First Amendment to the United States
Constitution. Uses the question of the
jurisdiction of the National Labor Relations
Board over parochial schools and the proposals
from the Interval Revenue Service to deprive
these same schools of tax-exempt status as case
studies and suggests and if implemented such
measures might well hamper the free exercise of
religion in parochial education.

823. Meyer, Fred. "Called to be Family." Lutheran
      Education 118 (March-April 1983): 224-232.

Demonstrates Lutheran commitment to
operating parochial schools in urban settings
in fourth of five articles. Sets up "family"
as model for individual classrooms and for
staff to work together in carrying out the
mission of the school. Outlines problems
(e.g., multi-racial makeup of the urban
classroom) and suggests ways to build
relationships.

824. Piel, Paul F. "Toward Accreditation."
      Lutheran Education 116 (January-February
      1981): 121-125.

Calls attention to public movement to make schools more "accountable" and argues in favor of accreditation as means of improving the quality of education in Lutheran schools. Suggests that accreditation process will sharpen perception of strengths and weaknesses in the program, unify staff, clarify purpose of schools, and enhance public confidence.

825.   Pies, Timothy. "Financing Lutheran Schools: Some Suggestions." Lutheran Education 120 (September-October 1984): 40-47.

Sets forth various tuition, special-gift, endowment, fund-matching, and consolidation schemes as creative methods of assuring funding of Lutheran schools in an era marked by inflation and depressed economic activity.

826.   Rietschel, William C. "Lutheran Schools and the Law." Lutheran Education 120 (March-April 1985): 230-233.

Focuses on "custodial" and "managerial" dimensions of the in loco parentis statutes governing public education and discusses their applications to Lutheran schools. Warns that while Bright v. Isenbarger sets forth fundamental concepts related to constitutional rights (e.g., emphasis on moral development and strict discipline) that distinguish private schools from their public counterparts, Lutheran educators must be mindful of "rights" to which their pupils remain entitled (e.g., schools conforming in fact to rules and regulations set forth in own literature).

827.   Senske, Al H. "Private Education and the Government." Lutheran Education 116 (March-April 1981): 217-226.

Seeks to reduce tensions regarding
government "encroachment" on Lutheran schools
in legal and service areas by advocating more
active involvement in the political process.
Advocates remaining informed and working with
public school administrators on entitlement
programs, coordinating efforts with other
private schools through Council for American
Private Education (CAPE), communicating
purposes and positions to government officials.

828.   "Text of U. S. Supreme Court Decision: St.
       Martin Evangelical Lutheran Church v. South
       Dakota." Journal of Church and State 24
       (Winter 1982): 205-216.

       Supplies text for crucial high court
       decision upholding exemption of parochial
       schools with respect to their employees from
       taxes imposed by the Federal Unemployment Tax
       Act (FUTA) of 1976.

829.   Zimmerman, Paul A.   "The Lutheran
       Teacher--Minister of the Church." Lutheran
       Education 116 (September-October 1980):
       40-54.

       Interprets the Bible and Lutheran
       Confessions in favor of viewing male and female
       school teachers of the Missouri Synod as
       "ministers" in the performance of specific
       church functions. Argues that such teachers
       are entitled to a "divine call," to view their
       positions as being in no way subordinate to
       pastors, to seek ordination if the church sees
       fit to allow this human practice.

CHAPTER 15
MENNONITE SCHOOLS
Albert N. Keim

Part I: Historical

830. Brubaker, Jacob Lester. "A History of the
Mennonite Elementary School Movement. Ed. D.
dissertation. University of Virginia, 1966.

Historical analysis of the Mennonite school
movement with critical suggestions for new
directions for the movement.

831. Graybill, J. Paul. Christian Day Schools for
Mennonite Youth. Scottdale, PA: Herald
Press, 1945.

Provides the rationale for Mennonite
education which led to the first surge of
growth in Mennonite Christian day schools after
World War II.

832. Harder, Menno S. "The Origin, Philosophy and
Development of Education Among the
Mennonites." Ph. D. dissertation.
University of Southern California, 1949.

The most comprehensive treatment of the
history of Mennonite schools and schooling
extant. Encompasses all eras and geographical
areas of the world where Mennonites have lived.
Appendixes include materials from Menno Simons,
a Hutterite school discipline, Russian
Mennonite school regulations, and Christopher
Dock's School Management.

833. Hartzler, John E. Education Among the
     Mennonites of America. Danvers, IL: The
     Central Mennonite Publishing Board, 1925.

     A historical treatment of Mennonite
     educational developments.

834. Hertzler, Silas. "Mennonite Education Today."
     School and Society 80 (August 21, 1954):
     59-60.

     Surveys the rationale for and character of
     Mennonite elementary and secondary schools in
     the United States and Canada

835. Massinari, Karl. "The Contribution of
     Christopher Dock to Contemporary Christian
     Teaching." Mennonite Quarterly Review 15
     (April 1951): 100-115.

     Christopher Dock's Schulordnung (1770) has a
     timely relevance for Christian day school
     teachers. The author finds seven basic
     pedagogical principles in Dock's handbook for
     teachers.

836. Studer, Gerald. Christopher Dock: Colonial
     Schoolmaster. Scottdale, PA: Herald Press,
     1967.

     Carefully written biography of an early
     Mennonite teacher. The author successfully

recreates the tone and temper of the colonial
milieu in which Dock worked and lived. An
appendix includes Dock's famous "School
Management" treatise.

837. Wenger, A. Grace. "Anabaptist Perspectives on
      Education." Gospel Herald (February 25,
      1975): 127-139.

      A skillful linkage of theological principles
      to educational goals. The author speaks from a
      long career of service in education.

838. Yoder, Paton. Toward a Mennonite Philosophy of
      Education since 1890. Elkhart, IN:
      Mennonite Board of Education, 1968.

      Summarizes the literature of Mennonite
      educational objectives and purposes as
      developed by Mennonite educators, institutions
      and study conferences.

Part II: Contemporary

839. Bernstein, Barbara. "A Cross-Cultural Study of
      Sixth-Graders' New Year's Resolutions:
      Middle-Class Versus Mennonite and Amish
      Youth." Social Behavior and Personality 5
      (February 1977): 209-14.

      Reports research results when comparing
      middle-class sixth-graders with Mennonite and
      Amish sixth-graders. Mennonite and Amish
      students resolved to try harder; middle-class
      youngsters resolved to do better.

840. Brubaker, Stanley K. Feed My Lambs: A Book
      About Christian Schools. Goshen, IN.:
      Pilgrim Publishers, 1979.

This book, by a teacher in the conservative
Mennonite tradition, captures, in a genuinely
accurate way, a wide range of intention and
practice, as well as the humble but thoughtful
spirit of this school movement within the
Mennonite parochial school community. Here one
finds a third alternative to the Amish on one
hand and the professional Mennonite educators
on the other.

841.   <u>Christian</u> <u>School</u> <u>Builder</u>.   Crockett, KY: Rod
and Staff Publishers.

Monthly magazine for Mennonite parochial
schools.

842.   Erb, Alta Mae.   <u>Christian</u> <u>Nurture</u> <u>of</u> <u>Children</u>.
Scottdale, PA: Herald Press, 1955.

Argues that Christian nurture of children
must be an intentional effort guided by basic
understanding of child development and
religious values.

843.   Hertzler, Daniel.   <u>Mennonite</u> <u>Education:</u>   <u>Why</u>
<u>and</u> <u>How</u>.   Scottdale, PA: Herald Press,
1971.

This volume comes as close to an official
statement of educational purpose and philosophy
as the Mennonite church has developed.   The
goal of Mennonite education must be Christian
maturity defined as faith in Christ in the
context of commitment to a Christian community.

844.   Hess, Ernest Mark.   "A Study of the Influence
of Mennonite Schools on Their Students in
the (Pennsylvania) Conference of the
Mennonite Church."   Ph.D. dissertation.
Ohio State University, 1975.

Do young Mennonite adults who attended
Mennonite schools hold beliefs and values
significantly different from those who did not
attend Mennonite schools? Yes, this study
concludes, but home religiosity, amount of
education and church service assignments are
powerful variants which make the educational
efforts somewhat inconclusive.

845. Hooley, William D. "A Comparison of the
       Values, Attitudes and Beliefs of Mennonite
       Youth Who Attended Church-Related High
       School and Those Who Attended Public High
       Schools." Ph.D. dissertation. Western
       Michigan University, 1974.

Concludes that on most values and beliefs
there are no statistically significant
differences between church related and public
school attendees. On several specific beliefs
church-related school attenders were more
aligned with Mennonite beliefs than public
attenders.

846. Hostetler, John A. , Gertrude Enders Huntington
       and Donald B. Kraybill. Cultural
       Transmission and Instrumental Adaptation to
       Social Change: Lancaster Mennonite High
       School in Transition. Final Report
       RO-20651. Washington, DC: U.S. Department
       of Health, Education and Welfare, 1974.

How does a tightly-knit ethnic high school
respond to rapid social and cultural change?
This is an excellent case study of the
strengths and limits of church-related
secondary education in the transmission of
religious values and purposes.

847. Kraybill, Donald Brubaker. Mennonite
       Education: Issues, Facts, and Changes.
       Scottdale, PA: Herald Press, 1978.

Interprets the work of a half-dozen recent research projects on the impact and effectiveness of Mennonite elementary and secondary schools. The Mennonite school is crucial, the author concludes, in articulating the vision which forms the Mennonite identity and faith.

848.   Kraybill, Donald Brubaker. "Religions and Ethnic Socialization in a Mennonite High School." _Mennonite Quarterly Review_ 51 (October 1977): 329-349.

Concludes that this Mennonite high school decreases assimilationist tendencies of Mennonite youth into the larger American society. Students become more compatible with normative social behavior espoused by their church and parents.

849.   Lederach, Paul M. _Mennonite Youth_. Scottdale, PA: Herald Press, 1971.

Summarizes research findings on Mennonite youth regarding a wide range of values. Provides a basis for Christian nurture and educational strategy for the Mennonite church.

850.   Lehman, Esther K. _Teachers' Guide: First, Second, Third Grade_. Harrisonburg, VA: Association of Mennonite Elementary Schools, 1959.

An attempt to bring the best pedagogical course designs and plans into coherence with Christian theological values. A thorough state-of-the-art document. A second volume treats grades four to six.

851. Meyer, Albert J. "Peoplehood Education."
      Mennonite Educator 4 (January 1974): 1-6.

      A seminal essay which brings into sharp
      focus the specific theological nexus from which
      Mennonite schools should derive their program
      and curricula.

852. Taddie, John A. "A Comparison of Academic
      Achievements of Mennonite Pupils Attending
      Mennonite Parochial Schools and Public
      Schools in Lancaster County, Pennsylvania."
      Ph.D. dissertation. Lehigh University,
      1970.

      Using standardized tests on ability and
      achievement, the author finds no significant
      difference between Mennonite children in
      parochial schools and those in public schools.

853. Weaver, Laura. "Forbidden Fancies: A Child's
      Vision of Mennonite Plainness." Journal of
      Ethnic Studies 11 (Fall 1983): 51-59.

      Autobiographical reflections on childhood
      training in a subculture's primary values - in
      this case, the enforced practice of "plain"
      dress.

854. Winter, Dorothy McCleaf. "An Ethnographic
      Study of a Mennonite Christian Elementary
      School in Lancaster County, Pennsylvania."
      Ph.D. dissertation. University of
      Pennsylvania, 1982.

      Provides descriptive analysis of classroom
      and other school activities which relate to the
      perpetuation of Mennonite religious beliefs and
      values. Focuses particularly on teacher
      awareness of roles' values in the school.
      Demonstrates that unity of purpose of school,

home and church makes the definition and
attainment of clear objectives possible.

855. Yoder, Gideon G. The Nurture and Evangelism of
     Children. Scottdale, PA: Herald Press,
     1959.

     The Anabaptist-Mennonite insistence on
     voluntary adult baptism creates special
     dilemmas for the nurture of children. The
     author searches for applications of practice
     appropriate to Mennonite theology.

CHAPTER 16
MORAVIAN SCHOOLS
Beatrice E. Naff

Part I: Historical

856. Blair, Marian. "Contemporary Evidence--Salem
      Boarding School, 1834-1844." North Carolina
      Historical Review 54 (July 1977): 142-161.

      Uses the letters received by the 1834
      academy principal to picture the life within
      the school and to provide insights on the
      conditions within the south which tended to
      affect the growth of the institution.

857. Brickman, William W. "Jan Amos Comenius
      (1592-1670), Cosmopolitan Citizen and
      Ecumenical Educator." School and Society 98
      (November 1970): 437-439.

      Part of special section "The Tercentenary of
      Comenius' Death." Excellent summary
      introduction.

858. Comenius, John Amos. The Orbis Pictus. New
      York: C.W. Bardeen, 1887.

      A 17th century encyclopedia of knowledge
      which introduces young children to the world of
      the senses through creative use of pictures and
      mneumonics.

859. Comenius, John Amos. The School of Infancy:
     An Essay of the Education of Youth During
     Their First Six Years. London: W.
     Mallalieu & Co. , 1958.

     Includes ten chapters of biographical
     information on Comenius. This 17th century
     Moravian educator's essay purports the
     sacredness of the child, the necessity of
     active learning, and the educational aim of
     moral development. Also gives specifics on
     teaching skillful use of language.

860. Cremin, Lawrence A. , ed. John Amos Comenius on
     Education. No. 33. Classics in Education.
     Columbia: Teachers College Press, 1967.

     Includes Jean Piaget's introduction, "The
     Significance of John Amos Comenius at the
     Present Time. "

861. Dobinson, C. H. Comenius and Contemporary
     Education. Hamburg: UNESCO Institute for
     Education, 1970.

     Educators from around the world celebrate
     the 300th anniversary of Comenius. Includes
     article by American John Sadler entitled
     "Comenius as an International Citizen. "

862. Fries, Adelaide. Historical Sketch of Salem
     Female Academy. Salem, NC: Crist and Kehln,
     1902.

     Earliest publication from local historian on
     beginnings of the academy.

863. Griffin, Francis. Less Time For Meddling: A
     History of Salem Academy and College
     1772-1866. Winston-Salem, NC: John Blair,
     1979.

Shows how the Moravian girls' school founded
on Comenian educational philosophy eventually
became a boarding school for girls from
prominent southern families.

864.   Hacker, H.H.   Nazareth Hall: An Historical
       Sketch and Roster of Principals, Teachers
       and Pupils.   Bethlehem, PA: Times
       Publishing Co. , 1910.

Adds to the earlier historical perspectives
of Levin and William Reichel.   Presents 150
years of academy's existence.   Includes
sketches of original buildings, accounts of
Count Zinzendorf, and important school
documents.

865.   Haller, Mabel.   "Early Moravian Education in
       Pennsylvania."   Transactions of the Moravian
       Historical Society 15 (1953): 1-409.

Contains exhaustive bibliography of primary
sources found within the Moravian Archives.
The history covers the development of
Bethlehem, Narareth, Lititz and other extinct
Moravian academies.   Also covers the Indian
missions and the Moravian educational
philosophy.

866.   Hamilton, Kenneth, ed.   Records of the
       Moravians in North Carolina.   Raleigh, NC:
       1966.

Contains volumes of historical information
on many facets of Moravian life.   Volumes 10
and 11 include information on education.

867.   Handler, Bonnie Silver.   "The Schooling of
       Unmarried Sisters: Linden Hall and the
       Moravian Educational Transition, 1863-1940.
       Ed.D. dissertation.   Pennsylvania State
       University, 1980.

Examines the history of curricular changes
at Linden Hall. Argues that the original
Moravian educational ideals had become
"decidedly unfashionable" by 1940.

868. Hixson, Ivy. "Academic Requirements of Salem
      College, 1854-1909." North Carolina
      Historical Review 54 (July 1977): 419-429.

Uses formal college catalogues and issues of
The Academy as well as Moravian histories to
show how the academy evolved into an
institution of higher learning.

869. Jelinik, Vladimier, trans. The Analytical
      Didactic of Comenius. By Jan Amos Komensky.
      Chicago: University of Chicago Press, 1953.

Presents Comenius' 17th century educational
methodology. Comenius provides certain
educational axioms and then gives examples for
support. For example, axiom XXI is as follows:
"You will find it difficult to teach one who is
unripe for instruction." He then explains that
it would be senseless to teach a child to run
before he/she can walk just as it would be
silly to teach a child grammatical rules before
he/she is a competent speaker.

870. Kurdybacha, Lukaxz. "Comenius Documents in
      Poland." School and Society 98 (November
      1970): 446.

Discusses some of the 695 documents in state
archives in Poznan. Documents include Comenian
letters and documents fromthe Leszno high
school.

871. Kyrinek, J. J. A. Comenius: Selections from
      His Work. Prague: Statni Pedagogicke
      Nakladatelstvi, 1964.

Sums up Comenius' educational methodology
and aim as a scientific pedagogy geared toward
making man an intelligent and loving being, an
image of the Creator.

872. Monroe, Will. Comenius and the Beginnings of
     Educational Reform. New York: Charles
     Scribner's Sons, 1912.

     Explains the impact Comenius had on European
     educational reformers like Franke, Rousseau,
     Pestalozzi, Frobel and Herbart.

873. Rights, Douglas L. "Salem in the War Between
     the States." North Carolina Historical
     Review 27 (July 1950): 227-288.

     Shows how and in what manner the Salem
     girls' school was able to remain open during
     the war.

874. Sadler, John Edward, ed. Comenius. London:
     Collier-Macmillan Limited, 1969.

     Looks at Comenius' thought from a
     philosophical, psychological and sociological
     perspective and then shows how his position was
     applied in curriculum, methodology and choice
     of instructional instruments. Includes
     annotated bibliography of translated works.

875. Sadler, John Edward. J. A. Comenius and the
     Concept of Universal Education. London:
     George Allen & Unwin Ltd., 1966.

     Discusses Comenius' universal concepts: his
     notion of the good man and the good society,
     encyclopedic knowledge, and the didactic
     process. Comenius believed universal education
     could be realized through the vehicles of
     schools, teachers, and books.

876.   Shields, R.E.   A History of the Moravian
       Seminary for Young Ladies in Hope, Indiana.
       Hope, IN: Bartholomew Co., 1916.

       Shows how this school began as a day school
       for girls in 1859 and then evolved into a
       boarding school by 1866.

877.   Wenhold, Lucy.   "The Salem Boarding School
       Between 1802 and 1822." North Carolina
       Historical Review 52 (July 1977): 32-46.

       Reconstructs the intimate life of the
       school's first two decades of existence.

878.   Zeisberger, David.   Diary of David Zeisberger,
       A Moravian Missionary Among the Indians of
       Ohio.   Trans. Eugene F. Bliss.   Cincinnati:
       Historical & Philosophical Society of Ohio,
       1885.

       A stirring account of early Moravian
       attempts to educate the American Indians.

Part II: Contemporary

879.   Comenius Medallion Presentation.   Mortimer
       Adler Convocation.   Bethlehem, PA: Moravian
       College, February 28, 1984.

       Each year Moravian College recognizes a
       renowned educator who in some way exemplifies
       the educational leadership of Comenius.
       Mortimer Adler and Elie Weisel have been recent
       recipients.   Tape recordings of the
       presentations are available in the college
       library.

880.   Pope, James D.   "Comenius Speaks to Modern
       Man."   School and Society 98 (November
       1970): 440-445.

Argues that Comenius could help educators
reconsider issues such as the proper
relationship between school and society, the
need for an international language, and the
role of education in preventing war.

881. Roberts, Paul C. "Comenian Philosophy and
      Moravian Education from 1850 to the Present
      Day." Ph.D. dissertation. Rutgers, 1979.

      Concludes that Comenian philosophy may still
      be present in the elementary schools but is
      less pervasive in the Moravian College.

CHAPTER 17
PRESBYTERIAN SCHOOLS
D. Campbell Wyckoff

Note: The line between the historical and the
contemporary is drawn at 1957, the year in
which the General Assembly of the Presbyterian
Church in the U.S.A. (one of the several
branches of Presbyterianism represented here)
issued its statement, The Church and the
Public Schools.

Part I: Historical

882.   Agnew, Edith J. , and Ruth K. Barber.   "The
Unique Presbyterian School System of New
Mexico." Journal of Presbyterian History 49
(Fall 1971): 197-221.

The Presbyterian system of elementary and
secondary education as it developed in northern
New Mexico, including the "plaza schools"
(elementary), the Allison-James School in Santa
Fe (junior high), and the Menaul School in
Albuquerque (senior high), serving mainly local
people of Spanish origin. The system has been
largely dismantled in recent years. Only one
or two of the plaza schools remain, and the
mission of Menaul School has been redefined.

883. Atkins, Carolyn C. "Menaul School, 1881-1930."
      Journal of Presbyterian History 58 (Winter
      1980): 279-298; and "Menaul School,
      1930-1981." Journal of Presbyterian History
      60 (Spring 1982): 1-22.

      Centennial articles on the Menaul School,
      which for ninety years was the "flagship" of
      New Mexico's Presbyterian educational system.
      Turned over to local control in 1971, the
      school continues to enjoy strong Presbyterian
      backing and support.

884. Burr, Nelson R. Education in New Jersey,
      1630-1871. Princeton, NJ: Princeton
      University Press, 1942.

      An independent account of Presbyterian
      parochial schools is given in a chapter
      entitled "The Good Old Presbyterian Plan."

885. Drury, Clifford Merrill. Presbyterian
      Panorama. Philadelphia: Board of Christian
      Education, Presbyterian Church in the
      U.S.A. , 1952, pp. 233-241.

      Summarizes briefly the history and
      development of national missions schools,
      highlighting those in Alaska, Indian areas, the
      Spanish-speaking region, the Intermountain
      states, the Southern Mountains, Cuba, and the
      black sections of the south.

886. Gaebelein, Frank E. Christian Education in a
      Democracy. New York: Oxford University
      Press, 1951.

      A thorough look at Christian education in
      all its facets, including its place in public
      education and a rationale for the independent
      school.

887. Gaebelein, Frank E. The Pattern of God's
     Truth. New York: Oxford University Press,
     1954.

     A study of the program and curriculum of
     Christian education as practiced in the total
     academic and community life of the Christian
     independent school.

888. Healey, Robert M. Jefferson on Religion in
     Public Education. New Haven, CT: Yale
     University Press, 1962.

     Cites Jefferson's paranoia over the
     possibility of Presbyterian hegemony in both
     state and school, mainly expressed in private
     correspondence.

889. Henderson, Robert W. The Teaching Office in
     the Reformed Tradition, A History of the
     Doctoral Ministry. Philadelphia:
     Westminster Press, 1962.

     Ways in which the teaching office (in
     parish, school, higher education, and
     theological education) has been defined and
     used in churches of the Presbyterian tradition
     from Calvin to the contemporary American scene
     are traced and analyzed. The author is
     convinced that the office needs rehabilitation,
     but indicates that its history cannot give much
     help in this task beyond showing its necessity
     and significance.

890. Hodge, Charles. "The Education Question."
     Princeton Review 26 (1854): 504-544.

     In the guise of a book review, Hodge gives
     the most complete exposition of his views on
     education. Argues the case for church schools,
     holding that education must be basically

religious in a particularistic sense. Sees
little hope for religion in the common schools.

891. Hodge, E. B. "Cortlandt Van Rensselaer, D. D. ,
      Founder of the Presbyterian Historical
      Society." Journal of the Presbyterian
      Historical Society 1 (1902): 213-235.

      Memoirs of the most effective advocate of
      Presbyterian parochial schools, which are seen
      as the distinguishing feature of his
      multifaceted career. A comprehensive
      bibliography indicates his writings on
      education.

892. Janeway, J. J. Report to the Synod of New
      Jersey on the Subject of Parochial Schools.
      Philadelphia, 1845.

      A brief report recommending the
      establishment of parochial schools by the
      churches of the Synod of New Jersey, presaging
      the General Assembly's action of 1847.

893. Kennedy, William Bean. The Shaping of
      Protestant Education. New York:
      Association Press, 1966.

      Recognizes that certain Presbyterian clergy
      (e. g. , R. J. Breckenridge, of Kentucky, who
      served for a time as Superintendent of Public
      Instruction in that state) were strong
      proponents of the common school, and that the
      common school movement owed much to the
      antecedent Sunday school movement.
      Nevertheless, establishes the fact of the
      predominant emergence of the dual system, in
      which the common school limited itself to
      general and moral education, with the church
      responsible for religious education.

894. Miller, Samuel. The Christian Education of
      Children and Youth in the Presbyterian
      Church. Philadelphia: Presbyterian Board
      of Publication, 1840.

      The 1839 General Assembly appointed a
      committee to suggest ways of improving
      Christian education. This is their report.
      Advocates the establishment of parish primary
      schools, infant schools, and Presbyterian
      academies, and places these recommendations in
      the context of a total Christian education in
      the parish and family.

895. Mulford, Roland J. History of the
      Lawrenceville School, 1810-1935. Princeton,
      NJ: Princeton University Press, 1935.

      A detailed account of the history and
      functions of one of the most enduring and
      successful of independent schools in the
      Presbyterian tradition.

896. Parker, Inez Moore. The Rise and Decline of
      the Program of Education for Black
      Presbyterians of the United Presbyterian
      Church, U.S.A., 1865-1970. San Antonio, TX:
      Trinity University Press, 1977.

      Immediately after the Civil War, the
      Presbyterian Church mounted a program for the
      education of the black people of the South.
      The work proliferated into many community-based
      schools, today consolidated into a few mission
      schools and colleges of high grade. This
      detailed history tells the story, school by
      school, stressing the impact of the schools on
      their communities.

897. Parochial Schools, Report of the Board of
      Education of the Presbyterian Church on

Parochial Schools. Philadelphia: Board of
Education, 1847.

By 1846, the General Assembly of the
Presbyterian Church in the U.S.A. had come to
the point where it was ready to ask for a full
report on the establishment of a system of
parochial schools. The 1847 report presents a
full rationale for such an educational system,
citing its educational and religious advantages
and its contributions to ministerial training
and to "the prosperity of the church." The
recommendations cover primary church school and
presbyterial academies, and include suggestions
for practical implementation.

898.   Schenck, Lewis Bevens. The Presbyterian
       Doctrine of Children in the Covenant. New
       Haven, CT: Yale University Press, 1940.

The rationale for church sponsored schools
is usually pragmatic -- the preservation of the
church through the cultivation of its future
constituency. In contrast, the theological
rationale is here discussed -- the church's
responsibility to the baptized child in the
covenant. While schooling is not specifically
dealt with, such reasoning was basic to the
Presbyterian parochial school movement.

899.   Sherrill, Lewis Joseph. Presbyterian Parochial
       Schools, 1846-1870. New Haven, CT: Yale
       University Press, 1932.

The major research source on Presbyterian
schools. Traces in detail the impetus of the
movement; the debates of its protagonists and
antagonists; the actual results in schools
opened and their duration, their leadership,
curriculums, and administrative arrangements.
Attributes the failure of the movement to

inability of the church to influence the
direction of national change in the period
under discussion. (More particularly, the rise
of the common schools, the division of the
church and the subsequent Civil War, and lack
of denominational consensus on the matter,
might be cited.) Concludes with prescriptions
for cooperation of churches among themselves
and with the public schools, while safeguarding
denominational distinctives.

900.   Smyth, Thomas. "Parochial Schools." Southern
       Presbyterian Review 2 (March 1849): 520-549.

       Ardent support for the 1847 report on
Presbyterian parochial schools.

901.   Spence, Thomas H. Catalogues of Presbyterian
       and Reformed Institutions. Montreat, NC:
       Historical Foundation Publications, 1953.

       Lists Presbyterian schools for which
catalogues were available to the author.
Useful as a partial guide to locating and
dating the schools, most of which have gone out
of existence. 37 of the schools are PCUS; 7,
PCUSA; 1, CP; and 1, joint PCUS-PCUSA.

902.   Thompson, Ernest Trice. Presbyterians in the
       South, Volume One: 1607-1861. Richmond,
       VA: John Knox Press, 1963.

       A chapter on "Schools for All" traces the
initiative and support of southern
Presbyterians in the establishment of public
elementary education in the region. Secondary
education was private, and detail is provided
on the early academies, their leaders, and
their curriculums.

903.   Trowbridge, John Edwards.   "Presbyterian
          Interest in Elementary Education in New
          Jersey, 1816-1866." Ph. D. dissertation.
          Rutgers University, 1957.

          Includes analyses of the contributions of
       Robert Baird, Theodore Frelighuysen, and John
       Maclean. Concludes that Presbyterians in New
       Jersey were instigators and supporters of
       public education, and that parochial schools
       were an aberration.

904.   Van Rensselaer, Cortlandt, ed.   Home, the
          School, and the Church.   10 vols.
          Philadelphia, 1850, 1852-1860.

          The Presbyterian periodical devoted to
       educational matters (elementary, secondary,
       higher, and theological) at the height of the
       parochial school movement. (Periodical reports
       on periodical schools and presbyterial
       academies are included.) Substantial
       contributions on educational theory and
       practice by such leaders as Robert J.
       Breckenridge, J. W. Alexander, Samuel Miller,
       Charles Hodge, James H. Thornwell, and Dr. Van
       Rensselaer himself.

905.   Vaughan, C. R.   A Review of the Doctrines of the
          Board of Education of the Presbyterian
          Church in upon the Relations of the Church
          to the General Interests of Education.
          Lynchburg, VA: Paxtion & Irving, 1854.

          Challenges the premises upon which the
       Presbyterian Church mounted its action on
       parochial schools. The church, it is argued,
       has a limited teaching commission -- that of
       teaching the gospel. Control of general and
       religious education of children belongs with
       neither church nor state, but to parents.

906.   Weyer, Frank E.   "Presbyterian Colleges and
           Academies in Nebraska."   Ph.D. dissertation.
           University of Nebraska, 1940.

           Contains information on Oakdale Seminary
           (1881), which continued for ten years, and
           Pawnee City Academy (1883), which had a twenty-
           five year history.

Part II: Contemporary

907.   Adams, Jay E.   Back to the Blackboard, Design
           for a Biblical Christian School.
           Phillipsburg, NJ: Presbyterian and Reformed
           Publishing Company, 1982.

           In exasperation over Christian schools that
           are mere copies of the secular school with
           cosmetic changes (Bible courses, prayer, etc.),
           a radical biblical model is proposed, one where
           the purposes and practices are sharply
           different, and in which home and school see
           themselves as involved in a common enterprise.
           Humanism is the bete noire.

908.   Barnette, Helen P.   Your Child's Mind, Making
           the Most of the Public Schools.
           Philadelphia: Westminster Press, 1984.

           Useful for parent groups interested in the
           purposes, program, and quality of public school
           education, and for parents in church day
           schools.

909.   Blake, James.   "Religion at Lawrenceville --
           the Liturgical and the Academic Experience."
           Lawrentian, November 1983, pp. 4-6.

           Describes in detail the religion program of
           the Lawrenceville School, which has a strong
           Presbyterian history.   The school maintains an

active worship life (now voluntary and
pluralistic) and a religion curriculum that
includes Bible study, ethics, various aspects
of the sciences of religion, philosophical
studies of religion, religion in literature,
approaches to religious living, and topical
studies of current interest.

910.   Christian Education on the National Missions
       School Campus. New York: Board of National
       Missions of the Presbyterian Church in the
       U.S.A. , 1957.

       Starts with the premise that the purpose of
       a national missions school is evangelistic and
       that the strongest influence leading persons
       into the Christian way of life is fellowship,
       and provides detailed guiding principles and
       guidelines for accomplishing this end through
       the weekday curriculum, Westminster Fellowship,
       devotions, chapel, and Spiritual Emphasis Week,
       together with an analysis of administrative
       responsibilities and relationships.   Detailed
       course outlines are provided on the Old
       Testament, the life of Christ, and the
       Christian church.

911.   The Church and Public Elementary and Secondary
       Education. Philadelphia: Board of
       Christian Education of the United
       Presbyterian Church in the U.S.A. , 1972.

       An official statement of the 184th General
       Assembly of the United Presbyterian Church in
       the U.S.A. (1972).   Seemingly an official
       response to the Open Letter (1969), reaffirms
       support of the public schools, strongly
       recommends compensatory education and social
       services through the schools, and urges such
       things as church volunteering for functions
       like tutoring, establishment of special

services (day care, career counseling, special
education for the handicapped), advocacy of
student rights, and less stringency about
"public funds for public schools" alone.

912. The Church and the Public Schools.
      Philadelphia: Board of Christian Education
      of the Presbyterian Church in the U.S.A.,
      1957.

      An official statement of the 169th General
      Assembly of the Presbyterian Church in the
      U.S.A. (1957). Affirms strong support of
      public education by the Presbyterian Church,
      analyzing the legitimate areas of religious
      life in the schools (moral and spiritual
      values, the common core, the influence of the
      religiously motivated teacher, and aspects of
      the guidance function), suggesting released-
      time and nursery schools and kindergarten as
      proper alternatives to parochial education, and
      advocating active dialogue between the church
      and public educators.

913. Earle, Clifford. "Fighting for Free Schools."
      Presbyterian Life, December 9, 1950, pp.
      11-12.

      Deals with the Dixon, New Mexico case in
      which nuns in garb were teaching in publicly
      supported schools, whose activities included
      overtly Roman Catholic activities. Indicative
      of the strong official opposition of the
      Presbyterian Church at that time to any
      sectarian activities in the public schools.

914. Fuoss, Robert. "Church, Children, and the
      Supreme Court." A.D., September 1972, pp.
      19-30.

Reviews the legal status of public support for non-public schools up to 1972, analyzes the various groups opposed to it, details the conflicting demands of various citizen groups (particularly black and Catholic) in favor of it, and concludes that while meeting their demands would wreck the public school system, there may be a middle way (hinted at by the 184th General Assembly's relaxation of support for public funds for public schools alone).

915.   King, Wayne. "In Rural Georgia, A Prep Boarding School for Blacks." The New York Times, November 24, 1976.

Cites Boggs Academy, Keysville, Georgia, as the only accredited, coeducational, predominantly black college preparatory school in the United States.

916.   Lynn, Robert W. Protestant Strategies in Education. New York: Association Press, 1965.

A historical analysis of American Protestant education in relation to total schooling, culminating in a rejection of current attempts to create a theologically oriented church education, and challenging the church to reopen vital communication with the national educational enterprise.

917.   Maxson, Theron B. "Religion in the Schools: A Presbyterian's View." In America's Schools and Churches, Partners in Conflict, pp. 48-52. Edited by David W. Beggs III and R. Bruce McQuigg. Bloomington, IN: Indiana University Press, 1965.

Reviews Presbyterian theology and developing policy in relation to public education.

Presbyterian logic, according to Maxson, sees
the public schools as performing the
educational functions inherent in its view that
"freedom to learn and to know" is the heart of
its educational mission.

918. Minutes of the General Assembly of the United
      Presbyterian Church in the U.S.A., 1977,
      Part 1, pp. 623-632.

      Typical of the Presbyterian approach to
      education in recent years. Focuses on public
      education, and advocates bilingual and
      bicultural (or multi-cultural) education, based
      on a report on "Education and Inclusion" from
      the church's Council on Church and Race.

919. Newbury, Josephine. Nursery-Kindergarten
      Weekday Education in the Church. Richmond:
      John Knox Press, 1960.

      Clear and detailed picture of the purposes,
      setting, activities, and leadership of the
      weekday church nursery school and kindergarten.
      Written by the director of the school conducted
      by the Presbyterian School of Christian
      Education, and based upon the experimental work
      done there.

920. Nichols, James Hastings. "Religion and
      Education in a Free Society." In Religion
      in America, pp. 148-167. Edited by John
      Cogley. New York: Meridian Books, 1958.

      Sees the schools as subject to a precedent,
      secularization of society, thus being, whether
      church or state sponsored, essentially secular
      in character. Religious schools are seen as
      risking irresponsibility in education by not
      being subject to the criticism and review of
      the community.

921.   An Open Letter: The Public and Its Education.
       Philadelphia: Board of Christian Education
       of the United Presbyterian Church in the
       U. S. A. , 1969.

       A strange tractarian document, released in a
       quasi-official way of the Boards of Christian
       Education of the United Presbyterian Church in
       the U. S. A. and the Presbyterian Church in the
       U. S. Claims that after the 1957 statement the
       situation changed drastically, and that the
       position the church must advocate is that of
       the schools as agents of "the formation of the
       public," a term whose meaning is hinted at in a
       variety of ways that seem to boil down to an
       inclusive political egalitarianism. A number
       of suggestions for the church are thrown in,
       such as abandonment of production of
       denominational curriculums in favor of support
       of public alternative educational experiments.

922.   Wilkins, Lewis. "Church and School: The Why
       and How of Reformed Involvement." Seventh
       Angel, October 1984, pp. 20-21, 23.

       Maintains that Presbyterians have been "up
       to their steeples in education" from the
       beginning, with an abiding commitment to
       education of the public as a high priority in a
       society reordered according to the Word of God,
       with a conviction that freedom of inquiry in
       educational institutions is essential if
       learning is to play a proper role in a society
       so reordered, and seeing the close connection
       between the church and the highest possible
       quality of education as a necessary consequence
       of right theology, not a tool for
       indoctrination into Reformation ideology.

CHAPTER 18
REFORMED SCHOOLS
Donald Oppewal

Part I: Historical

923. Beversluis, N. Henry. "A Biblical Approach to
      Educational Philosophy for the Christian
      Reformed Church." Ph.D. dissertation.
      Columbia University, 1966. Ann Arbor, MI:
      University Microfilms, Inc.

      A theologian-educator's analysis of the
      Reformed schools that arose out of the
      Christian Reformed Church. Includes critiques
      of such pivotal thinkers as William Henry
      Jellema and Cornelius Jaarsma, with the plea
      that a clarification of religious vision could
      bring closure between colliding views.

924. Cummings, David B. et al. The Basis for a
      Christian School. Phillipsburg, NJ:
      Presbyterian and Reformed Publishing
      Company, 1982.

      Several writers address facets of the role
      of parents in the Christian school, including
      constitutional rights and the principles of the
      Protestant Reformation as they bear on the role
      of parents.

925.   DeBoer, Peter P. Shifts in Curriculum Theory
          for Christian Education. Grand Rapids, MI:
          Calvin College Monograph Series, 1983.

          A study of curriculum theory as advanced by
       Reformed Christians over a thirty-year period
       from the 1950's to the 1980's. The author
       perceives subtle shifting from an earlier
       academic position ("Christian Traditionalism"),
       through a contrasting emphasis on the person of
       the child and his needs ("Christian
       Progressivism"), to a more recent effort at
       blending the best of both earlier positions
       ("Christian Revisionism").

926.   De Jong, James A. and Louis Y. Van Dyke, eds.
          Building the House: Essays on Christian
          Education. Sioux Center, IA: Dordt College
          Press, 1981.

          A mixture of essays on theological
       influences, like covenant, and legal-political
       questions, like the relation of government to
       church-related schools as seen through Supreme
       Court decisions. Includes a tribute to
       Emeritus Professor Nick Van Til, in whose honor
       the essays were written.

927.   De Jong, Jerome Bernard. "The Parent-
          Controlled Christian School: A Study of the
          Historical Background, The Theological Basis
          and the Theoretical Implications of Parent-
          Controlled Education in the Schools
          Associated with the Christian Reformed
          Church in America." Ph. D. dissertation.
          New York University, 1954.

          Encompasses both the Netherlands and the
       United States, and places the schools within
       the context of the Dutch and Reformed heritage
       supporting this type of education. Includes a

comparison of parent-controlled schools with
other Christian schools.

928. Jaarsma, Cornelius. The Educational Philosophy
      of Herman Bavinck. Grand Rapids, MI:
      Eerdmans Publishing Company, 1953.

      An adaptation of a doctoral dissertation
      done at New York University, it is a
      sympathetic analysis of a Dutch theologian,
      philosopher and psychologist who greatly
      influenced Jaarsma.

929. Jaarsma, Cornelius, ed. Fundamentals of
      Christian Education. Grand Rapids, MI:
      Eerdmans Publishing Company, 1953.

      A collection of speeches and periodical
      articles by those in the Reformed tradition,
      with several chapters contributed by the
      editor. Section one: "The Basis of Christian
      Education" has contributions by Reformed
      philosophers, like William Harry Lellema and
      Cornelius Van Til, and systematic theologian
      Louis Berkhof. Remaining sections contain
      contributions by the editor and other
      professional educators who deal with the
      organization and implementation of the school
      program.

930. Kuiper, Henry J. "The Two Pillars of Christian
      Education." Christian Home and School 53
      (November 1973): 6-8.

      A brief identification of the two pillars as
      the Reformed conception of covenantal theology
      and the doctrine of the kingdom of God, the
      latter being broader than the Church and
      extending to every domain of life. A reprint
      of an editorial from The Banner, August 25,
      1944.

931. McCarthy, Rockne, et al. Society, State, and
      Schools: A Case for Structural and
      Confessional Pluralism. Grand Rapids, MI:
      Eerdmans Publishing Company, 1981.

      Written by a team of scholars in the Calvin
      Center for Christian Scholarship, this volume
      contains historical, theological, and legal
      precedent in the case for subsidizing pluralism
      in education by funding equitably all schools
      and not just government schools. Argument
      includes evidence that secularism is a
      religion, and one that pervades public
      education textbooks. Culminates in plan for
      change through legislation about vouchers,
      court litigation, and a possible constitutional
      amendment.

932. Oppewal, Donald. The Roots of the Calvinistic
      Day School Movement. Grand Rapids, MI:
      Calvin College Monograph Series, 1963.

      An intellectual history of the movement up
      to the middle of the twentieth century,
      identifying in the soil of Calvin, its cultural
      roots in the Netherlands, its ecclesiastical
      roots in the Christian Reformed Church, its
      religious roots in the Bible, and emerging
      cultural roots in American democracy.

933. Oppewal, Donald and Peter P. DeBoer.
      "Calvinist Day Schools: Roots and
      Branches." In Religious Schooling in
      America, pp. 58-84. Edited by James C.
      Carper and Thomas C. Hunt. Birmingham, AL:
      Religious Education Press, 1984.

      Describes the historical development of what
      are called "Christian Schools," as well as
      supporting organizations such as Calvin College
      and Christian Schools International. A section

on biblical grounding identifies the major
Reformed doctrines that have shaped the
educational practices.

934. Palmer, Edwin. "Freedom and Equity in Dutch
      Education." In Educational Freedom and the
      Case for Government Aid to Students in
      Independent Schools, pp. 65-84. Edited by
      Daniel McGarry and Leo Ward. Milwaukee:
      Bruce Publishing Company, 1966.

      A historical account of the "school
      struggle" in the Netherlands over funding of
      religiously oriented schools there. Argues
      that the experience of Holland demonstrates
      that a system can be worked out whereby there
      is minimal government control that follows
      funding.

935. Ruiter, Michael. "Educaid - A Rationale and a
      Model for Granting Financial Aid to the
      Nonpublic School Students in Michigan."
      Ph.D. dissertation. Michigan State
      University, 1969.

      Defends "educaid" by exploring the
      philosophical premises which undergird the
      nature of education, and the meaning of
      educational freedom in the United States.
      Develops a philosophically and administratively
      defensible model for providing public financial
      assistance to the students attending the
      nonpublic schools in Michigan. A chapter is
      dedicated to the constitutionality question.
      Recommendations for subsequent action to
      benefit all school children in the state
      conclude the study.

936. Snapper, J. Marion. "Contributions of
      Independent Education." In Educational
      Freedom and the Case for Government Aid to
      Students in Independent Schools, pp.

103-121. Edited by Daniel McGarry and Leo
Ward. Milwaukee: Bruce Publishing Company,
1966.

A summary of the contributions to the social
good of private schools as a basis for
subsidizing them. Includes the contributions
of these schools in the inculcation of moral
and spiritual values, to democratic social
ideals, and to political freedom.

937.   Stob, George. The Christian Reformed Church
and Her Schools. Th. D. dissertation.
Princeton Theological Seminary, 1955.

While focusing mainly on Calvin College and
Seminary, it is invaluable for its use of
original, unpublished sources to make sense of
controversies that filtered down to elementary
and secondary schooling.

938.   Tiemersma, Richard. "Education in a Period of
World Crisis." Reformed Journal VIII (July-
August 1958): 10-15.

An avowed traditionalist argues that in the
wake of Russia's leap into space with Sputnik,
Christian schools ought to resist efforts to
educate the "whole man" and reaffirm the value
of liberal education, defined as "informing and
disciplining of the mind."

939.   Van Brummelen, Harro. "Molding God's Children:
The History of Curriculum in Christian
Schools Rooted in Dutch Calvinism." Ph. D.
dissertation. University of British
Columbia, 1984.

Investigates the schools' Dutch background,
their beginnings in nineteenth century America,
their Americanization between 1890-1920, their

"bulwark" mentality during the inter-war years, and their quest for purpose since World War II. Concludes that the schools have not yet demonstrated the possibility of fully implementing their leaders' vision of Biblical, Christian principles permeating the school's total program.

940. Vander Ark, John.   Twenty-two Landmark Years. Grand Rapids, MI: Baker Book House, 1983.

A description of the emergence and development of Christian Schools International (1943-65), the service organization and school board association of Calvinist day schools, including the influence of Canadian views, the struggle over government funding, and the battle over the creedal basis of CSI. An insider's view by the Director of CSI in these pivotal years.

Part II: Contemporary

941. Beversluis, N. Henry.   "First-Order Issues in Christian Philosophy of Education." Christian Educators Journal 10 (April 1971): 15-19.

Identifies the need for articulation of (1) religious vision, (2) major learning goals, and (3) the core curriculum of a Christian school as preceding the clarification of the many other, secondary questions of classroom pedagogy and school practice.

942. Beversluis, N. Henry.   Toward a Theology of Education. Grand Rapids, MI: Calvin College Office of College Relations, Vol. 1, No. 1 (February 1981).

Sets forth a religious vision for Christian
Schools, arguing for both piety goals and
culture goals. Identifies the doctrine of
covenant as an encounter and response model,
which is to be mirrored in Christian school
theory and practice.

943.   Beversluis, N. Henry. <u>Christian Philosophy of
       Education</u>. Grand Rapids, MI: National
       Union of Christian Schools (now Christian
       Schools International), 1971.

Sets forth a religious vision rooted in a
biblical view of man and faith, with major
attention to three learning goals:
intellectual, moral, and creative. Some
attention to curriculum pattern which comports
with the view of man and the learning goals.

944.   Blomberg, Douglas. "Curriculum Guidelines for
       the Christian School." In <u>No Icing on the
       Cake</u>, pp. 111-122. Edited by Jack
       Mechielsen, Melbourne, Australia: Brookes-
       Hall Publishing Foundation, 1980.

Argues for a third way beyond the subject-
centered and the child-centered curriculum,
called an integral, problem-posing curriculum.
Holds that all units of instruction begin with
life problems, but, acknowledging that creation
is law-ordered or structured, proceeds to
examine the created norms which reside in the
disciplines that relate to the problem.

945.   Blomberg, Douglas. "Toward a Christian Theory
       of Knowledge." In <u>No Icing on the Cake</u>, pp.
       41-60. Edited by Jack Mechielsen,
       Melbourne, Australia: Brookes-Hall
       Publishing Foundation, 1980.

Drawing on Hebraic and Old Testament meanings, he articulates a way of knowing that involves concrete experience and what he calls "distantial knowing," in both of which the subject-knower relation is maintained, where this relation includes the knower and the to-be-known.

946.   Blomberg, Douglas. "The Development of Curriculum with Relation to the Philosophy of the Cosmonomic Idea." Ph.D. dissertation. University of Sydney, Australia, 1978.

Chiefly a treatment of epistemology in the perspective of Herman Dooyeweerd, it surveys the views of Ernst Cassirer and Paul Hirst, finding both inadequate because of commitment to the autonomy of human rationality. It then argues for several kinds of knowing relevant for the school, and ends with three dimensions to the goal: Perspectives, Praxis, and Proficiencies. Includes specific courses for a secondary school.

947.   DeBoer, Peter P. "What's Your School's 'Social Quotient'?" Christian Educators Journal 24 (April-May 1985): 9-12.

Explores the social thought of three leading 20th century educational thinkers (Maritain; Dewey; Phenix) and some biblical foundations for a curriculum and pedagogy that envision a discipleship that, whenever necessary, can dissent from and seek to reform society.

948.   DeBoer, Peter P. "Toward a Responsibility Theory: Becoming Who We Are." In Christian Approaches to Learning Theory, pp. 119-136. Edited by Norman DeJong. New York: University Press of America, 1984.

949. De Jong, Judith. "The Calvinist Ethic in Two Generations: A Study of Personality Style Among Dutch Calvinists in the Midwest." Ph.D. dissertation. Catholic University of America, 1984.

Using three instruments which gauged personality and interpersonal relationship factors on both students and their parents in selected midwest Reformed day schools and Catholic schools, the study tested the Max Weber thesis that Calvinist dogma generated spiritual anxiety and existential insecurity about salvation. The study found no evidence in the sample population of the presence of the personality mechanism described by Weber.

950. DeJong, Norman. Education in the Truth. Phillipsburg, NJ: Presbyterian and Reformed Publishing Company, 1970.

Covers a wide range of topics, from anthropology to curriculum, with critiques of behaviorism in psychology as it relates to goals of education as well as classroom management.

951. DeJong, Norman, ed. Christian Approaches to Learning Theory (A Symposium). Lanham, MD: University Press of America, 1984.

A collection of papers delivered at Trinity Christian College by philosophers, psychologists, and professional educators on the general theme of learning theory. Some attention to epistemology as perceived by all three of the above specialists, and prescriptions for theory building focusing on responsibility theory, motivation, and research on learning theory.

952. De Koster, Lester. "Education for Freedom."
     Reformed Journal VIII (February 1958): 4-9.

     A plan for a curriculum which acknowledges
     both the theoretic and the practical, both
     "knowledge value" and "training-value." A case
     for a modified form of vocational education. A
     response to a critic appears in the May 1958
     issue which expands on the theme.

953. De Kruyter, Arthur H. "The Reformed Christian
     Day School Movement in North America."
     Master's thesis. Princeton Theological
     Seminary, 1952.

     Covers aspects of the Reformed day school
     movement, including its philosophy, purposes
     and objectives, organization and
     administration, and curriculum and methods.

954. Hoeksema, Thomas B. "The Rights of the
     Handicapped--An Act of Morality." Christian
     Home and School 57 (March 1978): 16-18.

     Argues that while Christian schools are not
     required by law to provide services for the
     handicapped, the belief that all are created in
     God's image and are part of the community of
     believers requires them. Details three
     alternative types of educational placement:
     mainstreaming in a regular class, a special
     class, and a resource room arrangement.

955. Hoekstra, Dennis. Christian Education Through
     Religious Studies. Grand Rapids, MI:
     Calvin College Monograph Series, 1985.

     An explication and defense of a revelation-
     response model for teaching religion. Opposes
     both intellectualism and moralism, and favors
     teaching for obedient decision making and

action in life. Includes contrasting lesson
materials to illustrate both what is opposed
and what is favored. This document is the
theoretic underpinning for what Christian
Schools International calls its Revelation-
Response Bible Curriculum.

956. Jaarsma, Cornelius. Human Development,
      Learning, and Teaching. Grand Rapids, MI:
      Eerdmans Publishing Company, 1961.

      With the sub-title of "A Christian Approach
      to Educational Psychology," it represents the
      author's most systematic treatment of the
      unitary nature of the learner and an
      experiential methodology. Includes analysis of
      competing theories of learning and child
      development. Much use of Scriptural material
      to support a Christian form of progressive
      education, rooted in a biblical theory of the
      "organic unity" of the learner.

957. Jaarsma, Cornelius. "French in the Christian
      Secondary School." Christian Educators
      Journal V (Fall 1965): 28-32.

      An application of a theory of personality
      enhancement as a goal of education, stressing
      French culture and its influence on character
      and interpersonal relationships over mastery of
      the structure of the French language.

958. Jellema, William Harry. "The Case for Foreign
      Language." Reformed Journal III (July
      1953): 7-9.

      Argues that foreign languages are justified
      as required subjects, but not for their
      practical usefulness in business or tourism,
      but for mind training in the logic of language.
      Favors Greek, Latin, German, and French as
      superior languages for this purpose.

959.   Kass, Corrine, E. "Toward a Theology of
        Learning Deviance." In Christian Approaches
        to Learning Theory, pp. 31-46. Edited by
        Norman DeJong. Lanham, MD: University
        Press of America, 1984.

        Considers teaching and learning from the
        perspective of a Christian developmentalist
        with a special interest in learning disability.
        Describes five stages through which the
        learning disabled move, with clues for
        remediation appropriate for each stage.

960.   Marsden, George. "The Christian and the
        Teaching of History." Christian Scholar's
        Review II (1973): 33-53.

        An extended statement about the difference
        in methods between a Christian historian and
        others. Warns against both a naive Christian
        evaluation of events and the dangers of a
        merely objective treatment of history.

961.   Oppewal, Donald. "Needed: An Educational
        Creed." Christian Educators Journal 10
        (April 1971): 11-14.

        Argues that ecclesiastical or church creeds
        are an inadequate basis for undergirding theory
        and practice in Christian education, and offers
        both a justification for, and examples of,
        items for an educational creed that focuses on
        educational questions and offers biblical
        support for them.

962.   Oppewal, Donald. "Organizing Literature by
        Theme: A Defense." Christian Educators
        Journal 5 (April 1966): 22-26.

After describing three ways of organizing
literary materials: (1) chronological, or
historical, (2) formological, or literary type
(genre), and (3) psychological, or thematic --
the essay argues the case for the thematic as
best fitting the proclaimed goals of Christian
education, which are described as "achieving a
commitment to a way of life, and not just
competence in collecting concepts."

963.   Oppewal, Donald. <u>Biblical Knowing and
       Teaching</u>. Grand Rapids, MI: Calvin College
       Monograph Series, 1985.

       Argues that an interactive model of knowing
       permeates Scripture and requires a teaching
       methodology that fits the biblical
       epistemology. Formulates a three step
       methodology of consider, choose, and commit
       phases. Includes a view of integrated
       curriculum that favors interdisciplinary
       problem-centered versions consistent with both
       the epistemology and methodology presented.

964.   Oppewal, Donald. "Parochialism in Christian
       Schools: Its Perils. <u>Reformed Journal</u> 20
       (September 1970): 12-14.

       In a plea for educational ecumenism the
       author warns about denominational identity
       reflected in courses in Reformed doctrine and
       in the ecclesiastical homogeneity of faculty
       and students. Deparochialization policies
       urged include changing the rules for voting
       members of school associations and active
       recruitment of students from the wider
       evangelical community.

965.   Reynolds, Larry. "Values Clarification: A
       Critique and Prescription." <u>Christian
       Educators Journal</u> 15 (May 1976): 15-18.

An assessment of both the theory and the strategies of the values clarification movement. Finds it to be sometimes inconsistent and poorly worked out as a theory, and lacking in empirical research, but nevertheless one which can help achieve goals of Christian education.

966. Slenk, Howard. "School Music: Solid or Vapor?" Christian Educators Journal 6 (February 1967): 29-32.

Argues that "an analytical and historical grasp of what occurs in great music" is being sacrificed when music studies focus almost exclusively on vocal and instrumental performance. In a "blueprint for change" he urges the establishment of academic courses, like those in science, English, and mathematics.

967. Snapper, J. Marion. "Motivation for Learning Faith-knowledge." In Christian Approaches to Learning Theory, pp. 53-170. Edited by Norman DeJong. Lanham, MD: University Press of America and Trinity Christian College, 1984.

Translates a biblical "Shalom" model of man into motivation theory. Uses Festinger's theory of cognitive dissonance to develop a paradigm for teaching with an action component through creation of cognitive dissonance.

968. Snapper, J. Marion. "The State and the Christian Schools." Reformed Journal XI (April 1961): 4-8.

Thesis is that whether one approves or not, all education is a governmental activity, as determined by both political precedent and legal decisions. Conclusion is that "if Christian day school education is governmental activity, and if such education is controlled by the state . . . then it would appear that it ought to have financial support from the state."

969.   Snapper, J. Marion. "Christian Education in 1989." Reformed Journal XIII (May-June 1963): 10-13.

A prophetic projection that in twenty-five years the Christian school movement will not be able to exist as a viable institution providing quality education without some form of government subsidy.

970.   Snapper, J. Marion. "The Content of Process." Christian Educators Journal 14 (January 1975): 6-11.

Develops the thesis that the process by which learning is achieved is as crucial to outcomes as is the content studied. Holds that distinctiveness in methodology for Christian educators consists in choosing for the inquiry method, no matter what content is studied.

971.   Steensma, Geraldine and Harro Van Brummelen. eds. Shaping School Curriculum: A Biblical View. Grand Rapids, MI: Signal Press, 1977.

A collection of writings which identify a curriculum design, provided by the editors, and examples of its application to ten curriculum areas provided by various experts in each field. Appendix contains examples of units of instruction judged to be expressions of integration of biblical insights and topics as diverse as "Trees" and "Statistics."

972. Stronks, Gloria Goris. "From Theory to
     Instruction: Implications for Christian
     Schools." Pro Rege XII (No. 3 1984): 25-35.

     Presents research findings which should have
     an effect on middle school instruction and
     curriculum development. A curriculum design
     for educating transescents in keeping with
     developmental findings is presented.
     Particular emphasis on helping students become
     responsible for their own learning as well as
     helping them understand their responsibility
     for the nurture and growth of others.

973. Stronks, Gloria Goris. "Stages of Intellectual
     Development: A Scheme." Pro Rege XI (No. 4
     1983): 14-23.

     Presents a description of the stages of
     intellectual and moral development in the late
     adolescent and early adult. Perry's research
     in this area is examined and critiqued.
     Describes educational implications for
     instruction in Christian high schools and
     colleges.

974. Tiemersma, Richard. "Sticking to One's Last:
     A Plea for Organizing Literature by Genre."
     Christian Educators Journal 12 (November
     1972): 25-28.

     Responding to the movement to organize
     literature by theme, a traditionalist offers
     reasons why that which is unique to literature,
     i.e., form, should govern sequencing, and in
     what way this would foster the intellectual
     goals of education.

975. Van Brummelen, Harro. "Towards a Radical Break
     with the Public School Curriculum." In To
     Prod the "Slumbering Giant," pp. 69-92.

Toronto, Ontario: Wedge Publishing
Foundation, 1972.

Argues for a curriculum which brings unity
to the curriculum, rather than a separate
cataloging of knowledge.   Holds that the goal
is preparation for a "many-sided calling" as
well as for analytic knowing.   Includes a
curriculum design for a "core" of
interdisciplinary studies.

976.   Van Dyk, John.   "Building a Curriculum with the
Kingdom Vision."   In To Prod the "Slumbering
Giant," pp. 46-62.   Toronto, Ontario: Wedge
Publishing Foundation, 1972.

Extension of the "philosophy of the
Cosmonomic Idea" (of Herman Dooyeweerd) to
curriculum.   Van Dyk holds that dualism,
aggravated by individualism, has fragmented the
curriculum into humanities and sciences and
argues for "the establishment and development
of an integral curriculum."   Appendix B of same
volume expands on the idea of modalities in
this philosophy of the Cosmonomic Idea.

977.   Wolterstorff, Nicholas.   Educating for
Responsible Action.   Grand Rapids, MI: CSI
Publications and Eerdmans Publishing
Company, 1980.

A treatment of what the author calls
tendency learning as a goal of Christian
education.   It stresses pedagogy in achieving
the goal of responsible action, devoting
chapters to discipline, modeling, and moral
reasoning (casuistry) as the appropriate means.
Views are based on selected psychological
research.   Includes some critique of values
clarification and other moral reasoning
strategies.

978. Wolterstorff, Nicholas. Curriculum: By What
      Standard? Grand Rapids, MI: Christian
      Schools International, 1966.

      An address to administrators in which goals
      for curriculum are stated in terms of their
      relevance for living the Christian life for the
      student in school and out, now and in the
      future. It rejects the view of man as
      exclusively rational and the view of faith as
      assent to propositions, in order to defend this
      action goal.

979. Young, Davis A. "Genesis One and Science
      Teaching." Christian Educators Journal 22
      (October 1982): 16-23.

      A geologist's critical view of some
      interpretations of Genesis that distort the
      texts to create a "biblical" view of creation
      and neglect the ordinances or laws in nature
      itself.

980. Zylstra, Henry. "Modern Philosophy of
      Education." In Testament of Vision. Grand
      Rapids, MI: Eerdmans Publishing Company,
      1958, pp. 81-89.

      A classic statement by an avowed
      traditionalist, identifying the theory of man
      as that which is at stake in the
      traditionalist-progressivest controversy in
      Reformed circles. Other essays in the same
      volume elaborate upon and extend the argument
      into curriculum and his position on formal
      discipline in the subject matter of the school.

CHAPTER 19
SEVENTH-DAY ADVENTIST SCHOOLS
George R. Knight

Part I: Historical

981. Ashworth, Warren S. "Edward Alexander
Sutherland and Seventh-day Adventist
Educational Reform: The Denominational
Years, 1890-1904." Ph.D. dissertation.
Andrews University, 1986.

Analyzes the life and work of Adventism's
most controversial educational reformer. Also
provides insight into Sutherland's contribution
to the denomination's elementary and secondary
school movements.

982. Brown, Walton J., comp. Chronology of Seventh-
day Adventist Education. 2nd ed.
Washington, DC: General Conference of
Seventh-day Adventists, Department of
Education, 1979.

Outlines, in the order of their development,
lists of Adventist schools, administrators,
gatherings of note, and educational
publications.

983.   Cadwallader, E. M.   A History of Seventh-day
          Adventist Education.   4th ed.   Payson, AZ:
          Leaves-of-Autumn Books, 1975.

          Despite its title, this is not a history of
          Adventist education.   It is more of a series of
          papers on Adventist secondary and collegiate
          institutions.   It does, however, have two
          chapters on the early history of the
          denomination's elementary schools.   The volume
          still has value for understanding Adventist
          education, even though later works have more
          fully explored many of the topics treated and
          in some cases invalidated its conclusions.

984.   Cadwallader, E. M.   Principles of Education in
          the Writings of Ellen G. White.   Payson, AZ:
          Leaves-of-Autumn Books, n. d.

          Presents an extensive collection of
          categorized quotations from Ellen White's
          writings on a wide variety of educational
          issues.   Not interpretive.   Based on the
          author's doctoral dissertation, completed at
          the University of Nebraska in 1949.

985.   Cady, Marion E.   The Education That Educates.
          New York: Fleming H. Revell, 1937.

          Develops a Seventh-day Adventist philosophy
          of education based on the Bible and the
          writings of Ellen White.

986.   Dick, Everett.   Union College of the Golden
          Cords.   Lincoln, NE: Union College Press,
          1967.

          Presents the history of one of the
          denomination's earliest schools.   Sheds light
          on the development of Adventist education in
          general, and also provides understanding of

specific issues such as the church's struggle
with accreditation in the 1920s and 1930s.

987. Gardner, Eva B. Revised by J. Mabel Wood.
      Southern Missionary College: A School of
      His Planning. 2nd ed. [Collegedale, TN],
      Board of Trustees, [1975].

      Presents the history of a school that was
      both secondary and collegiate for much of its
      history. Sheds light on conditions in
      Adventist education at the turn of the century.

988. Graybill, Ronald D. Mission to Black America:
      The True Story of Edson White and the
      Riverboat Morning Star. Mountain View, CA:
      Pacific Press Pub. Assn., 1971.

      Recounts the pioneering educational work of
      northern white Adventist missionaries to
      southern blacks in the 1890s.

989. Hodgen, Maurice, ed. School Bells and Gospel
      Trumpets: A Documentary History of Seventh-
      day Adventist Education in North America.
      Loma Linda, CA: Adventist Heritage
      Publications, 1978.

      Presents the most complete published
      collection of documents related to Adventist
      education. Introductory commentaries provide
      contextual understanding.

990. Hook, Milton R. "The Avondale School and
      Adventist Educational Goals, 1894-1900."
      Ed.D. dissertation. Andrews University,
      1978.

      Provides the history of the first six years
      of the school that Adventists look to as the
      "ideal model" of their brand of reform

education. Hook's analysis separates the
universal principles undergirding the Avondale
School from the particulars of time and place
that provided the school's immediate context.

991. Knight, George R. "Battle Creek College:
      Academic Development and Curriculum
      Struggles." Unpublished manuscript, Andrews
      University Heritage Room, 1979.

      Presents the catastrophic difference between
      the philosophy and the curriculum of
      Adventism's first academic institution in its
      historical context. The results of the issues
      faced at Battle Creek continue to influence
      Adventist education at all levels.

992. Knight, George R. , ed. Early Adventist
      Educators. Berrien Springs, MI: Andrews
      University Press, 1983.

      Presents the contributions of eleven of the
      most important educators to the denomination's
      educational system during its formative period
      (1867-1910). In lieu of a formal history, this
      volume is the most comprehensive treatment of
      nineteenth-century Adventist education
      available.

993. Knight, George R. "Oberlin College and
      Adventist Educational Reforms." Adventist
      Heritage 8 (Spring 1983): 3-9.

      Demonstrates that the "unique" aspects of
      Adventist educational reform in the period from
      1870-1900 had been tried and had been given up
      at Oberlin in the 1830s and 1840s. Further
      argues that Adventist education must not lose
      touch with its impulse to reform.

994. Knight, George R. "Seventh-day Adventist
     Education: A Historical Sketch and
     Profile." In Religious Schooling in
     America, pp. 85-109. Edited by James C.
     Carper and Thomas C. Hunt. Birmingham, AL:
     Religious Education Press, 1984.

     Summarizes the most salient features of the
     history of Adventist education from the 1840s
     through the early 1980s. Provides a profile of
     contemporary Adventist education.

995. Lindsay, Allan G. "Goodloe Harper Bell:
     Pioneer Seventh-day Adventist Christian
     Educator." Ed.D. dissertation. Andrews
     University, 1982.

     A well-documented account of the first
     "successful" Adventist teacher. Highlights not
     only Bell's contribution to the theory and
     practice of Adventist schooling, but also his
     contribution to the development of the
     Adventist Sabbath school and textbooks for
     English classes.

996. Lindsay, Allan G. "The Influence of Ellen
     White Upon the Development of the Seventh-
     day Adventist School System in Australia,
     1891-1900." M.Ed. thesis. University of
     Newcastle, 1978.

     Treats the roots of the Adventist elementary
     school movement. Although Lindsay's primary
     topic is Adventist education in Australia, he
     demonstrates that the stimulus for American
     elementary schools developed out of the
     experience of Ellen White in Australia. Thus
     this thesis presents valuable background
     material on the rationale for the establishment
     of Adventist elementary schools in the United
     States.

997.   Neff, Merlin L.   For God and C.M.E.:   A
       Biography of Percy Tilson Magan Upon the
       Historical Background of the Educational and
       Medical Work of Seventh-Day Adventists.
       Mountain View, CA: Pacific Press Pub.
       Assn. , 1964.

       Provides a biography of one of Adventism's
       most illustrious educational reformers.
       Presents the early Magan as a radical reformer
       of the Sutherland school ar:d the later Magan as
       the denomination's foremost educator of medical
       personnel.

998.   Neufeld, Don F. , ed.   Seventh-day Adventist
       Encyclopedia.   Rev. ed. Washington, DC:
       Review and Herald Pub. Assn. , 1976.

       Presents a large number of articles on
       Adventist educators and educational
       institutions.   Many of the other articles
       provide contextual understanding of the
       development of Adventist education.

999.   Pierson, Robert H.   Miracles Happen Every Day.
       Mountain View, CA: Pacific Press Pub.
       Assn. , 1983.

       Surveys in a popular style the origin and
       current status of many self-supporting (non-
       denominational) Adventist schools.

1000. Reye, Arnold Colin.   "Frederick Griggs:
       Seventh-day Adventist Educator and
       Administrator. "   Ph.D. dissertation.
       Andrews University, 1984.

       Analyzes the contribution of the Adventist
       administrator who had the most impact on the
       formation of the denomination's administrative
       and curricular development as its scattered

schools were developed into a system in the
first decade of the twentieth century.

1001.   Robinson, Dores Eugene. The Story of Our
        Health Message: The Origin, Character, and
        Development of Health Education in the
        Seventh-day Adventist Church. 3rd ed.
        Nashville, TN: Southern Pub. Assn. , 1965.

        Provides a history of the development of
        health-related topics in Adventism and the
        development of health education in the
        denomination.

1002.   Sandborn, William Cruzan. "The History of
        Madison College." Ed. D. dissertation.
        George Peabody College of Teachers, 1953.

        Discusses the development of the school
        that became the mother of a large number of
        self-supporting Adventist schools and medical
        institutions throughout the world, but
        particularly in the southeastern United
        States.

1003.   Schwarz, Richard W. John Harvey Kellogg, M. D.
        Nashville, TN: Southern Pub. Assn. , 1970.

        Treats the life, work, and thought of
        Adventism's foremost health educator. Kellogg
        influenced Adventist education at every level.
        An adaptation of Schwarz's doctoral
        dissertation, completed at the University of
        Michigan, 1964.

1004.   Schwarz, Richard W. Light Bearers to the
        Remnant. Mountain View, CA: Pacific Press
        Pub. Assn. , 1979.

        The most up-to-date history of Adventism.
        Devotes several chapters to understanding

Seventh-day Adventist education in the context of a developing church.

1005. Simmons, Marion Seitz. "A History of the Home Study Institute (Seventh-day Adventist Church)." M. A. thesis. University of Maryland, 1953.

The only history of the development of Adventist theory and institutions related to correspondence study at the elementary, secondary, and collegiate levels.

1006. [Spalding, Arthur Whitefield], "Lights and Shades in the Black Belt." [1913.] Unpublished manuscript, Andrews University Heritage Room.

A contemporary study of the development of black Adventist education in the South between 1890 and 1913.

1007. Spalding, Arthur Whitefield. Origin and History of Seventh-day Adventists, 4 vols. Washington, DC: Review and Herald Pub. Assn. , 1961-1962.

Offers an interpretation of the historical development of Adventist education within the context of general denominational history. Devotes several chapters to the growth of Adventist educational thought and institutions.

1008. Sutherland, E. A. Living Fountains or Broken Cisterns: An Educational Problem for Protestants. Battle Creek, MI: Review and Herald Pub. Assn. , 1900.

Argues that the hope of Protestantism and republicanism lies in the proper education of the youth, and that this education is to be found in the principles delivered to the Jews, demonstrated by Christ, and revived by the Reformation.

1009.   Sutherland, E. A.   Studies in Christian Education.   Nashville, TN: Nashville Agricultural and Normal Institute, 1915.

Argues that Adventists education must not make the educational mistakes of other Protestants, such as Oberlin College which backslid from its program of the 1830s and 1840s.   Contends that manual labor, self-supporting missionary work, the Bible, and simplicity in such areas as diet should be at the heart of Christian education.

1010.   Syme, Eric.   A History of SDA Church-State Relations in the United States.   Mountain View, CA: Pacific Press Pub. Assn. , 1973.

Chapter nine presents an overview of the Adventist position on church-state relationships that affect education.   Included are such issues as prayer in public schools and state aid to church-related schools.   The book is a revision of Syme's doctoral dissertation, completed at American University, 1969.

1011.   Thurston, Claude, et al.   60 Years of Progress: The Anniversary History of Walla Walla College.   College Place, WA: The College Press, [1952].

Presents the history of an institution that was as much a secondary school as a college for much of its early period.   Provides a great deal of human interest material regarding faculty, students, and life in

general at a late nineteenth and early
twentieth century Adventist school.

1012. Utt, Walter C. A Mountain, a Pickax, a
       College: A History of Pacific Union
       College. Angwin, CA: Alumni Association
       of Pacific Union College, 1968.

       Argues in the early chapters that
       Healdsburg Academy--which later became
       Healdsburg College and Pacific Union
       College--began with a reformed educational
       program that was not evident in the
       denomination's first educational
       institution--Battle Creek College.

1013. Valentine, Gilbert Murray. "William Warren
       Prescott: Seventh-day Adventist Educator."
       2 vols. Ph.D. dissertation. Andrews
       University, 1982.

       Discusses the role of Adventism's leading
       educator of the 1880s and 1890s. Analyzes
       Prescott's significant contributions to
       Adventist education during its formative
       period.

1014. Vande Vere, Emmett K. The Wisdom Seekers.
       Nashville, TN: Southern Publishing
       Association, 1972.

       Discusses the history of Adventism's first
       educational institution from its inception as
       a private non-denominational Adventist school
       in the late 1860s, through its development as
       Battle Creek College (1874-1901), Emmanuel
       Missionary College (1901-1959), and Andrews
       University (from 1960). Provides a great deal
       of necessary background for understanding
       Adventist education.

1015. Wehtje, Myron F. And There Was Light: A
       History of South Lancaster Academy,
       Lancaster Junior College, and Atlantic
       Union College. South Lancaster, MA: The
       Atlantic Press, 1982.

       Develops the history of an important early
       Adventist secondary school. The first few
       chapters shed light on the implementation of
       Adventist educational philosophy.

1016. White, Arthur L. Ellen G. White, 6 vols.
       Washington, DC: Review and Herald Pub.
       Assn., 1981-1986.

       Presents the biography of the most
       influential person in the development of
       Adventist educational theory and practice.
       Several chapters discuss education as their
       primary goal, while other chapters treat it
       incidentally.

1017. White, Ellen G. Counsels on Education: As
       Presented in the Nine Volumes of
       Testimonies for the Church. Mountain View,
       CA: Pacific Press Pub. Assn., 1968.

       Presents in one volume the educational
       writings of Ellen White that were published in
       Testimonies for the Church to guide
       Adventism's developing educational system
       between 1872 and 1909. Ellen White, it should
       be noted, was the most influential person in
       the development of the denomination's
       educational thought and practice. She
       continues to hold that position through her
       writings.

1018. White, Ellen G. Counsels to Parents,
       Teachers, and Students Regarding Christian
       Education. Mountain View, CA: Pacific
       Press Pub. Assn., 1913.

Sets forth the general principles of
Christian education. Focuses on the
application of principles.

1019.   White, Ellen G. Education. Mountain View,
CA: Pacific Press Pub. Assn., 1903.

Expounds upon a biblical philosophy of
education. The most important book in the
formation of Adventist educational ideals.
Holds that the purpose of Christian education
is the restoration of God's image in fallen
humanity.

1020.   White, Ellen G. Fundamentals of Christian
Education: Instruction for the Home, the
School, and the Church. Nashville, TN:
Southern Pub. Assn., 1923.

Sets forth the general principles of
Christian education. Focuses on the
application of principles.

Part II: Contemporary

1021.   Dudley, Roger L. Why Teenagers Reject
Religion and What To Do About It.
Washington, DC: Review and Herald Pub.
Assn., 1978.

Presents the basic causes of youth
alienation from Christian values. Forcefully
demonstrates, from an Adventist philosophic
perspective, the role of the home and school
in fostering a healthy attitude toward
religion.

1022.   Hilde, Reuben. Showdown: Can SDA Education
Pass the Test? Washington, DC: Review and
Herald Pub. Assn., 1980.

An evaluation of contemporary Adventist education by an official of the General Conference Department of Education. Basically defensive in regard to "the system." Argues against those who, like Raymond Moore, demand more radical approaches to educational reform.

1023. Knight, George R. Myths in Adventism: An Interpretive Study of Ellen White, Education, and Related Issues. Washington, DC: Review and Herald Pub. Assn., 1985.

Argues that if Adventism is to be faithful to its educational goals, it must separate the unchangeable principles enunciated at its founding from the particulars of time and place that formed its original context. These principles must then be applied with understanding to a late twentieth century context. Analyzes several misconceptions in Adventist education that are based on false assumptions, and illustrates the hermeneutical method it proposes in such areas as recreation and literary study.

1024. Knight, George R. Philosophy and Education: An Introduction in Christian Perspective. Berrien Springs, MI: Andrews University Press, 1980.

Surveys traditional and modern philosophies of education and evaluates them from a biblical perspective. Part III presents the biblical grounding for the Christian approach to education that forms the foundation of Adventist educational thought.

1025. Moore, Raymond S. Adventist Education at the Crossroads. Mountain View, CA: Pacific Press Pub. Assn., 1976.

Argues that Adventist education should be
more faithful to its philosophy as expounded
by Ellen White--especially in such areas as
work-study programs. This book is built upon
a skewed and inaccurate view of Adventist
educational philosophy, but it is important
because it represents the views of a sizable
portion of "fundamentalist" Adventists in the
tradition of E. A. Sutherland.

CHAPTER 20
SHAKER SCHOOLS
James C. Carper

1026. Taylor, Frank G. "An Analysis of Shaker
Education: The Life and Death of an
Alternative Educational System, 1774-1950."
Ph. D. dissertation. University of
Connecticut, 1976.

Describes the history and philosophy of
informal and formal Shaker educational
efforts.

CHAPTER 21
UNITED METHODIST SCHOOLS
L. Glenn Tyndall

Part I: Historical

1027. Bailey, Kenneth K. Southern White
       Protestantism in the Twentieth Century.
       New York, Evanston & London: Harper and
       Row Publishers, 1964.

       Gives a helpful view of the role of the
       Southern Methodists in trying to provide basic
       education for the masses (except blacks) in
       the late Nineteenth and early Twentieth
       Centuries. Notes that at the turn of the
       century, the role of the Church moved more
       toward cooperation in improvement of common
       schools in the rural South. Claims that
       Methodist efforts in southern education
       probably surpassed those of any other agency
       or group prior to 1900. States that many
       Methodist secondary schools flourished when
       public education in the South was little more
       than a hope for the future.

1028. Barclay, Wade Crawford. History of Methodist
       Missions. New York: The Board of Missions
       and Church Extension of the Methodist
       Church, 1950.

Reviews early Methodist education in
context of missions development. Describes
some early Methodist academies - Bethel in
Kentucky, Ebenezer in Virginia, Cokesbury in
North Carolina, and the first permanent
Methodist academy - Wesleyan in New Hampshire.
States that action of General Conference and
Annual Conferences in establishing schools was
in keeping with goals of early Methodist
leaders. Notes that as public education grew,
Methodists accommodated readily and became its
advocate. Also describes the development of
mission schools among the Indians, with 6
elementary schools and 2 high schools in New
Mexico alone in 1886.

1029. Behney, J. Bruce. The History of the
       Evangelical United Brethren. Nashville:
       Abingdon Press, 1979.

       Provides a history of the Evangelical
United Brethren and its predecessors, showing
in most respects a common history with the
Methodists regarding the development of
parochial schools. Notes that such schools
did not begin until after 1840, opening as
academies and either evolving into colleges or
ceasing to exist. Suggests support of common
schools, except in the domestic mission field.
Describes some successful examples of such
work, with Spanish-speaking persons in
Florida, with the Navajo in New Mexico, and
with poor whites in Kentucky.

       Boles, Donald E. The Bible, Religion, and the
          Public Schools. Ames, IA: Iowa State
          University, 1965.

       * See item 3.

1030. Brawley, James P. _Two_ _Centuries_ _of_ _Methodist_
       Concern. New York: Vantage Press, 1974.

       Provides a helpful understanding of the
       context in which the Freedmen's Aid Society
       originated. Notes that there were not many
       elementary schools in the South after the
       Civil War, even for whites. Describes the
       South as poor, defeated and not yet committed
       to universal education. Outlines the goal of
       the Freedmen's Aid Society as providing basic
       schools for Negro children and adults until
       the state would do so. Identifies main
       supporter of the schools of the Freedmen's Aid
       Society in the Methodist Episcopal Church as
       the Woman's Home Missionary Society.

1031. Bucke, Emory Stevens, ed. _History_ _of_ _American_
       Methodism. 3 vols. New York: Abingdon
       Press, 1964.

       Gives a valuable account in Volume I of
       early Methodist ventures in parochial
       education, citing Francis Asbury's views on
       elementary and secondary schools, involving
       reliance on the English model and strict
       religious discipline. Cites action of 1820
       General Conference, directing each Annual
       Conference to develop its own school and
       system for its control. Notes that 45 schools
       were begun by Methodists between 1784 and
       1844, with only 2 currently in existence.
       Gives an overview in Volume II of work by the
       Methodist Episcopal Church, South, following
       the Civil War, noting that 187 academies were
       started between 1860 and 1920. Points out
       that many other academies had Methodists as
       headmasters.

1032. Bugbee, Leroy E. _Wyoming_ _Seminary_ _1844-1944_.
       N. p. 194_?

Describes the establishment in 1844 of
Wyoming Seminary by the Oneida Annual
Conference of the Methodist Episcopal Church.
Outlines the structure of the seminary, which
started during the era of seminaries and
academies under the auspices of several
denominations. Shows that this college
preparatory school was pressured in the 1940's
to emphasize religious studies more, and even
become a theological seminary. Indicates that
this pressure was successfully resisted, and
Wyoming Seminary remained a typical academy.

1033.   Campbell, Richard C. Los Conquistadores.
        Santa Cruz, NM, 1965.

Gives a capsule view of the development of
McCurdy School in Espanola, New Mexico,
including a high school, a junior high school,
and an elementary. Cites McCurdy as an
example of a missionary school, founded by a
United Brethren missionary in 1912 in a
setting where there were no schools at all.
Notes that this school continued as one of the
strongest Evangelical United Brethren schools.

1034.   Course of Study: Navajo Mission Academy.
        Farmington, NM, 1985.

Gives a brief description of the historical
development of the Navajo Mission Academy, one
of the college preparatory schools currently
related to the United Methodist Church.
Recounts how at first the Navajo Methodist
Mission was established in 1891, with one of
its primary purposes the education of Navajo
youth. Relates that the Navajo Academy was
established in 1976 at a different location,
but two years later it moved to Farmington,
New Mexico, to combine forces with the Navajo
Methodist Mission.

1035. Crum, Mason. The Negro in the Methodist
       Church. New York: Editorial Department,
       Division of Education and Cultivation,
       Board of Missions and Church Extension, the
       Methodist Church, 1951.

       Gives an excellent account of the
       establishment of the Freedmen's Aid Society in
       1866. Notes concern felt by northern
       Methodists over the lack of educational
       opportunities for four million freed slaves, a
       concern not shared by southern Methodists.
       Calls the establishment of many schools for
       Negroes "one of the brightest chapters in
       Methodist history." Notes that fifty-one
       schools were organized in the first few years
       alone, and that the Methodist Church
       subsequently became a leading advocate for
       free public schools for Negroes.

1036. Cummings, Anson Watson. The Early Schools of
       Methodism. New York: Phillips and Hunt,
       1886.

       Focuses exclusively on Methodist schools
       during the Church's first century and thus
       provides an excellent resource. Uses the
       Kingwood School in England as a standard, and
       describes eight of the earliest Methodist
       schools in America. Includes a detailed
       description of the organization of Cokesbury
       College in Maryland, which was actually an
       academy and not a college. Notes that all of
       the early Methodist schools were academies or
       classical seminaries, with post-secondary
       schools coming later. Shows the extent to
       which the development of academies was a
       priority, especially prior to the Civil War.

       Curran, Francis X. The Churches and the
       Schools: American Protestantism and

Popular Elementary Education.   Chicago:
Loyola University Press, 1954.

* See item 188.

1037. DuBose, H. M.   A History of Methodism.
       Nashville: Smith and Lamar, Agents, 1916.

Provides a good survey of Methodist schools
in the southern United States during the
denomination's first century. Cites several
instances where Methodist academies have gone
on to become established colleges and
universities, such as Union Institute (Trinity
College and Duke University), and Cokesbury
School in South Carolina (Wofford College).
Offers excellent background of a general
historical nature, but is weakened by the
absence of footnotes or bibliography.

1038. Elliott, T. Michael, et al., ed.   To Give the
       Key of Knowledge: United Methodists and
       Education 1784-1976. Nashville: National
       Commission on United Methodist Higher
       Education, 1976.

Describes background of early Methodist
involvement in American education. States
that basic literacy was the primary concern at
first, so most of the early Methodist schools
were elementary schools and academies. Notes
that as the level of literacy rose, Methodists
moved their emphasis to higher education and
the education of ministers. Makes clear that
while a number of excellent elementary and
secondary schools continue to be related to
the Church, this became secondary to higher
education as the church moved into its second
century.

1039. Fair, Harold L. "Southern Methodists on
       Education and Race: 1900-1920." Ph.D.
       dissertation. Vanderbilt University, 1971.

       Assesses southern Methodist concern for two
       critical issues in the early Twentieth
       Century, education and race. Describes in
       Chapter Two how post-Civil War Methodists
       chose to establish private schools when Bible
       teaching was removed from the public schools.
       Outlines in Chapter Four the development of
       church-supported schools for the Negro in the
       South after the Civil War, at first focusing
       on basic literacy, and later on secondary and
       post-secondary level.

1040. Ferguson, Charles W. Organizing to Beat the
       Devil: Methodists and the Making of
       America. Garden City, NY: Doubleday and
       Co., Inc., 1971.

       Shows the development of early Methodist
       schools in its historical context as related
       to other attempts to fight sin and spread
       "Scriptural holiness" since the earliest days.
       Gives a brief account of Cokesbury,
       Methodism's first American School, as an
       excellent example. Treats education as a
       primary means of overcoming sin, although in
       spite of its importance, it is given
       relatively little attention in this volume.

1041. Fish, John Olsen. "Southern Methodism in the
       Progressive Era: A Social History." Ph.D.
       dissertation. University of Georgia, 1969.

       Focuses on several social issues in the
       South, including education, during the early
       Twentieth Century. Gives a view of the
       denomination's hopes for the development of
       Christian character with its support of

emerging public school movement. Notes that
in 1878 there were 95 Methodist institutions
in the South, including 35 high schools, with
total number increasing to 136 by 1902.
Relates that 1902 Episcopal Address called on
the Church to support public high schools, and
help secure Christian teachers. Notes that
academies and high schools began to be phased
out in the period 1900-1915.

1042. Gross, John O. The Beginnings of American
       Methodism. New York and Nashville:
       Abingdon Press, 1961.

       Provides in Chapter 9 a helpful account on
"The Methodist Church and Education." Relates
early educational development in America to
John Wesley's views on education for all,
especially through academies. Gives a capsule
view of the rise and fall of Asbury College in
Maryland during the latter part of the
Eighteenth Century. Shows that Francis Asbury
was interested in schools, not colleges; he
wanted each Annual Conference to have its own
academy and helped five of them organize their
own. Maintains that early Methodist schools
were not sectarian, but simply tried to offer
education to a broader population.

1043. Hagood, L. M. The Colored Man in the Methodist
       Episcopal Church. Westport, CT: Negro
       Universities Press, 1970.

       Focuses primarily on the life of non-white
people in the Methodist Episcopal Church since
its inception. Gives a helpful view to the
needs of "Freedmen," or freed slaves,
following the Civil War, especially their need
for basic education. Makes clear the
desperate straits of the Freedmen, and the
absolutely vital role played by the northern

Church in providing basic education in the
South until the development of the common
schools. Shows that the last half of the
Nineteenth Century was a period of great
growth in church schools for the Freedmen,
while at the same time the role of other
Methodist schools was declining.

1044. Hunt, Thomas C. "Methodism, Moral Education,
       and Public Schools: A Look into the Past."
       Methodist History 19 (Winter 1981): 84-98.

       Describes from a Roman Catholic perspective
       the darker side of Nineteenth Century
       Methodist support for public schools as
       agencies for imparting Protestant Evangelical
       morals. Suggests that once the public schools
       became thoroughly secular, the Methodists lost
       their enthusiasm. Uses the context of
       Wisconsin in the late Nineteenth Century to
       show the conflict between Roman Catholic and
       Methodist interests. Questions whether United
       Methodists in later years have continued to
       support the public schools.

1045. Lansman, Quentin Charles. Higher Education in
       the Evangelical United Brethren Church.
       Nashville: Division of Higher Education,
       United Methodist Church, 1972.

       Describes early concerns for education by
       the United Brethren in Christ (a forerunner of
       the Evangelical United Brethren and United
       Methodist denominations). Notes that the main
       concern of the United Brethren in Christ at
       first was the education of preachers. States
       that, in 1847, Otterbein "University" was
       organized as an academy, becoming a college
       two years later. Notes that the United
       Brethren had five academies in 1891. Also
       gives a description of the work of the

Evangelical Association (another forerunner),
especially stressing teaching in German.
Describes the development of Albright Seminary
in 1853.

1046. McTyeire, Holland N. A History of Methodism.
      Nashville: Southern Methodist Publishing
      House, 1884.

Describes opening of Cokesbury College,
Methodism's first academy, in 1785, including
a physical description of the property.
Mentions Francis Asbury's strong preference
for schools - not colleges. Marks 1820 as the
important year in renewal of interest by
Methodists in education after early failures.
Describes support for church schools by
Bishops and District Superintendents, though
the support within the church structure was
not universal. Gives a thorough description
of mission schools and schools for Indians,
some of which continue until the present.

1047. The Methodist Trail in New Jersey. The New
      Jersey Annual Conference of the Methodist
      Church, 1961.

Gives a descriptive history of the
Pennington School as one part of an account of
Methodist history in the New Jersey Annual
Conference. Notes that the Annual Conference
had expressed the need for an educational
institution in 1838, agreeing to place the
school in the New Jersey community that
subscribed to the largest amount of its
original support. Relates that the school
opened in 1840 as the Methodist Episcopal Male
Seminary, changing its status to coeducational
some years later, and changing its name to the
Pennington School in 1942 after several name
changes.

1048.   Moore, Raymond S. "Protestant Full-Time
        Weekday Schools." In Religious Education:
        A Comprehensive Survey, pp. 236-246.
        Edited by Marvin J. Taylor. New York and
        Nashville: Abingdon Press, 1960.

        Gives historical perspective on development
        of Protestant day-school education. Notes
        that once public education became established
        by 1850, Methodists as a denomination were
        among its strongest supporters. States that
        in recent times Methodist support has been
        buttressed by the fear that growing parochial
        education might erode the quality of the
        public system. Notes that although there has
        been a marked increase in Methodist nursery
        schools and pre-schools in recent years,
        Methodists have not figured significantly (if
        at all) in the proliferation of Protestant and
        evangelical day schools in the mid-Twentieth
        Century.

1049.   Randolph-Macon Academy. Front Royal, VA,
        1985.

        Gives a brief historical sketch of the
        development of Randolph-Macon Academy, a
        military-preparatory boarding school under the
        auspices of the United Methodist Church.
        Notes how the school opened its doors in Front
        Royal, Virginia, in 1892, after preparation
        and approval by the Baltimore Annual
        Conference. States that the military emphasis
        was developed in response to the First World
        War. Notes that the academy has broadened
        itself in recent years, having become co-
        educational since 1980.

1050.   Schaeffer, Roberta. The Story of Red Bird
        Mission - Its Beginnings and Growth.
        Beverly, KY: Red Bird Mission, Inc., 1980.

Gives a close and detailed look at the
development of Red Bird Mission (including Red
Bird School) in southeastern Kentucky. Notes
that the Red Bird School originated in 1924 in
an isolated area where children often could
not travel to the nearest public school.
Shows that the Red Bird School has become a
successful example of a religious school
related to the United Methodists, although it
was started by the Evangelical United Brethren
(which merged with the Methodist Church in
1968). Offers a view of the history of the
Mission and the School that is often more
testimonial and devotional than historical,
for the book is without documentation of any
kind.

1051. "Statement to Our Church and the World."
       Messages of the Council of Bishops of the
       Methodist Church/United Methodist Church
       During its First 40 Years 1939-1979.
       Compiled by the Office of the Secretary of
       the Council of Bishops of The United
       Methodist Church, 1979.

Provides a collection of statements by the
Bishops since the Methodist Church was formed
from three predecessor denominations in 1939.
Gives recognition to the right of churches to
establish elementary and secondary schools if
they meet requisite standards, but without
government support. Reaffirms Methodist
opposition to diversion of public funds to
private institutions, and calls upon
individual Methodists to support this
position.

1052. Sweet, William Warren. Methodism in American
       History. New York and Nashville: Abingdon
       Press, 1953.

Gives quick review of early Methodist
ventures in parochial education and Francis
Asbury's philosophy of education, especially
his stress on academies and not colleges.
Shows how this important Methodist emphasis on
elementary and secondary education thrived and
then gradually evolved into a system of higher
education. Gives passing notice to Methodist
schools for blacks through the Freedmen's Aid
Society and the Methodist Episcopal Church
(North). Includes biased information in later
chapters on Protestant and Catholic tensions
over public support of parochial education.
Contains a bibliography and sparse footnotes.

1053.   Third Annual Report of the Freedmen's Aid
        Society of the Methodist Episcopal Church.
        Cincinnati: Western Methodist Book Concern
        Print, 1869.

Gives rationale of Methodist Episcopal
Bishops for establishment of Freedmen's Aid
Society in 1866 for the basic education of
freed slaves. Notes that in 1869 the Society
through the Methodist Episcopal Church had 105
teachers with 10,000 pupils in day schools.
States that the emphasis was on basic
education with sixty primary schools. Makes
clear that the Methodist Episcopal Church
would accept the role of educating Negroes
until the southern states would accept the
responsibility.

Part II: Contemporary

1054.   The Book of Discipline of the United Methodist
        Church. Nashville: The United Methodist
        Publishing House, 1984.

Gives the official position of the United
Methodist Church on theological,

ecclesiastical and social issues. Makes clear
in the paragraph on education that the current
stance of this large denomination is strongly
in favor of public schools, although the
United Methodists continue to embrace a small
number of quality elementary and secondary
schools, some of which came from the
Evangelical United Brethren.

1055. The Book of Resolutions of the United
       Methodist Church: 1980. Edited by the
       United Methodist Communications.
       Nashville: 1980.

       Represents official United Methodist policy
       as of 1980. Gives evidence of United
       Methodist support for universal public
       education and public educational institutions.
       Recognizes the right of private schools to be
       formed meeting public standards of quality.
       Stresses opposition to expanding or
       strengthening private schools with public
       funds. Opposes the establishment of private
       schools that jeopardize the public system or
       thwart public policy. Opposes tuition tax
       credits for support of religious schools at
       primary and secondary level.

1056. College Bound: A Guide to United Methodist
       Colleges, Universities, and Schools.
       Nashville: General Board of Higher
       Education and Ministry of the United
       Methodist Church, 1982.

       Includes a profile of each of the eleven
       elementary and secondary schools remaining of
       the 261 documented as having been at one time
       affiliated with the United Methodist Church
       and its predecessors. Notes that the schools
       have been of two types: mission oriented and
       college preparatory. Includes information on

enrollment, fees, accreditation, etc., for each
of these schools: Kents Hill School (Maine),
Lydia Patterson Institute (Texas), McCurdy
School (New Mexico), Navajo Mission Academy
(New Mexico), the Pennington School (New
Jersey), Randolph-Macon Academy (Virginia),
Red Bird School (Kentucky), Robinson School
(Puerto Rico), Tilton School (New Hampshire),
Wyoming Seminary (Pennsylvania), and St. Paul
United Methodist Elementary School (Florida).

1057. Conn, Robert H. "College Preparatory Schools:
       United Methodism's Other Educational
       System." Into the Third Century: United
       Methodist Ministry in Higher Education.
       Nashville: Division of Higher Education of
       the Board of Higher Education and Ministry,
       1985.

       Gives a brief overview of nine current
       college preparatory secondary schools related
       to the United Methodist Church, some having
       been inherited from the former Evangelical
       United Brethren Church. Helps the reader to
       discover how these unique schools are related
       to the larger system of educational
       institutions within the denomination.
       Provides helpful insights even though it is a
       denominational and promotional piece. Makes
       especially clear the value of United Methodist
       secondary opportunities for Hispanics, Blacks,
       and Native Americans.

CHAPTER 22
STATEMENTS ON RELIGIOUS SCHOOLS
Charles R. Kniker

A. By Public Educators/Advocates

Part I: Historical

1058. American Humanist Association. "A Reply to
the Bishops of the United States."
Progressive Education 33 (September 1956):
155, 160.

Opposes Bishops' position that Catholic
education is an integral part of the American
public school system. Objects to public tax
support for religiously-sponsored schools.

1059. Benjamin, James M. "Lester F. Ward and Public
Education." Journal of Thought 11 (July
1976): 252-256.

Suggests that Ward's Dynamic Sociology was
instrumental in providing a positive rationale
for public schools as opposed to the frequent
negative attacks on nonpublic schools in the
nineteenth century.

1060. Brickman, William W. "Public and Private
Education as Co-Partners in the Formation
of American Society, 1875-1964." Religious
Education 49 (July-August 1964): 294-304.

Sees a place for both public and private
(independent and religiously-sponsored) school
systems; provides extensive historical
background (facts and figures rather than
interpretative materials).

1061. Conant, James B. My Several Lives: Memoirs
      of a Social Inventor. New York: Harper &
      Row, 1970.

      Includes the chapter, "Are Private Schools
      Divisive?" that discusses his famous 1952
      speech to the American Association of School
      Administrators which declared that
      "independent schools could be a threat to
      democratic unity."

1062. Cubberley, Ellwood P. Public Education in the
      United States. Boston: Houghton Mifflin
      Company, 1919.

      Assumes that public schools are superior to
      sectarian schools; provides historical account
      of the "battle" to overcome sectarianism.

1063. "Denominational Schools--A Symposium." The
      Journal of Proceedings and Addresses of the
      National Educational Association, 1889.
      Topeka: Kansas Publishing House, 1889.

      Includes speeches of four educational
      leaders debating the merits of nonpublic
      schools and relationship to public schools.
      Catholic leaders Keane and Gibbons offer
      rationale for Catholic schools, claiming that
      they are a vital part of Christian
      civilization. They maintain that secular and
      religious aims can be easily combined in
      Catholic education. Edwin Mead and John Jay
      disagree, stating that parochial education
      will be narrow and likely to undermine the
      public schools.

1064. Erickson, Donald A. "On the Role of Non-
       public Schools." School Review 69 (Autumn
       1961): 338-353.

       Reviews state laws and includes comments by
       public school defenders. Concludes that laws
       should treat nonpublic schools more equitably.

1065. Fisher, William H. "New Interpretation of
       Church-State, Relations." Education 89
       (April-May 1969): 344-347.

       Favors accommodation of government to
       religion, especially aid to nonpublic schools
       because it is consistent with the pluralistic
       goals of American education.

1066. Kniker, Charles R. "Reflections on the
       Continuing Crusade for Common Schools:
       Glorious Failures, Shameful Harvests, or
       ...?" In Religious Schooling in America,
       pp. 169-206. Edited by James C. Carper and
       Thomas C. Hunt. Birmingham, AL: Religious
       Education Press, 1984.

       Suggests that the common school movement
       had five major goals and reviews statements by
       public school and parochial school leaders on
       what ways the religious schools added to or
       detracted from these common goals. Touches on
       the future relationship of public and
       religiously-sponsored schools.

1067. Landon, Elliott. "The Evolving Church-State-
       Education Policies of the National
       Education Association, 1961-66." Ed. D.
       dissertation. Columbia University, 1968.

       Concludes that the NEA changed its policies
       regarding categorical aid to nonpublic

elementary and secondary schools during this
period, under the leadership of William Carr
and James E. Russell. Argues that while it
accepted limited aid to such schools, the NEA
also lessened its concern that there be
judicial reviews of congressionally-mandated
programs.

1068. Lawn, Evan. "Fundamental Differences between
the Philosophies of Public and Parochial
Education: A Socio-Historical Study."
Ph.D. dissertation. The University of
Connecticut, 1959.

Posits that a particular secular philosophy
(Prometheanism) has taken over the public
schools and courts. This philosophy, which is
religious, contains definitions of the ideal
person and society. Because of how firmly it
is rooted, it is difficult for alternative
philosophies (such as found in religious
schools) to be accepted by the courts.

1069. Mann, Horace. Annual Reports of the Secretary
of the Board of Education. Boston: Dutton
and Wentworth, 1849.

Defends the emerging common school against
a variety of opponents in twelve annual
reports to the Massachusetts Board of
Education. Argues (in the first report)
against the logic of those who send children
to sectarian schools because of the problems
found in the common schools. Attacks the
leaders of parochial schools in twelfth report
who don't think public schools can offer moral
education or "religious" education.

1070. Mann, Horace. "Parochial Schools, Are They in
Harmony with the Spirit of American
Institutions?" Proceedings of the National

Teachers' Association. Syracuse, NY: C.
W. Bardeen, 1858.

Sees no way in which parochial schools aid
the nation in preparing future citizens.

1071. McCluskey, Neil G. Public Schools and Moral
        Education: The Influence of Horace Mann,
        William Torrey Harris, and John Dewey. New
        York: Columbia University Press, 1958.
        (Reissued: Westport, CT: Greenwood
        Publishers, 1975.)

Compares the views of three prominent
educators, concluding that Horace Mann was the
most critical of the three regarding religious
schools and John Dewey the least critical.
Finds that William T. Harris, despite his
personal opposition, permitted released time
programs when he was superintendent of St.
Louis schools.

1072. Meyer, Agnes E. "Public and Private
        Education." Proceedings of The National
        Education Association. Washington, DC:
        National Education Association, 1952.

Contains a ringing defense of public
education and includes numerous criticisms of
religious schools. Includes numerous
references to the opinions of public school
educators.

1073. National Education Association. Proceedings
        of the National Education Association.
        Washington, DC: NEA, 1972.

Indicates in resolutions that the public
schools must be supported and that no
financial support should be given to nonpublic
schools.

1074. "Religion and the State--A Symposium." <u>Law</u>
      <u>and Contemporary Problems</u> 14 (Winter 1949):
      1-169.

      Includes eight articles, most by attorneys
      who are separationists. Discusses James
      Madison's opposition to parochial schools (M.
      Konvitz); educational cooperation between
      church and state (A. Mielkejohn); and
      significance of the <u>McCollum</u> case.

1075. "Religious Instruction in Public Schools."
      <u>The American Journal of Education</u> 2 (August
      1856): 153-172.

      Incorporates a number of comments, many
      negative, about private schools by advocates
      of the public schools.

1076. Smith, B.O. "What Do the Sectarians Want?"
      <u>Progressive Education</u> 26 (February 1949):
      121-124, 128.

      Opposes financial aid to parochial schools.
      Discusses consequence of financial aid:
      disintegration of public school system that
      would contribute to collapse of American
      culture--"the public schools have helped with
      the "purification of the American soul."

1077. Thayer, V.T. <u>The Attack Upon the American</u>
      <u>Secular School</u>. Boston: The Beacon Press,
      1951.

      Advocates public schooling and criticizes
      nonpublic schools. Includes a number of
      quotations from past public school leaders and
      educational theorists.

1078. U.S. Bureau of Education. <u>Report of the</u>
      <u>Commissioner of Education for the Year</u>

1894-1895. Vol. 1. Washington, DC: U.S. Government Printing Office, 1895.

Reports on status of nonpublic schools, concludes that they are "experimental schools for the public."

Part II: Contemporary

1079. Bell, Terrell, H. "Catholic Schools Are An Important National Resource." Momentum, September 1984, pp. 10-11.

Advocates financial support for religious schools.

1080. Everhart, Robert B., ed. The Public School Monopoly: A Critical Analysis of Education and the State in American Society. Cambridge, MA: Ballinger Publishing Co., 1982.

Contains 14 essays, many historical. Supports alternative schooling and indicates reasons why the public school system has never reached the lofty goals set for it in the nineteenth century. Offers support for programs designed to help religious and independent schools gain public tax monies.

1081. Finn, Chester E., Jr. "Catholic and Public School Cooperation: It's Imperative!" Momentum, May 1983, 6-9.

Applauds Catholic schools for being "good" academically. Asks Catholic school leaders to think of ways to promote collaboration with public schools so both will increase excellence.

1082. Finn, Chester E., Jr. and J. Porter. "Public
      Policy and Private Education: A Future of
      Harmony or Discord?" Compact 15 (Fall
      1981): 14-15+.

      Debate the changes in the meaning of the
      terms private and public. Discusses what
      assumptions can be made about the nature of
      the two systems today. Shows that the major
      issue for many is still funding for private
      (religious and independent) schools.

1083. Jones, Tom. Public v. Nonpublic Education in
      Historical Perspective. Palo Alto, CA:
      Stanford University Institute on Research
      on Finance of Government Report TTT-6,
      February 1982.

      Argues that the disagreements between
      public and religious schools historically may
      be overstated. Provides examples of
      cooperation at the local level, especially in
      funding situations.

1084. "Nonpublic School: A Public Service." A
      symposium edited by Sidney Marland, Jr.
      NASSP Bulletin 66 (March 1982): 1-104.

      Assumes that nonpublic schools do
      contribute to the public good; however, while
      most authors delineate the excellent work of
      such schools and some call for public tax
      monies, others oppose such aid.

B. By Religious Educators/Religious School Advocates

Part I: Historical

1085. Blake, Eugene C. "Strategies for Making
      Adequate Provision of Religious Education
      for All Our Young." Religious Education 49
      (March 1954): 100-103.

Views parochial schools as "the last ditch
defense against a completely secular society."
Claims they are inferior because they tend to
be poorly financed, more interested in piety
than intellect, and are too narrow in meeting
society's needs.

1086. Bodo, John R. The Protestant Clergy and
Public Issues, 1812-1848. Princeton, NJ:
Princeton University Press, 1954.

Argues (pp. 170-172) that mainline
Protestant leaders (Presbyterians, Lutherans,
etc.) in the 1840s-1860s began to favor
sectarian schools when they realized they
could not control the curriculum chosen for
the common schools, a position changed by many
in the 1880s.

1087. Brownson, O. A. "Schools and Education."
Boston Quarterly Review XI (July 1854):
354-376.

Compares the public and Catholic systems,
with the Catholic system being the better
because of its central religious purpose.

1088. Brownson, O. A. "Public and Parochial
Schools." Boston Quarterly Review XVLI
(July 1859): 324-342.

Details many faults of the public system,
concluding again that the Catholic system is
superior.

1089. Coe, George Albert. Education in Religion and
Morals. Chicago: Fleming H. Revell
Company, 1912.

Believes that the religious schools shared
a task with public schools--preventing society
from being overcome by "secular
encroachments." Dismisses the claim of
private schools for public fundings, despite
their common mission to educate the whole
child. In tone, surprisingly sympathetic for
its time.

1090. Ireland, John. "State Schools and Parish
Schools--Is Union Between Them Possible?"
The Journal of Proceedings and Addresses of
the National Educational Association, 1890.
Topeka: Kansas Publishing House, 1890.

Endorses public schools, but the majority
of his speech is a defense of and rationale
for Catholic schools. Announces Poughkeepsie
plan.

1091. Jenkins, Thomas J. The Judges of Faith:
Christian versus Godless Schools.
Baltimore: John Murphy and Co., 1886.

Assumes that public schools are "godless"
because they are not offering religious
instruction.

1092. Johnson, F. Ernest, ed. American Education
and Religion. New York: Harper and Row,
1952.

Mirrors a conciliatory tone, with
spokespersons from various faiths addressing
what is being done in various parochial
systems and what can be done with religion as
part of the general education in the public
schools. Addresses the specific role and
responsibilities of parochial schools briefly.

1093. Lannie, Vincent P. "Sunlight and Twilight:
Unlocking the Catholic Educational Past."
Notre Dame Journal of Education 7 (Spring
1976): 5-17.

Reveals numerous sources on history of
Catholic education and reviews statements of
famous leaders who compare Catholic and public
schools.

1094. Mayo, A.D. "Object Lessons in Moral
Instruction in the Common School." The
Addresses and Proceedings of the National
Educational Association, 1880. Salem, OH:
National Educational Association, 1880.

Defends the public schools, claiming that
the Pope and leaders of Catholic education
want to "capture or destroy the unsectarian
common-school system of this republic."

1095. McCluskey, Neil G. Catholic Viewpoint on
Education. Garden City, NY: Hanover
House, 1959.

Contains chapters on the evolution of
secular school, Catholic school in theory, and
Catholic school in operation. Interprets the
"price of pluralism" for America.

1096. McDonnell, James M. "Orestes A. Brownson:
Catholic Schools, Public Schools, and
Education--A Centennial Reappraisal."
Notre Dame Journal of Education 7 (Summer
1976): 101-122.

Summarizes the writings of Brownson and
analyzes the debates that he had with
defenders of the public schools. Offers a
critique of Horace Mann's second annual report
that contains numerous references to religious
schools.

1097. Meiring, Bernard J. "Educational Aspects of
the Legislation of the Councils of
Baltimore, 1829-1884." Ph.D. dissertation.
University of California, Berkeley, 1963.

Reviews the correspondence, papers,
pronouncements related to the American Roman
Catholic Councils, including the arguments for
parochial education and the criticisms of
public education.

1098. Moehlman, Conrad H. School and Church: The
American Way. New York: Harper and
Brothers, 1944.

Endorses public schools
enthusiastically--"the greatest cultural
achievement of the United States." Argues
that parochial schools are an island within
American life.

1099. Moehlman, Conrad H. The Wall of Separation
Between Church and State. Boston: The
Beacon Press, 1951.

Extolls the public schools through
statements by public and religious school
leaders, which also include, directly and
indirectly, many comments about religious
schools. Includes many references to specific
programs such as released time and shared time
plans.

1100. Nielsen, Niels C. , Jr. GOD In Education: A
New Opportunity for American Schools. New
York: Sheed and Ward, 1966.

Focuses mainly on higher education, but
contains a historical overview of Protestant
attitudes toward elementary and secondary
parochial education.

Ognibene, Richard. "Catholic and Protestant
Education in the Late Nineteenth Century."
Religious Education 77 (January/February
1982): 5-20.

* See item 195.

1101.   Reilly, Daniel F. The School Controversy,
1891-1893. Washington, DC: The Catholic
University of America Press, 1944; reprint
ed. Arno Press and The New York Times,
1969.

Concentrates on the complex relation of
Catholic schools to public education during
this critical three year period. Covers such
issues as public funding, right of the state
to control education, and the nature of the
public and parochial curriculum.

1102.   Ryan, Mary Perkins. Are Parochial Schools the
Answer? New York: Holt, Rinehart and
Winston, 1964.

Lists reservations about the need for
parochial schools, especially in large cities.
Claims that public schools can be more
effective academically due to financial
problems of Catholic schools.

1103.   Stewart, George, Jr. A History of Religious
Education in Connecticut to the Middle of
the Nineteenth Century. New Haven, CT:
Yale University Press, 1924.

Contains chapter on the growth of the
Catholic school system, including statements
by such Protestant religious leaders as Horace
Bushnell who were strongly opposed to such
schools.

1104. Tyack, David. "The Kingdom of God and the
      Common School." _Harvard Educational Review_
      36 (Fall 1966): 447-469.

      Details Protestant clergy's active
      involvement in starting and maintaining public
      schools from the 1850s to 1890s. Suggests
      that the general concern for religion in the
      curriculum meant that there was more
      cooperation than competition between public
      and nonpublic schools at the local level than
      is usually indicated in the literature.

Part II: Contemporary

1105. Neuhaus, Richard John. "Educational Diversity
      in Post-Secular America." _Religious
      Education_ 77 (May-June 1982): 309-320.

      Encourages discussion on the meaning of
      public education today. Believes that
      parochial schools are part of public education
      and that alternative schools should receive
      public funds. Other articles in this issue
      treat religious schooling and public
      education.

1106. Smith, Robert L. "Private Education and
      Public Policy." _Religious Education_ 75
      (November/December 1980): 647-653.

      Urges that fresh thinking be brought to
      bear so that the combined resources for public
      and private education will be used to insure
      the education of all children.

CHAPTER 23
FORMAL AND INFORMAL INTERACTIONS OF
PUBLIC AND RELIGIOUS SCHOOLS
Charles R. Kniker

Due to the large numbers of entries possible for
this category (released time programs, dual
enrollment or shared time programs, shared
facilities, to name the most common), it has been
decided to exclude, with few exceptions, those found
in Albert J. Menendez (see item 1144). Further,
references to studies comparing the performance
levels of students in public and religious schools
are not included.

Part I: Historical

1107.   Arnold, Richard Jennings. "A Comparison of
        the Attitudes of Three Groups Toward
        Released Time for Religious Instruction in
        Oregon." Ed.D. dissertation. Oregon State
        University, 1978.

        Surveys reactions of citizens, public high
        school teachers, and church leaders to a 1977
        Oregon law allowing five hours a week for
        released time programs. Attempts to learn
        subjects' knowledge of law, level of interest
        for establishing programs, potential impact on
        high schools, and potential changes in church-
        school relationships. Finds that there is

interest but little implementation, with
church leaders more in favor than the other
groups.

1108. Athearn, Walter S. Religious Education and
American Democracy. Boston: The Pilgrim
Press, 1917.

Discusses the correlation of weekday
religious schools and public schools (pp.
27-142). Contains many brief descriptions of
cooperative (shared time) programs around the
country following the author's critique of
parochial schools, which he regards as a
threat to democracy because of the need to
have the nation's students do "collective
thinking."

1109. Beggs, David W., ed. America's Schools and
Churches: Partners in Conflict.
Bloomington: Indiana University Press,
1966.

Focuses on the administrative tasks of
shared time programs, including curriculum
development, faculty scheduling, and
extracurricular activities. (Marvin Heller is
author of this section, pp. 163-174.)

1110. Bond, Donald Edward. "The Practice of Shared
Time in Ohio Schools." Ph.D. dissertation.
The Ohio State University, 1969.

Based on a 1968 21-item survey of 269
public school superintendents and 9 nonpublic
superintendents and follow-up of selected
respondents, concludes that shared time
programs occurred in 57 Ohio schools. Over 80
percent of respondents viewed the program as
successful for students, stating that shared
time programs did not weaken the public school

curriculum; specific advantages and disadvantages are also discussed.

1111. Caliguire, Arthur John. "A History of Cooperation Between the Cleveland Public Schools and the Cleveland Catholic Diocesan Schools, 1966-1976." Ed. D. dissertation. The University of Akron, 1980.

Finds that the Elementary and Secondary Education Act of 1965 was a catalyst in furthering cooperative efforts between the Catholic and public school systems of Cleveland. Compares years prior to 1966, when cooperation was mainly in athletics, with the following decade (1966-1976) when the systems worked together in programs for disadvantaged students, library materials, counseling services, and transportation.

1112. Callam, James Monroe. "A Study of the Impact of the Elementary and Secondary Act of 1965 Upon Shared Time Programs in Selected School Districts in New Jersey." Ed. D. dissertation. Rutgers University-The State University of New Jersey, 1968.

Reports that shared time programs were greatly increased after 1965, with the large majority of nonpublic schools administrators surveyed approving of the new efforts. Shows that some public school leaders were concerned about possible violation of the wall of separation.

1113. Cloud, Don Anthony. "The Historical and Legal Aspects of Religious Influences as They Affect the Public Schools of California." Ed. D. dissertation. University of Southern California, 1970.

Employs interviews with superintendents as well as historical documentation to reach conclusion that there is wide discrepancy among superintendents as to the proper relationship of religious schools and public schools. Contains comments by administrators admitting bias on a number of public school/religion issues, including released time.

1114. "Cooperation Between Public and Nonpublic Schools." Religion and the Schools: From Prayer to Public Aid. Washington, DC: National Public Relations Association, 1970.

Contains references to specific communities that have had cooperation programs. Reveals that the most frequent are shared time and released time although many others are cited in the Education U.S.A. survey.

1115. Corcoran, Gertrude Beatty. "Social Relationships of Elementary School Children and the Released-Time Religious Education Program." Ed.D. dissertation. Stanford University, 1960.

Finds that degree of participation in released time program, based on three sociometric measures, did not correlate with the social status of elementary (6th grade) children, contradicting the expectation that such participation would negatively influence social status.

1116. DePillo, George Bernard. "Shared Time Relations of Public and Parochial Schools." Ph.D. dissertation. The University of Michigan, 1966.

Uses historical methods to investigate the shared time concept, finding that it can be effective for both school systems.

1117. Dierenfield, Richard Bruce. "An Examination of the Current Relationship Between Religion and American Public Schools." Ed. D. dissertation. University of Colorado, 1958.

Studies the parochial school movement and its relationship to public education through surveys, policy statements of church bodies, and opinion of authorities, concluding that sectarian groups are pressing for more religious instruction in public schools, released time programs are growing in popularity, and Roman Catholic groups are seeking public tax funds.

1118. Dierenfield, Richard Bruce. "The Extent of Religious Influence in American Public Schools." Religious Education 56 (May-June 1961): 173-79, 167.

Discovers that a large majority of superintendents believe that the teaching of moral and spiritual values is provided for in the curriculum (99 percent and 78 percent respectively). Support by the surveyed superintendents (in 400 communities) for cooperative practices have much lower percentages: released time (29%), bus transportation (19%), public school classes held in church buildings (7%), and members of religious orders teaching in public schools (6%).

1119. Fichter, Joseph H. Parochial School: A Sociological Study. Notre Dame, IN: University of Notre Dame Press, 1958.

Presents a case study of one parochial
school that includes a description of the ways
that it interacted with the public school
system--Chamber of Commerce teacher
appreciation dinners, athletic contests,
scheduling, PTA meetings (pp. 446-449)

1120. Friedlander, Anna Fay. Shared Time Strategy.
St. Louis: Concordia Press, 1966.

Provides an overview of selected shared
time strategies.

1121. Gibbs, James E. Dual Enrollment in Public and
Nonpublic Schools. Washington, DC: U.S.
Office of Education, Circular No. 722,
1965.

Analyzes case study information from nine
communities, revealing that two organizational
patterns have emerged: (1) students from the
parochial schools study only one or two
courses in public schools; (2) parochial
students are spending approximately 50 percent
of their day in each system. Adds extensive
bibliography.

1122. Hamant, Nancy Rusell. "An Historical
Perspective on Religious Practices in
Selected Ohio City School Districts."
Ed. D. dissertation. University of
Cincinnati, 1967.

Covers four city school districts
(Cincinnati, Lockland, Chillicothe, and St.
Bernard), finding some differences in degree
of cooperation with religious schools.
Discovers that released time is the most
common practice of the public schools.

1123. Hittner, Eunice. "A Study of the Nature and Extent of Cooperation Between Public and Nonpublic Schools in Title III PACE Projects." Ph.D. dissertation. The Catholic University of America, 1969.

Examines the actual working relationships in Projects for the Achievement of Creativity in Education (PACE), noting that while there was an increase in cooperation to plan and implement PACE programs between the systems, the actual involvement of nonpublic students was minimal.

1124. Hoppe, Lawrence Louis. "Theological and Political Considerations of An Expanded Share-Time Secondary Education Program." Ph.D. dissertation. University of Pittsburgh, 1973.

Describes 13 aspects of shared time programs, including staff, financing, and administration. Includes a number of recommendations for restructuring shared time to make it theologically more defensible and workable in current situations.

1125. Labrake, John Richard. "A Cooperative Public-Parochial Secondary School Venture: A Case Study." Ph.D. dissertation. University of Maryland, 1977.

Explores how one predominantly Catholic community in northern Vermont carried out a Title III Federal Planning Grant for a "Projects that Advance Creativity in Education" (PACE) program.

1126. Locigno, Joseph. "A Study of the Basic Principles Governing Church and State in Shared Time Education." Ph.D. dissertation. Boston College, 1965.

Offers a basic description of the meaning
of shared time as well as the effects of
shared time in practice.

1127. Lotz, Philip Henry. "A Survey of Week-Day
Religious Education." Ph.D. dissertation.
Northwestern University, 1924.

Contains much factual material about
programs throughout the country, along with
curriculum analysis.

1128. Lucker, Raymond Alphonse. "Some
Presuppositions of Released Time." Ph.D.
dissertation. University of Minnesota,
1969.

Examines the rationale for released time,
studies the history of the movement, reports
on court cases, and analyzes arguments for and
against it.

1129. McCluskey, Neil G. Catholic Education Faces
its Future. Garden City, NY: Doubleday
and Company, 1968.

Engages in brief discussions of released
time and shared time programs from the
Catholic perspective.

1130. McInnis, Francis Leo. "Administrative
Problems Involved in Shared Time Programs
in Selected Public and Nonpublic Schools
with Implications for Implementation."
Ph.D. dissertation. Michigan State
University, 1967.

Analyzes administrative problems in 26
school districts using shared time through
questionnaires and interviews. Finds that no

major problems exist, regardless of setting;
also, reports that science and industrial arts
courses are most commonly chosen courses in
shared time programs.

1131.   Morrissey, Timothy H.   "Archbishop John
        Ireland and the Faribault-Stillwater School
        Plan of the 1890's: A Reappraisal."   Ph.D.
        dissertation.   University of Notre Dame,
        1975.

        Posits that Ireland sought to provide
        Catholics with a legitimate alternative to the
        separate parochial school system.   Points out
        that the proposal of Ireland was not new, that
        a variety of factors caused a vehement
        reaction, and that resistance to the
        Archbishop's plan was viewed by many Catholics
        as the final straw in trying to cooperate with
        the public education system.

1132.   Myles, Mary.   "Relations with Public Schools."
        The Catholic Educator 25 (March 1955):
        416-417, 420, 422.

        Suggests numerous techniques for keeping
        the lines of communication open between
        religious and public schools.

1133.   Phillips, Richard Lee.   "A Content Analysis of
        the Cooperative Weekday Religious Education
        Curriculum of the National Council of
        Churches."   Ed.D. dissertation.   Syracuse
        University, 1965.

        Analyzes 49 texts used in weekday religious
        education classes.   Concludes that content
        about God, Jesus, and church is relatively
        non-doctrinal in the Protestant-sponsored
        schools.   While Jews are portrayed in a quite
        favorable light, Catholic life and practices

tend to be viewed in neutral or negative terms.

1134. Prickett, James Russell. "Religious Practices in the Public Schools of Pittsburgh, Pennsylvania, 1834-1965." Ph.D. dissertation. University of Pittsburgh, 1970.

Concludes that there has been extensive "friendly cooperation" between the public schools and religious schools in Pittsburgh throughout its history. Shows that the primary ways of cooperation include sharing of facilities and participation in released and shared time programs.

1135. Provost, Sterling Roylance. "The Scope of National Church Programs of Secondary School Released Time Religious Education in the United States." Ed.D. dissertation. Brigham Young University, 1966.

Ascertains that national religious denominations have supported released time programs and have made available resource materials. Reports, however, that use of materials at the local level appears minimal and the scope of programs at the local level is difficult to gauge.

1136. Rittweger, Louis Robert. "An Analysis of Virginia's Public School Policies on Religion: From Historical, Public Policy, and Evangelical Christian Perspectives." Ed.D. dissertation. Virginia Polytechnic Institute and State University, 1978.

Seeks to show how evangelical Christian perspectives have not been included in local school decisions, but should be (based on

historical study followed by questionnaire);
ends with possible policy recommendations on
correct relationship between religion and
public education.

1137. Smith, Timothy L. "Parochial Education and
American Culture." In History and
Education: The Educational Uses of the
Past, pp. 192-211. Edited by Paul Nash,
New York: Random House, 1970.

Dispels myths about parochial education in
America's heritage. Shows gradual evolution
of parochial schools and makes the point that
at the local level, public schools often
reflect the dominant sectarian perspective.

1138. Week-Day Classes in Religious Education.
Bulletin No. 3, Federal Security Agency,
U.S. Office of Education, 1941.

Reveals that after a quarter-century of
experimentation, enrollments in released time
programs were declining at that time.

1139. Woodcock, George Clifford. "Guidelines of the
AASA and Certain Practices in the School
and Curriculum Related to Religion." Ed.D.
dissertation. University of Missouri-
Columbia, 1973.

Concludes from a survey of administrators
in seven midwestern states that they were
encouraging, according to AASA guidelines,
"reciprocal" relations with nonpublic schools
in separate courses.

340   Religious Schools in America

Part II: Contemporary

1140. Hansen, Kenneth H. "Public Education and
       Private Schools: Service Without
       Entanglement." Portland, OR: Northwest
       Religion Lab, September 1981. (ED 226 406)

       Offers guidelines to administrators who
       must provide certain programs from block
       grants to both public and private (religious
       and independent) school students. Suggests
       that details be kept simple and that, whenever
       possible, everything that can be shared, such
       as personnel, services, materials, be done on
       neutral ground, i.e., the public school
       setting.

1141. Hollar, Warren Lynn. "The Legal Aspects of
       Private Use of Public School Facilities."
       Ed.D. dissertation. The University of
       North Carolina at Greensboro, 1984.

       Contains rationale for state decisions.
       Finds that generally decisions by local
       authorities are made first in light of state
       statutes and state constitutions.

1142. Hook, Ormand G. "A Study of the Public and
       Nonpublic School Relationship in Michigan."
       Ed.S. thesis. Central Michigan University,
       1982.

       Claims, in light of historical, legal, and
       philosophical parameters, that there is a
       growing likelihood of confrontation between
       church-operated schools and the State
       Department of Education. Concludes that it is
       still unclear to what degree the state can
       regulate the nonpublic, church-operated
       schools.

1143. "Issues in Religion and Public Education." A
       symposium. <u>Religious Education</u> 77
       (May/June 1982): 251-320.

       Contains three articles (by Thayer S.
       Warshaw, Charles R. Kniker, and Richard John
       Neuhaus) that speak indirectly to issues
       related to the interactions of public and
       religious schools.

       McCarthy, Martha M. <u>A Delicate Balance:</u>
            <u>Church, State, and the Schools</u>.
            Bloomington, IN: Phi Delta Kappan
            Educational Foundation, 1983.

       * See item 119.

       McCarthy, Martha M. "Church and State:
            Separation or Accommodation?" <u>Harvard</u>
            <u>Educational Review</u> 51 (August 1981):
            373-394.

       * See item 120.

1144. Menendez, Albert J. <u>School Prayer and Other</u>
            <u>Religious Issues in American Public</u>
            <u>Education</u>. New York: Garland Publishing,
            1985.

       Contains several chapters pertinent to
       interaction between public and religious
       schools. See pp. 97-109 on released time
       (approximately 150 references) and pp. 111-121
       for sources on religious instruction and
       weekday religious education. Other sections
       may also be relevant.

1145. Smith, Robert L. "New Challenges for Private
            Schools in the Eighties." <u>Lutheran</u>
            <u>Education</u> 116 (September 1980): 32-37.

Claims that private schools will be greatly challenged by religious and secular movements of the eighties.

1146. Veverke, F. "The Ambiguity of Catholic Educational Separatism." Religious Education 80 (Winter 1985): 64-100.

Discusses the contemporary and historical ramifications of the Catholic school system as a preparer of children in the faith and a contributor to the common good.

1147. Zakariya, S.B. "Here's How Boards Are Coping with the Equal Access Act." American School Board Journal 172 (May 1985): 37-39.

Makes clear that school boards have a difficult time in trying to give equal access to religious groups because two principles are involved: separation of church and state and free speech; includes examples of what several school districts are doing.

CHAPTER 24
THE EDUCATION OF THE PUBLIC
Charles R. Kniker

Part I: Historical

1148. "Education of the Public." Religious
Education 74 (July-August 1979): 338-401.

Contains four articles that relate to the
theme of the education of the public.
Includes Donald Miller, "Religious Education
and Cultural Pluralism," Thomas C.
Hunt, "Public Schools and Moral Education: An
American Dilemma," and Richard Bruce
Dierenfield, "Religion in the America
Secondary School Curriculum," and Ronald
Kronich, "Adjusting Jewish Education to
America."

1149. Bridgers, Raymond Bradley, Jr. "The Purposes
of American Public Education as Discerned
in the Works of Selected Writers on
Curriculum." Ed. D. dissertation. Duke
University, 1958.

Reports that a study of the writing of
eight curriculum authorities revealed that the
experts propose two primary and six secondary
purposes for American education; "education
for citizenship" was held to be the primary

purpose by five; "education for self-realization" was held to be the primary purpose by the other three.

1150. Carr, William G. "Public and Private Schools
Talk It Out." America, XCV, May 26, 1956,
pp. 222-223.

Offers guidelines to advocates and defenders of both public and private schools that minimize hostility; assumes that both have role to play in the education of the public.

1151. Clabaugh, Gary Kenneth. "The Fundamental
Protestant Radical Rightists: Their Views
and Influences on American Public
Education." Ed. D. dissertation. Temple
University, 1972.

Limits his critique to the "Fundradists," those who are from the Fundamental Protestant Radical Right. Notes that they are motivated by a strong ideology that emphasizes a conspiracy theory and is anti-democratic; explains how they pressure public schools to adopt values which are not compatible with a truly public school system.

1152. Cremin, Lawrence A. "The Public School and
The Public Philosophy." Teachers College
Record 59 (March 1956): 354-359.

Recalls the Western heritage that includes these common values: the worth and dignity of human personality, moral responsibility of the individual, common consent, devotion to truth, respect for excellence, and the freedom to develop and exchange ideas. Argues that the principal thrust of the common school, and its successor the public school, has been on

emphasizing that these are related values and
must be taught to all. Suggests that the
debate about the role of private schools has
hinged on the degree to which such schools can
embrace the "common" goals.

1153. "Current Criticisms of Public Schools, and
What Answer?" The Journal of Proceedings
and Addresses of the National Education
Association, 1888. Topeka: Kansas
Publishing House, 1888.

Reports, in a special thematic section,
that public schools are criticized for three
faults: they fail to teach morality and to
cultivate the religious sentiment; they fail
to give an adequate mastery of the subjects of
instruction, and they do not offer suitable
preparation for the duties of the active life.

1154. DeRemer, Richard Ward. "The Attitudes of
Public School Patrons and Non-public School
Patrons toward Public Education." Ed.D.
dissertation. University of Pittsburgh,
1954.

Finds differences in attitude in the two
classes of patrons, most significantly
concerning continuance of the principle of
church-state separation. Also notes the most
striking difference among the patrons
themselves is found in those who attended
public schools and those who did not.

1155. Dewey, John. The Public and Its Problems.
Chicago: Swallow Press, 1954.

Offers a theoretical basis for discussing
the meaning of the concept "public"; points
out that there are many "publics" and that the
concept that is most commonly thought of as
public may be in eclipse.

1156. Dewolfe, Norman Scudder. "New Perspectives on
       Religious Pluralism and Their Implications
       for Public Education." Ed. D. dissertation.
       Columbia University, 1971.

       Focuses on religion in public education;
       expands the concept of religious pluralism
       which too often considers only legal
       dimensions; promotes diversity of religious
       expression in schools.

1157. Diffley, Jerome Edward. "Catholic Reaction to
       American Public Education, 1792-1852."
       Ph. D. dissertation. University of Notre
       Dame, 1959.

       Explains that Catholic criticism of public
       schools was based on two perceptions: (1) the
       Protestant nature of the schools and (2) the
       philosophy of liberalism in American thought.
       Indicates that liberalism was understood as
       rationalism in thought, naturalism in
       religion, and an exaggerated humanitarianism
       in social action.

1158. Fischer, John H. "Public Education
       Reconsidered. Today's Education 61 (May
       1972): 22-31.

       Reacts to critics of the school, such as
       Ivan Illich, by defending the concept of
       public education. Deplores the voucher plan
       and is opposed to aid to religiously-sponsored
       schools. Ends by stating that public schools,
       while they have flaws, have been better than
       their critics contend, and stating they will
       meet their mission if they remain "free, open,
       and hospitable to all."

1159. Fister, James Blaine. "Protestant Policy
       Statements and Programs of Adult Education
       About Public Education." Ed. D.
       dissertation. Columbia University, 1965.

       Analyzes 47 official policy statements of
       13 Protestant denominations on public
       education; the pros and cons are tabulated and
       categorized. Determines from a survey that
       there is strong support of public education
       and 19 specific issues that are addressed in
       the statements. Summarizes the major
       additional pros and cons as follows: teaching
       about religion and urging persons to consider
       teaching as a career were frequently mentioned
       positively; use of public funds for nonpublic
       schools was most frequently opposed.
       Concludes that despite interest and
       pronouncements, little was done in terms of
       curriculum.

1160. Hunt, Thomas C. "Religion, Moral Education,
       and Public Schools: A Tale of Tempest."
       High School Journal 67 (April/May 1984):
       260-271.

       Reviews the ways in which religion has been
       treated in public schools--frequently a point
       of conflict. Argues that public schools
       should be places where religious pluralism can
       be expressed more openly than it has been in
       the past with a greater respect for the
       diversity of backgrounds.

1161. Hutchins, Robert M. "The Role of Public
       Education." Today's Education 63 (November
       1973): 80-83.

       Offers a brief statement on the philosophy
       of public education--"its primary aim ... is
       to draw out the common humanity of those

committed to its charge." Disagrees with a
number of the critics, especially those who
advocate alternative forms of education.
Defines public schools as those that "start
their pupils toward an understanding of what
it means to be a self-governing citizen of a
self-governing political community."

1162. Kaestle, Carl F. "Moral Education and Common
       Schools in America: A Historian's View."
       Journal of Moral Education 13 (May 1984):
       101-111.

       Recalls moral education's changing role in
       common schools and public schools, first as a
       pan-Protestant curriculum, then non-sectarian
       lessons that became more secular; with today's
       pluralistic student population, moral
       strategies are more relativistic. Predicts
       that there will be more clashes with those who
       favor traditional, local, parental, and
       sectarian perspectives in moral education.

1163. Keenan, James Park. "The Public Educational
       Thought of Selected American Big-Business
       Leaders, 1860-1917." Ed.D. dissertation.
       Columbia University, 1972.

       Examines and analyzes public pronouncements
       by 85 business leaders, finding that by 1870
       there was almost universal support for a
       publicly-financed educational system for all.
       Discovers that by 1890 businessmen "came to
       support both private and public secondary
       education of a multi-purpose nature to train
       young men and women." Discounts the
       stereotype of the "robber baron."

1164. Lannie, Vincent P. "Church and State
       Triumphant: The Sources of American
       Catholic Educational Historiography."

History of Education Quarterly 16 (Summer
1976): 131-146.

Contains references to numerous articles
showing disapproval of public schooling for
two major reasons: its secular nature and the
burden of double taxation. Collects the
comments of Catholic spokespersons about the
leaders of public schools. Argues that a
broader definition of public could have been
accepted.

1165. Meggers, John F. "Expectations for the Role
       of the Board of Education held by
       Parochial- and Public-School Oriented
       Parents." Ph.D. dissertation. The
       University of Wisconsin, 1966.

       Concludes that there are significantly
       different expectations of and satisfaction
       with the local public school board by parents
       of public-school and parochial-school parents.
       Finds that Roman Catholic parents, more than
       Lutheran, support efforts to provide shared
       time opportunities, transportation, and summer
       school programs (for both public and religious
       school systems).

       Menendez, Albert J. School Prayer and Other
           Religious Issues in American Public
           Education: A Bibliography.

       * See item 1144.

1166. Mercieca, Charles. "An Investigation into the
       Applicability of Dewey's Methodology in All
       American Schools, Public and Private."
       Ph.D. dissertation. University of Kansas,
       1966.

Concludes that Dewey's theories and methodologies could be employed in all schools.

1167. O'Neill, William. "The Protestant Principle and Its Relevance to the Survival and Renewal of the American System of Public Education." Ph. D. dissertation. Bradley University, 1962.

Advises readers that the Protestant principle (defined as the belief that all human institutions are to be subjected to the judgment of reason informed by faith) should still be operative in charting the mission of the public school. Suggests that readers repudiate religious bodies or individuals who claim special consideration for their schools that are to be exempt from public scrutiny.

1168. Pratte, Richard. The Public School Movement: A Critical Study. New York: David McKay Co., 1973.

Indicates that the lines which separate public and private (religious and independent) schools are blurring; discusses what criteria might be used to come up with a new definition of public education.

1169. Reese, William J. "Public Schools and the Great Gates of Hell." Educational Theory 32 (Winter 1982): 9-17.

Presents a general profile of the development of public schools, indicating that there has been constant pressure by various members of the public to keep the schools religious.

1170. Ryan, William Granger. "No Place for Private
       Schools?" The Commonweal, LXII, April 15,
       1985, p. 40.

       Posits that private (independent) and
       religious schools are part of the "public"
       system of education.

1171. Scott, Andrew Kieran. "Public Religious
       Education: The Encounter of Education and
       Religion in Contemporary Culture." Ed. D.
       dissertation. Columbia University,
       Teachers College, 1978.

       Argues that religious education has been
       compartmentalized (been made into a private
       enterprise); suggests that it has certain
       analytical tools and pedagogical tasks that
       should put it more in the public arena.

1172. Sumner, William Henry. "A Study of the
       Perceptions of Public, Independent, Free,
       and Catholic Elementary School Parents
       Regarding Selected Programs and Practices
       in the Public Elementary Schools of
       Michigan." Ph. D. dissertation. Michigan
       State University, 1971.

       States that there are differences between
       attitudes of various parents, especially in
       the areas of instructional trends and concepts
       about what constitutes effective teaching.
       Urges educators to be concerned about the
       various "publics" that are interested in the
       future of schooling.

1173. Tigert, John T. "The Faith of the American
       People in Public Education." Addresses and
       Proceedings of the National Education
       Association, 1925. Washington, DC:
       National Education Association, 1925.

Stresses that the public school is the place where students learn best what America's common values are. States that "the public school is more distinctively the expression of the faith of all the people than the church."

Part II: Contemporary

1174. Coleman, James S. "Public Schools, Private Schools, and the Public Interest." American Education 18 (January/February 1982): 17-22.

Compares how public school students and private school students have done academically and socially, attempting to show that some reported differences are not as pronounced as earlier suggested.

1175. Coleman, James S. "Quality and Equality in American Education: Public and Catholic Schools." Phi Delta Kappan 63 (November 1981): 159-164.

Clarifies what he regards as the distinctive goals of public education and how Catholic schools fit such a mission today. Reviews findings from his earlier studies.

Gaffney, Edward M., Jr., ed. Private Schools and the Public Good: Policy Alternatives for the Eighties.

* See item 11.

1176. Giroux, Henry A. "Public Philosophy and the Crisis in Education." Harvard Educational Review 54 (May 1984): 186-194.

Raises concerns about the linkage of the needs of the business community to the goals

of public education, as presented in such
national reports as A Nation at Risk.
Advocates the teaching of critical literary
skills and civic courage.

1177. Goodlad, John I., and T.G. David, eds. "The
Common School in a Multicultural Society."
Education and Urban Society 16 (May 1984):
243-353.

Offers a variety of positions about the
goals needed in education to meet the need of
the nation's diverse populations (a
symposium).

1178. "Religious Education and the Education of the
Public." Religious Education 80 (Winter
1985): 5-147.

Contains a symposium that questions how
society perceives public education today and
what roles the churches are to take in better
addressing public issues.

1179. Seymour, Jack, Robert T. O'Gorman, and Charles
R. Foster. The Church in the Education of
the Public: Refocusing the Task of
Religious Education. Nashville: Abingdon,
1984.

Explores the shift in both Protestant and
Catholic religious education during the mid-
nineteenth through early twentieth centuries
from a concern for shaping public life to a
preoccupation with building the life of the
church. Suggests that the development of a
sacramental imagination in addressing common
life issues is the instructive contribution of
the church in the education of the public.

1180. Tyack, David, and Elizabeth Hansot. "Conflict
       and Consensus in American Public
       Education." Daedalus 110 (Summer 1981):
       14-23.

       Recalls that both conflict and consensus
       efforts have been part of the establishment of
       American public school efforts. Suggests that
       there has been more cooperation between public
       and nonpublic schools on the local level than
       usually reported in history of education
       accounts.

1181. Warford, Malcolm. The Education of the
       Public. New York: Pilgrim Press, 1981.

       Expands the concepts of Lawrence Cremin and
       Robert W. Lynn in understanding what the
       "public" means. Calls for more cooperative
       efforts between public and religious schools.

CONTRIBUTORS

Contributors are listed in order of their appearance
in the book.

THOMAS C. HUNT received the Ph. D. from the University
of Wisconsin. He is Professor of Foundations of
Education at Virginia Tech. His major interest is
history of American education with an emphasis on
religion and schooling. He is the co-editor of
Religion and Morality in American Schooling (1981),
and co-edited Religious Schooling in America (1984).
His articles have appeared in Educational Forum, The
Journal of Church and State, Momentum, The Catholic
Historical Review, Paedagogica Historica, Journal of
Presbyterian History, Religious Education, Methodist
History, National Association of Episcopal Schools
Journal, and High School Journal.

JAMES C. CARPER earned the Ph. D. from Kansas State
University. He is Associate Professor of Foundations
of Education at Mississippi State University. His
articles have appeared in Kansas Historical
Quarterly, Mid-America, Educational Forum, Journal of
Church and State, Review Journal of Philosophy and
Social Science, and Journal of Thought. He recently
co-edited (with Thomas C. Hunt) Religious Schooling
in America. His scholarly interests include the
history of American education and religious schools,
particularly Christian day schools.

CHARLES R. KNIKER received the Ed. D. from Teachers
College, Columbia University. He is a Professor of
Education at Iowa State University where he teaches
foundations of education courses. He has published
extensively on values education, religion in public
schools, the historical interactions of public and
private schools, and is editor of Religion & Public
Education. His books include You and Value Education
(1977) and, with Natalie A. Naylor, Teaching Today
and Tomorrow (1981; 2nd edition, forthcoming). He is
currently involved in research on assessment of
students in teacher education programs.

DONALD E. BOLES is a Professor of Political Science
at Iowa State University in Ames, Iowa. He has been
chairman of the Iowa Commission on Human Rights and
the Iowa Advisory Committee to the U. S. Civil Rights
Commission. He is the recipient of the Meritorious
Achievement Award of the Regional Executive Council
on Civil Rights, and the Iowa Civil Liberties Union
Annual Award for his work in the field of Civil
Liberties. Among his books in the field of church-
state relations are: The Bible, Religion and the
Public Schools and The Two Swords: Commentaries and
Cases in Religion and Education. He is a frequent
contributor to journals in the fields of law and
education on church-state problems as they affect
areas of education. He is presently at work on a
book dealing with the views of Justice Rehnquist on
Church and State.

ROBERT W. PEARIGEN is a Phi Beta Kappa graduate of
the University of the South in 1976. He holds a
Masters degree in Political Science from Duke
University (1982) and presently is a Ph. D. candidate
completing a doctoral dissertation titled,
"Governmental Liability for Constitutional Torts: A
Study of Judicial Creativity and Congressional
Neglect." Formerly an Instructor at Duke University,
North Carolina State University, and Virginia
Polytechnic Institute and State University where he

received the Pi Sigma Alpha award for "Outstanding
Teacher of 1984-84.[?]. Presently he is an Assistant
Professor of Political Science at Hillsdale College.

ALBERT N. KEIM is Professor of History at Eastern
Mennonite College, Harrisonburg, Virginia. He
received the Ph.D. from Ohio State University in
recent American History. He is the author of
Compulsory Education and the Amish: The Right Not To
Be Modern (Beacon Press, 1975) and numerous articles
on church-state issues.

BRUNO V. MANNO is Director of Research and In-Service
Programs for the NCEA in Washington, D.C. One of his
responsibilities as Director of Research involves
coordinating the annual statistical reports on
Catholic elementary and secondary schools. He has
worked with NCEA since 1979. (Bruno Manno recently
assumed the post of Director of Planning for the
Office of Educational Research and Improvement (OERI)
of the U.S. Department of Education.)

MATTHEW R. WILT is Executive Director of the Catholic
Library Association, a post he has filled since 1960.
His position keeps him in the forefront of
developments in Catholic education, particularly on
the elementary and secondary levels.

CLAYTON L. FARRADAY received the A.B. from the
Swarthmore College, and the M.Ed. at Temple
University. He is a retired teacher of biology and
assistant Headmaster at Friends' Central School in
Philadelphia. He served as Chairman of the Executive
Committee of the Friends Council on Education, and is
a member of the Board of Directors of Council for
American Private Education (CAPE). He is past
president of the Pennsylvania Association of Private
Academic Schools (PAPAS).

BRUCE S. COOPER is Associate Professor of
Administration at the Graduate School of Education at

Fordham University. He received his Ph.D. from the
University of Chicago. Professor Cooper has been
active in studying the American private school for a
number of years. He has published extensively on
private schools and public policy both in books and
in a number of journal articles.

MURRAY L. WAGNER is Professor of Historical Studies,
Bethany Theological Seminary, Oak Brook, Illinois,
and Adjunct Professor of Religion. Elmhurst College,
Elmhurst, Illinois. He studied at the Free
University, Berlin; Comenius Theological Faculty,
Prague; and received the Th.D. at the Chicago
Theological Seminary.

THE REVEREND JOHN PAUL CARTER, Ph.D., D.D., is Rector
of St. John's Episcopal Church, Ellicott City,
Maryland. From 1952 until 1977, he was engaged in
the educational work of the church -- as Episcopal
Chaplain to the University of Texas, Secretary for
college work in the Mid-Atlantic States, and for
twelve years as the Executive Secretary for the
National Association of Episcopal Schools. He is one
of the founders of the Council of American Private
Education and served on the governing board of the
National Catholic Educational Association. He holds
degrees from the College of William & Mary, the
Virginia Theological Seminary, The University of The
South, and the University of Virginia.

JON DIEFENTHALER received the Ph.D. from the
University of Iowa and is Visiting Professor of
Church History at Lutheran Theological Seminary,
Gettysburg, Pennsylvania, and Pastor of Bethany-
Trinity Evangelical Lutheran Church in Waynesboro,
Virginia. His major fields of interest are the
history of American Christianity and American
Lutheranism. Mercer University Press will publish
his book, H. Richard Niebuhr: A Lifetime of
Reflection on the Church and the World. He has
contributed scholarly articles to Church History and
Currents in Theology and Mission.

BEATRICE E. NAFF is a doctoral student in education
and supervises student teachers at Virginia
Polytechnic Institute and State University. She also
holds a Masters in Theology from Bethany Theological
Seminary. She has taught for four years in the
Virginia public schools and two years in the Chicago
Network of Alternative Schools.

D. CAMPBELL WYCKOFF is Thomas W. Synnott Professor of
Christian Education, Emeritus, Princeton Theological
Seminary. Having studied at New College, Teachers
College, Columbia University (1934-38), he graduated
from the School of Education, New York University
(1939, 1941, 1948), and took postdoctoral work at the
New School for Social Research. Annually since 1960
he has prepared the "Bibliography in Christian
Education and Related Fields for Seminary and College
Libraries" for the Association of Theological
Schools.

DONALD OPPEWAL received the Ph.D. from the University
of Illinois. He is Professor of Education at Calvin
College, where he teaches graduate and undergraduate
philosophy of education. He has been Editor of the
Christian Educators Journal, curriculum policy
consultant to Christian Schools International, and
research associate for the N.I.E. Project on Equity
In Values Education. He has co-authored Society,
State and Schools: A Case for Structural and
Confessional Pluralism, and published articles in
Educational Forum, Education Week, Reformed Journal,
Christian Educators Journal, and Christian Legal
Society Quarterly. His present research interests
include vouchers, and textbook analysis for religious
bias.

GEORGE R. KNIGHT is currently a professor of church
history in the Seventh-day Adventist Theological
Seminary at Andrews University in Berrien Springs,
Michigan. Prior to his current assignment, he served

as a professor of educational foundations for nine
years at the same institution. He has written
several books in the field of Adventist educational
history and philosophy.

LESLIE GLENN TYNDALL serves as United Methodist
Campus Minister at Virginia Polytechnic Institute and
State University in Blacksburg, Virginia. Tyndall, a
native of Kinston, North Carolina, received the A.B.
Degree in History from Duke University (1963), and
the Master of Divinity from the Duke Divinity School
(1966). In 1977 he received the Master of Arts
Degree in Church History from Wake Forest University.
Tyndall is married to LaVina Stevens and they have
two children.

AUTHOR INDEX

Abbott, Walter 231
Ackerman, Walter I 709
Adams, Alice C. 654
Adams, Jay E. 907
Adar, Zvi 710
Adiv, Ellen 751
Agee, James 571
Albright, Raymond W. 561
Agnew, Edith J. 882
Alcorn, Bruce K. 655
Alexander, Kern 100
Allen, Douglas L. 656
Allison, Kenneth L. 657
Alper, Michael 711
Amendolara, Loraine 356
Arden, G. Everett 773
Arnold, Eberhard 160
Arnold, Richard Jennings 1107
Arons, Stephen 101, 127
Ashworth, Warren S. 981
Athearn, Walter S. 1108
Atkins, Carolyn C. 883
Attridge, Terrence 483
Auburn, Davis Ashburn 558
Auchinclos, Louis 572
Augenstein, John 510

Baca, Leonard 223
Bailey, Kenneth K. 1027
Bailyn, Bernard 546
Bainton, Denise M. 128
Baker, Michael D. 129
Baldwin, A. Graham 563
Ball, Earl John, III 617
Ball, William B. 130, 131
Ballou, Richard Boyd 547
Ballweg, George E., Jr. 658
Bank, Adrianne 752
Banta, Forrest D. 636
Banzhaf, Richard F. 578
Baradon, Eunice 712
Barber, Ruth K. 882
Barclay, Wade Crawford 1028
Barnds, Mary Lynch 357
Barnette, Helen P. 908
Barr, David L. 2
Barton, Jean 242
Bauch, Patricia 433
Baum, William 484

361

SUBJECT INDEX